Internationalizing and Privatizing War and Peace

Internationalizing and Privatizing War and Peace

Herbert Wulf

First published in 2005 by
PALGRAVE MACMILLAN
Houndmills, Basingstoke, Hampshire RG21 6XS and
175 Fifth Avenue, New York, N.Y. 10010
Companies and representatives throughout the world.

PALGRAVE MACMILLAN is the global academic imprint of the Palgrave Macmillan division of St. Martin's Press, LLC and of Palgrave Macmillan Ltd. Macmillan® is a registered trademark in the United States, United Kingdom and other countries. Palgrave is a registered trademark in the European Union and other countries.

ISBN-13: 978–1–4039–4917–2 hardback
ISBN-10: 1–4039–4917–4 hardback

This book is printed on paper suitable for recycling and made from fully managed and sustained forest sources.

A catalogue record for this book is available from the British Library.

Library of Congress Cataloging-in-Publication Data

Wulf, Herbert, 1939–
    Internationalizing and privatizing war and peace / Herbert Wulf.
      p. cm.
    Includes bibliographical references and index.
    ISBN 1–4039–4917–4 (cloth)
      1. Security, International. 2. World politics – 21st century. I. Title.

JZ5588.W85 2005
322′.5—dc22   2005045255

10 9 8 7 6 5 4 3 2 1
14 13 12 11 10 09 08 07 06 05

Printed and bound in Great Britain by
Antony Rowe Ltd, Chippenham and Eastbourne

Contents

vi *Contents*

List of Tables and Figures

Tables

Figures

Box

Acronyms

ACRF	African Crisis Response Force
ACRI	African Crisis Reaction Initiative
AMIB	African Mission in Burundi
ANC	African National Congress
APMC	Convention on the Prohibition of the Use, Stockpiling, Production and Transfer of Anti-Personnel Mines and on their Destruction
ASEAN	Association of South-East Asian Nations
AU	African Union
BICC	Bonn International Center for Conversion
BMZ	Bundesministerium für wirtschaftliche Zusammenarbeit und Entwicklung (Ministry for Economic Co-operation and Development)
BTWC	Biological and Toxin Weapons Convention
CFSP	Common Foreign and Security Policy
CIMIC	Civil–Military Co-operation
CPA	Coalition Provisional Authority
CTBT	Comprehensive Nuclear Test-Ban Treaty
CWC	Chemical Weapons Convention
DCI	Defence Capabilities Initiative
DRC	Democratic Republic of Congo
ECOWAS	Economic Community of West African States
ESDP	European Security and Defence Policy
EU	European Union
GNP	Gross National Product
ICRC	International Committee of the Red Cross
IAEA	International Atomic Energy Agency
IHL	International Humanitarian Law
IISS	International Institute for Strategic Studies
IPOA	International Peace Operations Association
IRA	Irish Republican Army
MAOW	Military Actions other than War
NATO	North Atlantic Treaty Organization
NEPAD	New Partnership for Africa's Development
NPT	Nuclear Proliferation Treaty
NRF	NATO Response Force

OAS	Organisation of American States
OAU	Organization of African Unity
OCHA	UN Office for the Coordination of Humanitarian Affairs
OECD	Organisation for Economic Co-operation and Development
OSCE	Organisation for Security and Co-operation in Europe
PFI	Private Finance Initiative
PPP	Public Private Partnership
PRT	Provincial Reconstruction Teams
SADC	Southern African Development Community
SANDF	South African National Defence Forces
SAS	Graduate Institute of International Studies, Small Arms Survey
SIPRI	Stockholm International Peace Research Institute
UN ECOSOC	United Nations Economic and Social Council
UN	United Nations
UNDP	United Nations Development Programme
UNGA	United Nations General Assembly
UNHCR	United Nations High Commissioner for Refugees
UNHLPT	United Nations High Level Panel on Threats, Challenges and Change
UNIASC	United Nations Inter-Agency Standing Committee Work Group
UNSG	United Nations Secretary General
USAID	United States Agency for International Development
USGAO	United States General Accounting Office
WEU	West European Union

Acknowledgements

This publication is the result of a research project funded by the Volkswagen Foundation. I would like to thank the foundation for their generous support, especially Alfred Schmidt who gave me useful comments already during the concept phase of my research. It was important for me to carry out this work with the institutional affiliation to the Bonn International Center for Conversion (BICC); this was made possible be the Director Peter Croll. I am grateful for his assistance. I would like to thank especially Michael Brzoska, my long-time colleague, who accompanied the research from the beginning with critical and constructive suggestions; he also read the full manuscript and I owe him thanks for many useful pieces of advice for revision. I would also like to thank Wilhelm Nolte for his suggestions and Craig Bennett for his edit during the final part of the process. Parts of the manuscript and earlier versions of chapters which I presented at conferences or in informal discussions were read and commented by Corinna Hauswedell, Andreas Heinemann-Grüder, Mary Kaldor, Edward Laurance and Laurie Nathan as well as my daughter Andrea Wulf. They raised numerous questions and made valuable suggestions which helped me to develop arguments and structure the book. My sincere thanks go to all of them. I would also like to thank Guy Lamb who was an important partner during my research at the Centre for Conflict Resolution at the University of Cape Town and Sebastian Wachendorf at BICC for his internet search. I am deeply indebted to my wife Brigitte for many discussions and for her patience and support over a long period of time. Tim Shaw encouraged me to publish this book at Palgrave MacMillan in their International Political Economy series which he edits. My thanks go to him as well as to Jennifer Nelson, the Editor, Political Economy at Palgrave, who directed me through the process of producing the manuscript and Vidhya Jayaprakash copy-editing this publication.

Despite all these helpful comments by attentive readers, all mistakes that remain are mine.

Preface

In 1996, two years after the Rwandan genocide and when yet another catastrophe of war refugees was in the making in the Great Lakes' region of central Africa, experts at UN headquarters in New York looked into the possibility of hiring troops from private military companies to stop the atrocities. Despite urgent calls for peacekeeping force contributions most UN members declined their participation. Executive Outcomes, a South African private military company which recruited members of the Special Forces of the former Apartheid army, offered to create safe havens for the refugees. The company had been active before in Angola and Sierra Leone assisting besieged governments. Within two weeks the company would be able to deploy their first soldiers in Rwanda; and within six weeks a contingent of 1500 soldiers would be stationed there, supported by Executive Outcomes' own logistics. The total cost for the UN, at US$600,000 per day, was much less than a UN peacekeeping mission itself would cost. Yet the Security Council was neither willing to pass a resolution for a UN peacekeeping mission nor to accept the company's offer. Kofi Annan, at the time in charge of the UN Department of Peacekeeping Operations, concluded: 'The world may not be ready to privatise peace.'[1]

The world however seems ready to privatize war. Ever more non-state actors are involved in fighting violent conflicts and wars. War lords, organized crime, militias, rebel groups, youth gangs and child soldiers spread violence, create insecurity and contribute to the failure of states; though child soldiers are of course more a victim than a cause of this insecurity. Many governments are no longer capable of guaranteeing law and order. Their police and military forces are too weak, too corrupt or unwilling to exercise the rule of law and the state monopoly of violence. This type of bottom-up privatization of violence offers attractive economic gains.

A second type of privatization, top-down, is based on the outsourcing of military functions undertaken by a number of governments. The US armed forces have been reduced since the end of the Cold War from 2.3 million to 1.5 million men and women. Yet today these forces are increasingly burdened with various deployments in conflict, war and post-war, such as in the Balkans, in Afghanistan and Iraq. They have consequently come to depend more and more on private military companies for logistic support, training, the repair and maintenance of weapons systems and other military equipment, for the collection of intelligence information, for interrogation of prisoners of war, and for supplying mail, food and clean uniforms.

Hundreds of new private military and security companies have been established to grab a share of this new bonanza – not only in the United States. It's the new Wild West! The issue exploded into the public consciousness with the pictures of four murdered US contract employees in Fallujah in Iraq at the end of March 2004. At the time contractors had filed claims for 94 deaths and 1164 injuries since the beginning of the war in Iraq (Isenberg 2004). It is estimated that the US authorities have hired at least 60 private security companies with 20,000 security guards in Iraq. In fact it is the second largest armed contingent in Iraq behind only the 135,000 US troops, and it is larger than all other coalition troops combined. The big companies are active in many countries of the world in pre-war preparation, in war, and in post-war programmes, and at issue is that this trend is largely outside the control of parliaments and only partially controlled by governments.

When I first planned to publish this book, I had the idea of analyzing the completely changed role of the armed forces after the end of the Cold War. At that time I had never heard about private military companies. The military was in search of new vocations and wanted to demonstrate its *raison d'être*. The military threat between East and West was gone, the Warsaw Pact dissipated. NATO's enemy had disappeared. Many soldiers had been demobilized, not just in Europe but in many developing countries as well. At the same time, the UN engaged an increasing number of Blue Helmets in the various different conflicts around the world. Soldiers were no longer primarily deployed to defend their country but to keep warring groups apart and possibly to disarm them. On the one hand the UN was desperately looking for more peacekeepers, and on the other most armed forces were still struggling to restructure and reduce their troop strength.

Many questions arose. What was the structure of the restructured armed forces and their capability to cope with their new missions? Would they be able to contribute to the new world order that US President George Bush had proclaimed in the early 1990s? Could they quickly reform and reinvent themselves, or would they be completely demobilized in some countries?

The UN was called upon to intervene to prevent or stop war. But the organization had to struggle with numerous shortcomings and bottlenecks in its organization and the overriding lack of political will be shown by many member countries. In areas such as the control of arms transfers usually only insufficient compromises in negotiations among the UN members were possible, despite detailed and convincing knowledge about the negative effects of weapons proliferation in crisis regions. This situation has not changed to this day as the inability of the UN Security Council to mandate sanctions against Sudan at the end of 2004 proves. The interest in Sudan's oil and in weapons deliveries to the Khartoum government (by France, Russia and China) prevents such actions.

South Africa's experience was much more positive than in most other African countries. The government of Nelson Mandela initiated a transformation process of the armed forces immediately after the country freed itself form apartheid in 1994. This transformation worked extremely well, especially when compared to the predictions of many sceptics. But South Africa's oversized military and defence complex could not be reduced overnight. Employees at Armscor, the giant defence producer and procurement agency in Pretoria, lost their jobs. It is therefore no surprise that former South African military officers were the first to found a private military company, Executive Outcomes. With fighting experience from the wars in Southern Africa the members of former elite units possessed the fighting know-how that could be marketed in other conflict areas. Executive Outcomes had its headquarters in South Africa until a 1999 law on military assistance forced the company to leave and to establish offices in the UK and the US.

It was anticipated at the end of the Cold War that many defence firms would disappear from the world's weapons markets and that others would diversify into non-military production; only the core companies would continue as large defence producers and make profits. However, the possibility to create an entirely new type of companies to meet the state's military inadequacies, took political analysts completely by surprise. In many cases former high-ranking military officers formed companies that were prepared to take over any kind of service required by the military. This new concept was so successful that booming small and medium sized companies are now the object of take-overs by large defence companies. Today these new military companies have emerged as a new branch with high growth rates. The reason for this economic success is the result of the over-burdening of the armed forces with new international jobs in crisis situations, and at the same time this trend has been facilitated by the promotion of the notion of market liberalization and the concept of the lean state. The power of privatization embraces the privatization of power too (Singer 2003). The neo-liberal economic policy does not stop outside military barracks.

This book looks at the interdependence of internationalizing and privatizing wars as well as peace efforts. The military is undergoing dramatic changes. Outsourcing to the private sector takes missions away from the military, but the shift towards international intervention adds new, wider functions to the traditional role of territorial defence. These include: international peacekeeping or peace enforcement duties, providing humanitarian assistance and emergency aid, separating warring groups, resettling refugees, post-conflict reconstruction as well as combating transnational crime and terrorism. As a result the organization of the armed forces is internationalized – in UN peace missions, in coalitions of the willing and occasionally in partly integrated forces as presently practiced in the European Union.

This book addresses, in a similar way as the two different types of internationalization (increasing international interventions and internationalizing the organization of armed forces), two types of the privatization of violence and military functions: the bottom-up privatization of non-state actors and the top-down outsourcing to private military companies. The first form of privatization has been dealt with extensively in other literature. In this book it is an important reference point but it is not the main focus. The focus of this book is the deployment of the private military sector in international wars and crises. The broad public recognized, with some surprise, the private military companies' activities only after the war in Iraq when company employees were used in dubious interrogation practices conducted on prisoners' of war. Is that the real face of these companies? Will they do *any* job if they are paid? What does this mean for international law, especially the Geneva Conventions that relate to the protection of civilians in wars and prisoners of war? During the war between Ethiopia and Eritrea at the end of the 1990s, Ethiopia leased a small but modern air force from the Russian aircraft manufacturer Sukhoi, including the modern Su-27 fighter jets with pilots and maintenance crew, that operated from the Mekele airbase in the country's north-east. This air force flew hardly any sorties during the war. Eritrea had equally hired Ukrainian aircraft and pilots, but the companies on both sides did not want to risk their assets and the pilots' lives. Is this risk avoidance strategy of private companies possibly a new and completely unexpected barrier to the engagement in fighting? Or is the profit motif of the companies a conflict accelerator?

I am interested in the internationalization and privatization of war and peace in order to find answers to two questions: First, what does the internationalization of the armed forces mean for their democratic control? Political analysts identify a democratic deficit, for example, in the European Security and Defence Policy (ESDP). If such a deficit poses problems in the case of mature democracies how problematic is this in other countries? The second question concerns the erosion of the state monopoly of force, which had been established in Europe with the treaty of the Peace of Westphalia in 1648. Is this progress in civilisation questioned by the massive privatising of military functions? This publication addresses both conceptually as well as in case studies the internationalization and privatization of war and peace: the causes, the motives and the effects. If the present trends continue important security functions will be out of the control of national governments and international authorities and the state monopoly of violence is itself at stake.

Introduction: New Wars and the Bumpy Ride to Peace Building

The internationalization and privatization of war and peace efforts are already realities in today's world. Privatizing violence and international peace support missions are part of, and a reaction to, what have become known as the 'new wars'. Today, not only the United Nations but also 'coalitions of the willing' have decided to intervene with military means more quickly and more often than in the past. While Blue Helmet operations or peace enforcement missions were exceptions until the end of the Cold War, they are now squarely on the international agenda, although both disagreements or blockades in the UN Security Council and the lack of resources of the UN has equally prevented them in recent times. In a few cases, such as in 1999 in Kosovo, a number of Western governments felt the responsibility to respond militarily when the Security Council failed to mandate a UN operation. Such interventions, it was argued by its proponents, were needed because of humanitarian concerns, for example the prevention of genocide, ethnic cleansing or other gross human rights violations, the promotion of democracy or a change of regime, and the need for nation-building. In these cases the military is supposed to act as a stabilizing factor. The 'responsibility to protect', as it is termed by a commission reporting to the UN (International Commission on Intervention and State Sovereignty 2001), quickly turned into an attitude that Bary Buzan (2002) aptly described with the question of 'who may we bomb'?

This policy has enormous effects on the organization of the armed forces and the role of private actors in war. The armed forces are faced with new, expanded missions; they are more often deployed not just in war but also in crisis prevention and post-conflict reconstruction programmes. Most of these missions are carried out jointly between forces from various countries. On the one hand, non-state actors in war and

1

conflicts have clearly intensified their activities, and on the other hand, private sector companies are considered to be an important support for the military. As in so many other traditional public functions, private firms are also used in promoting security.

I distinguish between two forms of the internationalization of the armed forces and, similarly, between two forms of privatizing violence, as is illustrated schematically in Table I.1.

The question arises if there is a causal relationship between privatization and internationalization or if these are two parallel processes that accidentally seem to have developed at the same time. A complicated network of associations and causal relations characterizes the different developments and their principal actors. I presume that the following causal relations shape the present trends: The numerous international crises and the growth of violence markets (described as privatization I) is one of the key root causes for the international community to engage in military interventions (internationalization I). Other factors for intervention are, as so often in history, dictated by the interests of the big powers. International military interventions result in the need for organizational and structural changes in the military (internationalization II). Here again, a whole range of other factors, including the disarmament of weapons and demobilization of soldiers after the end of the Cold War,

Table I.1   Internationalizing of armed forces and privatizing violence

	'New Wars'	**'New Armed Forces'**
Internationalizing	1) military missions (internationalization I) intervention, peacekeeping operations, peace enforcement	2) organization of armed forces (internationalization II) UN troops (Blue Helmets), coalitions of the willing, supra-national armed forces
Privatizing	3) violence market bottom-up (privatization I) non-state actors: warlords, organized crime, gangs, terrorists, rebels, militias, child soldiers	4) outsourcing top-down (privatization II) private military companies, private security companies, private service companies, defence producers, mercenaries

Notes: The term 'new armed forces' is – similar to the term 'new wars' – an overemphasis of the newness of this trend. Governments, of course, do not create completely new armed forces. Rather, this classification denotes that the traditional forces structure requires fundamental change.

play a role in the need for restructuring forces. The burden on the armed forces, due to military interventions and reductions in force levels, leads to efforts to outsource military functions (privatization II). The boom in the creation and turnover of the private military companies is also part of a general trend to privatize state functions.

This general structure with its causal relationships can be graphically presented as Figure I.1 illustrates. The two forms of internationalization are closely related: International military interventions require internationally organized forces. The two forms of privatization are principally different, and partly contradictory, since privatization in violence markets is exercised bottom-up through non-state actors, while outsourcing is a government planned top-down process.[2] However the two forms of privatization are not always easy to separate, since warlords, rebel groups etc., occasionally clash in fights with private military companies, particularly when besieged governments turn to the companies for protection or when governments deploy militias for their defence, as was the case, for example, in Zaire under President Mobuto Sese Seko shortly before his fall. As mentioned in the preface, many of the activities and motives of non-state actors in the use of violence and their roles in wars, conflicts and post-war societies (privatization I) have been described in great detail. Thus, this trend is only a point of reference here. The core of this book addresses international military interventions (internationalization I), the internationally oriented reorganization of the military (internationalization II) and outsourcing of military functions to private companies (privatization II).

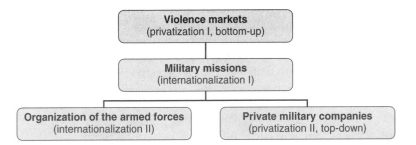

Figure I.1   Internationalization of the armed forces and privatization of violence

Politics and economics of new wars

A characteristic of recent wars is the disruption or loss of the state monopoly of violence,[3] as it can neither be adequately exercised nor can the rule of law be maintained. According to numerous scholars, we have apparently entered an era of new wars. These new wars are often also called internal, intra-state, local or regional, civil wars, low-intensity conflicts etc.,[4] and it is uncontested that the majority of these conflicts during the last few decades have not been inter- but intra-state wars. As rationale to be defined as something new, it has aptly been noted by Kaldor (1997, 1999) that in these new wars the very nature of conflict and the effects on the population in war-torn societies have changed (Münkler 2002, Duffield 2001). Criticism has been raised against the use of this term, arguing, for example, that the types of conflict are not so new at all (Gantzel 2002).

An ingredient of the changes in wars and conflicts is that today more people die of common and organized crime and violence than in state wars. Internal insecurity in societies and violent conflicts are the reason for the international community to try to pacify these conflicts – also by applying military means. The overall consequence is the long-term trend in the increasing burden of wars on civilians. In 'classical' wars of the past soldiers fought against soldiers; in today's wars the civilian population is an important target and the majority of the casualties are civilians. Civilians often have to leave their homes to avoid the fighting. The UN High Commissioner for Refugees (UNHCR) reports the number of 10.4 million foreign refugees and 2.4 million internally displaced persons in 2003 (UNHCR 2003). A large part of these refugees had to flee from their country because of wars. Often, the United Nations and its special agencies are not only called upon to provide humanitarian assistance but also to deploy troops. Such interventions by UN troops have regularly been requested; until early 2005 60 peace missions had been mandated, the vast majority of them since the end of the Cold War. One of the consequences of this demand on the UN is the internationalization and privatization of the military that I address in this book.

These recent developments are closely related with the globalization of almost all sectors of society. Integration into the world market has led to internal economic and political disruption and it follows that the military is requested to pacify internal violent conflicts.

When looking at the proliferating scholarly work on the new type of conflict two aspects, both rooted in deep shifts in the global political and economic order, feature prominently: economic globalization and the declining role of the state. Both of these trends have dramatic effects on the state monopoly of violence. Let us look at these two trends:

The effects of globalization

Economic globalization replaced state-led development through market liberalization with free trade, producing new opportunities not only for economic growth but also for the more systematic self-financing of combatants in wars. The pursuit of war has become economically attractive for many who participate in it, notwithstanding the cumulative societal destructiveness (Ballentine and Sherman 2003). Resources are not only used to fund wars, wars are also fought to extract these resources.

In the past, when economic factors were identified as root causes for intra-state violent conflicts, analysis tended to focus on the economic deprivation, underdevelopment and resource scarcity that prevented development and exacerbated conflict (Ballentine and Sherman 2003, Pugh and Cooper 2004). In recent years the emphasis has shifted from the economic scarcity argument to conflict-promoting economic factors such as economic interest in the continuation of conflict. This paradigmatic shift has been captured most graphically by the term: greed or grievance (Berdal and Malone 2000, Collier 2000a, 2000b, Collier and Hoeffler 2001, Collier *et al.* 2003). The dispute between political analysts who argue that resource scarcity causes conflict and those who argue that rich resource availability is the problem remains unresolved. Explanations for such wars propelled by greed are: war economies, loot seeking and plunder, resources and war, violence markets, violence entrepreneurs, shadow economies, network wars etc. (Duffield 2000, 2001, Elwert 1999, Keen 1998, Jean and Ruffin 1999, Kurtenbach and Lock 2004, Pugh and Cooper 2004, Reno 2000, Trotha 1997). Usually, the effects of globalization and their consequences to the state's ability to exercise its monopoly of violence feature prominently in such explanations.

The erosion of the nation state

The key to the Westphalian modern nation state was the monopolization of legitimate force (or organized violence). One of the central functions of the modern state is to guarantee the security of its citizens by establishing the rule of law, qualified by Max Weber as an achievement of civilization. The state in Europe became the monopolist of what Weber (1919) called the legitimate physical violence. In today's modern state the authority to exercise legitimate violence rests on the legality of this authority. The political leadership is democratically controlled and accountable for using the instruments of legitimate force. This authority is based on good governance.

This Weberian notion of the state is reflected, as Kaldor (1997) argues, in the elimination of private armies, internal pacification, the emergence of a state system with organized and centralized war-making activities in a given territory, and the rise of state-controlled regular professional armies. What is the relevance of these four factors in today's conflicts?

First, the disruption of this carefully balanced nation state system has led to 'new wars' with new actors. As the state is no longer capable of exercising the state monopoly of force, private groups or organizations act in conflicts usually without or expressly against the consent of state authorities. The result of the economic and political activities of these non-state actors, which either directly involve or implicitly threaten violence, is widespread insecurity. As a consequence of this insecurity other private actors, especially private military companies and private security companies, are increasingly hired by governments and international organizations to carry out tasks previously undertaken by the armed forces and the police (Cilliers and Mason 1999, Singer 2002, 2003, Lilly 2000b, Lock 2001, Musah and Fayemi 2000, Mair 2004, Münkler 2001, Wulf 2003).

Second, state authorities in many countries cannot guarantee internal pacification and the establishment and implementation of law and order because organized mafia-like crime, spiralling day-to-day robbery or militias create a situation of insecurity. As a consequence, people that can afford it try to organize their own security without having to resort to underfunded, incompetent or corrupt state authorities (Cilliers and Mason 1999, Eppler 2002), whilst those who cannot either have to live with the insecurity or might themselves resort to violence in their fight for survival. Zones of asymmetric security have emerged, or rather zones of insecurity for the poor and zones of relative security provided for people and their wealth by private companies. While the international norm of a state guarantee for the public good of 'security' still exists, its implementation, in reality is no longer possible.

Third, the idea of the undisputed national entity no longer exists as national boundaries have been increasingly broken down or lowered due to the general trend of globalization. Many actors today operate outside the boundaries dictated by the logic of territoriality. Economics, politics and culture are increasingly denationalized. Although wars might be manifest at the local level, the political economy of armed conflicts has effects on a whole region and conflicts are fuelled from beyond national borders. Market liberalization, deregulation and neo-conservative economic agendas have contributed to a freer flow of goods and services, including the financing of wars. Conceptually and in reality state functions are reduced and states are being emptied of functions – this also occurs by the outsourcing of the state's monopoly of violence to private actors, either by default or by design.[5] In societies where conflict is endemic and peace fragile, the neo-conservative economic strategy can increase poverty, crime and social unrest and thus contribute to challenging the state monopoly of force.

The only partial integration of some societies into the world economy has led to cross-border spill-over of violence and economic and military spin-in effects. Outside funding, cross-border sanctuaries for combatants, external reservoirs of violence and military inputs of finance, personnel and weaponry are now important ingredients in these wars (Jean and Ruffin 1999, Reno 2000). Duffield (2001) has defined wars that are fuelled by and rely on such external factors as network wars. This term points to the fact that not only NGOs but also warlords act locally and think globally.

Fourth, although many regular professional armies have been drastically reduced and soldiers have been demobilized in the millions during the last 15 years, the existence of professional armed forces is not principally questioned (BICC 2004). However, the two forms of the internationalization of the armed forces (e. g. in international missions and in the international orientation of UN peace operations, in coalitions of the willing and emerging supra-national forces such as the EU) go beyond national borders despite the fact that these forces are still organized nationally (Ku and Jacobson 2003a, Born and Hänggi 2004). This leads to a certain tension between the international orientation of missions and the national organization of the military.

The apparent trend towards the outsourcing of military functions in order to compensate for budgetary constraints or to cope with weapons modernization processes results in a shrinking scope of military missions while, at the same time, the number of military missions increases. The clear distinction between war and peace, war and violence, or military activities and organized crime can no longer be recognized, and wartime has gradually carried over into relative or fragile peace and vice versa (Debiel 2002). Kaldor argues (1997) that it is difficult to distinguish between internal and external wars because all wars are globally influenced and have effects beyond national state borders, and yet they are at the same time fought locally. This mishmash of violent situations does not mean however that those categories of violence and war have to be given up as Lock (2004) argues and Brock (2004) criticizes.

Terrorism as a new threat

Besides the effects of two strong economic and political factors of globalization and the erosion of the state, a third element is perceived as a central threat: The terrorist attacks of 11 September have changed the security landscape. Present day strategic thinking and planning are geared primarily to counter the terrorist threat. Yet the European and American reactions are quite different. The US government stresses its willingness to counter terrorism militarily, even if this means the toppling of a regime or elimination of movements that support terrorism. The strong (emotional) reactions to this criminal act are natural, but the declaration of 'war against terror' accords terrorists a status as combatants and a kind of dignity and almost diplomatic recognition (Howard 2002, 8). The 2001 attacks on Washington and New York or the 2004 bombings in Madrid and in Riyadh are criminal acts but not war.

European governments perceive terrorism primarily as criminal acts that are facilitated by diverse political, social and economic crises as well as by differences in culture and religion. These different perspectives in the United States and in Europe lead to divergent conclusions. The success of the US military approach is questioned and it is a view maintained among many European governments that the root causes of terrorism cannot be fought primarily with military means. A broadly based concept of judicial measures against criminal acts is required, and political, cultural and economic programmes to reduce the clashes in attitudes are needed too. Both these assessments, with their primarily judicial or military reactions, have important consequences for the means and methods of exercising the state monopoly of violence. Criminal acts are most effectively countered by police and judiciary actions, in which the military can, at best, play a supportive role.

The first phase of the 'war against terror' aimed at punishing and destroying Al Qaeda and its supporters. A second phase began before this first phase was concluded. The US government insisted that it would not tolerate the unholy trinity of terrorism, weapons of mass destruction and 'rogue states' (Gordon 2004). (The possible role of the military in fighting terrorism is analyzed in Chapter 7.)

Another consequence of 11 September is the international interest in countries that did not get much attention previously or which had lost attention. So-called basket cases, such as Somalia, Afghanistan and Sudan, are now of interest to the international community since they could possibly function as 'safe havens' for terrorists. To prevent terrorists from operating from their territory, in the opinion of some, notably in the US such countries would consequently then require regime change and a stabilization strategy involving nation-building, which has experienced a renaissance in recent years (Matthies 1995, Hippler 2003). This notion about international threats has direct effects on the way armed forces are deployed or on the implementation of international assistance programmes. To legitimize the deployment of the Bundeswehr in Afghanistan, for example, German Minister of Defence, Peter Struck, has tried to argue that Europe's 'security is also defended at the Hindukush' (according to Mutz 2004).

International interventions

Limited reactions

Given the experience of the post–Cold War years in conflict prevention, peacekeeping, post-conflict reconstruction and nation-building, there was never a magic bullet or a panacea to ensure the security of people, the prevention or resolution of conflicts or the restoration of the state monopoly of force. On the contrary, the instant cure-all approaches usually have long-term negative effects and have often exacerbated conflicts. The present military operations in Iraq are a case in point. Yet, due to public pressures and ethical considerations, the international community usually treats conflicts as urgent and short-term problems that have to be solved as soon as possible through conflict management and mediation, humanitarian intervention with civil and military means, emergency relief and aid, peacekeeping, peace enforcement and peace building, post-conflict reconstruction and nation-building, democratization and development etc. (Pape 1997, Debiel and Nuscheler 1996, OECD/DAC 2001). Most of these efforts are based on genuine humanitarian concerns. But a critical evaluation of the strengths and weaknesses of these approaches in concrete conflicts does not provide very encouraging results. Programme planning usually promises more than what implementation can provide since time limitations and orientation towards immediate success stories usually overlook the complexity of conflicts. The reasons for these limitations are the programme-inherent contradictions and the shortcomings of the proposed remedies.

The chosen geographic focus is often too narrow, especially in post-conflict reconstruction. Reactions are then confined within sovereign state borders, although conflicts usually have external spill-over and spin-in effects. Economic agendas introduced on the coat tails of international intervention have tended to disregard crucial aspects of war economies, especially their regional linkages and the functional aspects of shadow economic activity (Pugh and Cooper 2004). Ignoring these linkages often results in partial and fragile settlements.

Since the end of the Cold War the international community has responded with humanitarian interventions against violent conflicts more often than before. More importantly, it is increasingly difficult to distinguish in field programmes between military intervention and humanitarian assistance. The use of private military and security companies in such programmes results in a complete blurring of roles and responsibilities. As a result, complications in overcoming crises and the emergence of competition between different actors are not uncommon – to the detriment of those in need of assistance.

Whether military protection for civilians in war and war-like situations is possible at all, remains an open question. In Rwanda for example, a robust military intervention could have prevented the worst atrocities. Yet in contrast, the air attacks of NATO in Kosovo, bombings intended to stop the flow of refugees and lead to the provision of shelter to them, actually exacerbated the refugees' agony. Despite the fact that there are many threats in societies that cannot be countered by military force, governments have tended to pursue progressively more military-based policies (Buzan, Waever and de Wilde 1998).

The UN peacekeeping force in Somalia in 1992, for example, was legitimized on humanitarian grounds. The aim of the UN troops was to protect convoys that delivered food to the starving population. New and alternate motives, not necessarily mandated by the UN resolution, were, however, quickly added. US troops, which were never under the command of the UN, declared, with public fanfare, the capture of the warlord General Mohamed Farah Aideed as their main aim. The humanitarian concerns were transformed step by step into a security postulate and a symbolic and prestigious political and military objective (Wulf 2002, 102).

Armed forces need to be reorganized for the new tasks abroad, even those armed forces that have long since co-operated internationally, such as the NATO forces as their tasks are mainly outside NATO countries' territories. Other forces also engage more than before in international co-operation or are being transformed into integrated international armies. Mandates for such missions are not always clear, rather diffuse and not always democratically legitimized. On the one hand, policy makers and non-state actors use military power and violence more and more as a political and economic tool; while on the other hand, the outsourcing of military functions to private companies constitutes a withdrawal of the state's responsibility, namely to provide security to its people.

Inconsistencies of interventions

The quest for security, prevention of violence and re-establishment of the state monopoly of force in weak states has come up against and also reinforced a series of inconsistencies and contradictions:

First: the UN applies the enforcement of liberal and democratically motivated humanitarian interventions selectively. The Security Council does not mandate UN troops for peacekeeping or peace enforcement missions in all pertinent circumstances, for well known reasons of political compromise that are not always rational and for a lack of financial, human and material resources.

Second: many empirical cases illustrate that democratization, although a cherished value, has often coincided with new forms of militarism, violent conflict and insecurity. This is probably no accident. One reason is that democratization raises the level of political and economic expectations. It is, however, resisted, often forcibly, by those whose power and privileges are questioned (Cawthra and Luckham 2003). Problems worsen if the expectations of democracy and development are not fulfilled and when the process of democratization fails to deliver the initial promises. Equally, as European history shows, periods of intense violence such as the French Revolution preceded the establishment of stable democratic and peaceful political structures.

Third: the increased number of international interventions is primarily the result of increased demand: to protect victims of wars such as refugees, to prevent genocide or ethnic cleansing, or to re-install a toppled government. However, there are also non-altruistic supply side motives that have facilitated the trend towards increasing numbers of so-called humanitarian actions. After the Cold War the military was in search of new vocations and needed to demonstrate a *raison d'être* (Wulf 2002). Armed forces suddenly had excess capacities that humanitarian organizations lacked, especially in air transport and logistics. It seemed natural for the military to offer its services and for governments to call on them to provide assistance. Hence, military mission creep played a role too, not just humanitarian necessity.

Fourth: in reality, although humanitarian assistance may be delivered with impartial and neutral intent, civil or military actions always have political and sometimes military repercussions. They are an intervention into other societies and the political and humanitarian goals cannot be separated from each other (Weiss 1999, 214). In complex emergencies especially, for example in running a refugee camp, humanitarian aid can exacerbate conflict by supporting the war economy or providing legitimacy to combatants (Anderson 1999). The collateral damage of well-intended assistance can be enormous, particularly since the continuation of fighting will always affect civilians.

Fifth: humanitarian organizations pursue their own agendas too; they do not have only pure humanitarian motives. They are interested, for example, in receiving a large share of the collected donations. Humanitarian assistance is the business of numerous organizations. They are not guided exclusively by the requirements of the needy but have their own organizational interests and goals too.

Sixth: two paradoxes of conflict prevention and post-conflict reconstruction can be observed. The present trend of humanitarian interventions and especially post-conflict rehabilitation, such as in Afghanistan, leads to more and more primarily police, not military, tasks for the military – yet that is not what they have been trained for. And, paradoxically, the armed forces are more involved in war fighting in the *name* of prevention of conflicts and in reconstruction programmes than before.

Seventh: despite the predicted demise of the state and the dire experiences with weak, collapsed or failed states, it is still national governments which remain critical in international actions, whether it is a decision to fight war, intervene in conflicts, arm or disarm. Notwithstanding the intensification of globalization, the quest for global governance, international norm building, and the growth of civil society and multinational corporations, international policy remains decidedly state-centric (Zartman 1995, Schlichte 1996 and 1998, Milliken 2003).

Finally: difficulties in conflict prevention, peace settlements and post-conflict reconstruction are often underestimated or purposely downplayed and, in the absence of full-fledged peace treaties, partial settlements remain fragile and are easily disrupted if reservoirs of violence remain or peace spoilers are not under control. These peace spoilers pursue a course of continued fighting for a variety of economic, political and social reasons since they feel they can profit more from continued war than from a peace settlement and the re-establishment of the monopoly of violence. The tragic experiences of numerous failed peace treaties and ceasefires in many African conflicts (Angola, Sudan, Sierra Leone, DRC) are proof of the negative role that peace spoilers can play. They are the main hindrance to the establishment of the state monopoly of violence (Pugh 2003). In cases of post-conflict reconstruction, peace spoilers draw their strength from sources often from within their society, such as the warlords and war entrepreneurs in Afghanistan who also function as drug dealers. It is always a dilemma of either disregarding economic criminals or co-opting them into state building (Pugh and Cooper 2004).

Premises and hypothesis

In spite of all these inconsistencies, contradictions and paradoxes certain stopgap measures seem necessary to prevent the worst. Military interventions are not an alternative to diplomacy nor the only and unavoidable alternative to end violent conflicts. Governments have not always used all possible political means before the military was used 'as a last resort'. The primacy of political processes is essential before a conflict turns violent or escalates into war and also during post-conflict reconstruction, since the demonstration or deployment of military power through external intervention can exacerbate conflicts and worsen the situation of people who are meant to be protected through this very military intervention.

If the aim is to control violence, force may have to be used. The so-called Brahimi Report (UNGA 2001a) concludes in the executive summary, that '... no amount of good intensions can substitute for the fundamental ability to project credible force if complex peacekeeping, in particular, is to succeed'. But the criteria for the use or non-use of force need to be clearly spelt out. Despite numerous reports, the Security Council of the United Nations, the highest organ for peace and security in the world, does not apply such criteria in its decision-making process when deciding for or against the use of force.

Economic reconstruction is a means to make societies (not necessarily the nation state) functioning again. Economic development can prevent conflicts and crises. One of the conditions is that the population can participate in this development and that the development is not concentrated exclusively in rich but isolated zones in a sea of poverty.

The realities in many countries often mean that there will be no peace without a reform of the security sector. Security sector reform aims at improving the security of the population. To expect peace and to stabilize a society without touching the security-sector is wishful thinking. Security-sector reform addresses in particular the breakdown of law and order and the loss of the state monopoly of violence. Since the military, police and judiciary are the ultimate agents of the organized institutions of state force it is essential to make them efficient and accountable. Security is important for governance and inappropriate security structures can contribute to weak governance and intensified violent conflicts. Security sector reform tries to improve the situation through institutional reforms.

Democratic, civilian control over security forces is crucial for the provision of security in the interests of the population (Ball *et al.* 2003, Hendrickson and Karkoszka 2002, Brzoska 2003, OECD/DAC 2001 and 2004).

The premise of this book is that both internationalization of the armed forces and outsourcing military functions bear certain risks for the maintenance of the state monopoly of violence or for its re-establishment in weak states or in post-war societies. The monopoly of violence does not exist in countries with looming violence markets. Outsourcing of military missions undermines the monopoly of force even in stable and democratic societies. Figure I.1 earlier maintains that privatization in violence markets (privatization I) contributes to the need for military interventions (internationalization I). These military deployments necessitate internationalizing the organization of the armed forces (internationalization II). Outsourcing military functions to the private sector is then a top-down reaction (privatization II) to cope with the increasing number of military missions abroad.

Privatization of violence and of military tasks may not be the cause of conflicts. However, it has influenced the way and means of how violence is exercised and how national and international authorities try to prevent violence. Privatization is the most direct method to give up or to be forced to abandon the state monopoly of force. The trend of privatizing is particularly worrying since neither the actors in violence markets nor private military companies are democratically controlled. Their role in the wars in Africa, the Middle East and in the Balkans contributes to the anxiety over a potentially long-lasting damage to the state monopoly of force.

It is expected that the traditional military tasks (defence of the home territory) will continue to decrease or may even be totally abandoned in some countries or regions. International military commitments, in contrast, will continue to increase. Armed forces that are deployed simultaneously in several conflicts and are tasked with multiple interventions might easily be over-burdened. This is especially relevant in cases when armed forces have not been systematically restructured and are still oriented to Cold War organizational structures and doctrines. Strains on the armed forces are not merely a temporary phenomenon. It is also a question of the size of the armed forces and its capacity too. With the general tendency in many countries to put a cap on the personnel size of the military, it seems that governments, in the face of numerous interventions in conflicts, will consider and deploy private companies as a viable alternative.

Nationally organized armed forces are inadequate to prevent or end international conflicts in crises regions or to counter terrorism. Furthermore, democratic and civilian controls are not properly instituted in such international deployments – not even if the military interventions are mandated by the highest international authority on peace and security, the Security Council of the United Nations. Nationally organized armed forces are outdated, given the new international tasks. But considerations of prestige and pride, and national political and economic interest, are a barrier to establishing a truly integrated international armed force. However, gradual processes of such internationalization do take place in UN or regionally formed peace missions or in coalitions of the willing. The EU is presently moving, although only to a certain extent, in the direction of establishing supranational armed forces.

The democratic control of internationalized armed forces is more complex than of national forces. Tasking private military firms with military tasks complicates the democratic control even more or might make it impossible in certain situations. However, armed forces tasked with international interventions in the name of the defence of human rights, the promotion of democracy and the prevention or ending of war are only credible if they operate on the basis of effective democratic control. Otherwise, there is the danger of misusing the armed forces for purposes other than humanitarian.

The need for efficient state structures in post-conflict societies is obvious. International interventions and reconstruction programmes are geared to facilitate the creation or re-establishment of such central state authorities. The initiators of these international activities often ignore the strengths and weaknesses of local structures and the effects of globalization. It is questionable if nation-building is the adequate concept for all post-conflict societies and the only means to overcome crises. The notion of failed states and erosion of state authority presupposes the necessity, practicability and functionality of structures of the nation-state. But such structures are weak in many regions or have never existed in others. The Western perception of nation-building, democracy, and of providing the public goods of security and welfare are often alien in conflict-prone societies. The experiences in nation-building of the last few years prove that nation-building is no shortcut or an alternative to a long-term process of overcoming violent structures. The process of establishing state structures or nation states is too narrow a focus and an approach that overlooks cultural and societal structures. The idea of re-establishing the *state* monopoly of force at the nation state level is nowadays especially insufficient. The concept of global governance and the establishment and enforcement of international norms require a *public monopoly of force* at the local, national, regional and global levels.

Part I
Concepts

1
Internationalizing Armed Forces and their Deployment

The war in Iraq that commenced in spring 2003 is a reminder that the application of violence and military power continues to be an important element in international relations. Moreover, the actions of the war coalition under the US leadership are a graphic expression that the unilateral initiation of war, without a mandate of the United Nations (UN), is by no means a thing of the past.

Despite the war experience in Iraq, which rather serves imperial power politics than multilateral co-operation based on international law, two trends have emerged since the end of the 1980s: *First*, international military interventions have evidently increased, particularly those led by the UN and also by regional organizations such as the Economic Community of West African States (ECOWAS), NATO, the European Union (EU) and most recently by the African Union (AU) too. This policy is an obvious diversion from intervention policies during the Cold War. The East–West antagonism had led on numerous occasions to blockades in the UN Security Council; vetoes prevented UN peace missions. Yet today international military interventions have emerged as the primary task of armed forces, normally carried out in ad hoc alliances or coalitions of the willing. I have classified the rising number of outside international military interventions in the introductory chapter as 'internationalization I'. *Second*, this development is a challenge for the armed forces since they are confronted with new types of missions, requiring a new organization and new doctrines. To cope with these new challenges, international co-operation and an international orientation of the military organization are vital. I have classified this trend as 'internationalization II'.

John F. Kennedy called for a new world order on the basis of an assertive multilateralism, which envisioned, with similar optimism as

Kant, a pacified world. Pessimists, in contrast, see barbaric conflicts and anarchy, asymmetric wars and the need for military power to control conflicts. Independent of either the optimistic or the pessimistic perspective as a guide to international politics, the armed forces must be reformed and restructured if they are to prevent conflict for humanitarian reasons or to react to the new wars. International democratic control of the armed forces has not developed in parallel to the international military interventions and the reorganization of the forces. A culture of accountability of the decision-makers is glaringly absent. Democratic control, if exercised at all, takes place at the national level as in the past but not internationally. This is one of the central arguments in this book. Of equal importance is the description of the privatizing of the central, state instruments of violence, which is described in Chapter 2.

Which authority has the legitimacy to authorize the multilateral use of armed forces, and who can exercise such a mandate to apply military force in international peace enforcement most effectively? Are the rules, regulations and norms to control the military created during the last few centuries in democratic nation states sufficient for the new international necessities or should they be adjusted to comply with democratic values? Modern armed forces developed in parallel to the formation of the nation state (Tilly 1990). Private armies disappeared during this process and standing armies, based on citizen armies, have developed since the French revolution. Yet even citizen armies were never exactly as they were ideally modelled; they were never pure citizen armies, since they had a professional officer corps as their backbone.

The creation of the state monopoly of force was an important part of the establishment of nation states. At the same time, civilian control over the armed forces and the accountability of the executive strengthened democratic rules. The promoters of democracy challenged the monarchs' rights to make decisions about the recruitment, financing and deployment of armed forces. The control over the monopoly of force was a decisive factor for the democratization of societies in Europe.

Nowadays, the authority for decision-making about the deployment of troops has been progressively delegated to international organizations. Even though national governments reserve the right to eventually decide about the deployment of their armed forces, the international expectations and pressures, especially among allies and coalition partners, is so immense that a refusal to participate in peacekeeping, peace enforcement or other interventions will disturb foreign policy relations. To satisfy the notion of global governance those parts of national sovereignty that are delegated to international bodies should actually fall under international, civilian and democratic control. The creation and establishment of new instruments and methods to control the armed forces and other institutions of the state monopoly of force are a prerequisite if a centralized organization of a society, the nation state, changes due to internationalization and globalization. This is however presently not the case as the results of the chapters on the United Nations and the European Union in this book (Chapters 3 and 5) suggest, and it is not foreseeable that this gap in democratic control will soon be closed.

The changed role of the military

The role of the military in the nation state is fundamentally changed both by globalization and by the growing number of new international interventions. More and more countries have given up their conscript armies since the end of the Cold War. They rely on professional forces comprising specialists who want to fulfil a military career. Moskos, William and Segal (2000b, 1–5) classify the present development of the professional armed forces as *post-modern*. They are a product of today. The types of *modern armies* that date from the nineteenth century up to the end of the Second World War were based on the concept of citizen soldiers. The *late modern* types of armed forces, as they are termed by Moskos, William and Segal, prevailed from the mid-twentieth century until the end of the Cold War. They were mass-conscripted armies with a strong professional military component. The frequently used term 'post-modern' questions established wisdom and fixed values and introduces relativism. Constituent parts of post-modernism are pluralism, fragmentation, heterogeneity and deconstruction. Post-modern armed forces orient themselves around these varied developments in today's society, and in doing so this questions traditional military values. A case in point is the possibility for women to enter the military in many European countries. Equally, armed forces no longer stress so much on patriotism as was the case in most of the previous century, though patriotism is not completely absent nowadays either. In parallel to globalization and internationalization, military values of the past have eroded. The ideal that the armed forces are citizen soldiers is no longer; they have been through a process of professionalization and developed a professional ethos.

Moskos, William and Segal (2000b, 2) characterize post-modern armed forces through five major organizational changes: 'One is the increasing interpenetrability of civilian and military spheres, both structurally and culturally. The second is the diminution of differences within the armed services based on branch of service, rank, and combat versus support roles. The third is the change in the military purpose from fighting wars to missions that would not be considered military in the traditional sense. The fourth change is that the military forces are used more in international missions authorized (or at least legitimated) by entities beyond the nation state. A final change is the internationalization of military forces themselves'.

Whether the classification into modern, late modern and post-modern is convincing or not is not of importance here. For this book it is interesting that the authors describe a changed role of the armed forces in a changed world. The first change mentioned by Moskos, Williams and Segal, the increasing interpenetrability of civilian and military spheres, as well as the fourth and fifth changes, namely international deployment and the internationalization of forces (which I have called internationalization I and II), are of great interest for this book. I address these issues in Chapters 3 and 6 and I also take up the third aspect, the change from the fighting role of the military to new or less traditional missions. Their second point about change, the diminution of differences within the armed services, is not of interest in this book.

Statistical evidence verifies the increase in international military interventions. This trend is clearly visible. But truly internationalized military institutions and structures are still not very common; though a beginning of this development can be seen in the efforts of the European Union to create a rapid reaction force.[6] The UN Charter of 1945 calls for the establishment of UN military structures, a truly international force; this however has never materialized. Further, the UN standby forces requested in the UN Agenda for Peace of 1992 did not find many supporters among the UN members either.

Naturally, different military traditions result in different concepts of the future roles of the armed forces in the international arena. A certain scepticism about standing and conscript armies in Britain and the United States at the end of the nineteenth century contrasted distinctly from French military history (Damrosch 2003, 45). Germany's armed forces broke with their tradition after the end of the Second World War. The Soviet Union and their allies had completely different experiences, and both the colonial powers as well as the anti-colonial history of many armies in developing countries were strongly influenced by the period of colonization and the anti-colonial struggle. The following examples, though far from complete, illustrate the variety of different philosophies of the general trend towards the internationalization of armed forces.

The military in some countries, for example in the Netherlands, has been somewhat marginalized due to drastic cuts in military expenditures and reductions of personnel strengths. In other countries, such as in Israel and in Switzerland, the conscripted armed forces remain visibly nationally orientated and geared to territorial defence; they are obvious exceptions to the general trend. The Canadian military was the first to formally dismiss traditional territorial defence missions; they were restructured on the basis of unambiguous political guidelines and concentrate today no longer on internal defence missions but rather on intervention in international crises, especially on UN-sponsored peace missions (Hampson 2003). Although the government in Germany presently still holds on to the model of a conscript army (and thus it does not fulfil one of the criteria for a post-modern force), it is in a process of restructuring, which, similar to the Canadian experience, gives up territorial defence and prioritizes international deployments. Ireland has undergone a similar development, in which the government speaks about a 'culture of peacekeeping' (quoted in Mingst 2003, 69). Considering their military recruiting practices and the gradual switch from territorial defence to selective engagements in crises regions, both Germany's and Denmark's military concept can be classified as selective, optional and ad hoc.[7] Most transformation countries that have become or aspire to become members of NATO and/or the EU orient their armed forces towards participation in international operations (Heinemann-Grüder 2003, Karkoszka 2003). The Indian armed forces too are prepared to respond quickly to calls from the UN (Thakur and Banerjee 2003), and in some countries, for example in Bangladesh and Fiji, participation in international peace missions are a method of financing the military budget from UN payments. The ECOWAS forces in West Africa have been deployed in several countries of the region as UN peacekeeping and peace enforcement troops, and, after much hesitation, the South African government has finally decided to take over regional responsibility in African conflict regions (for a case study on South Africa see Chapter 4).

The larger the military power and the capabilities of the armed forces (as in the United States), the more the military is in the societal driving seat (as in China), and the more the armed forces are a project of national prestige (as in Russia), correspondingly the more are these armies an instrument to pursue national interests and a symbol of great power ambitions. Hence, it is no surprise that internationalization of the armed forces in these countries is far from the model described earlier.

Civil–military relations and the control of the armed forces

Civil–military relations concern the role of the military in society, and civilian control of the military means that civil authorities are in charge of and are responsible for decisions in security and defence policy. This includes the deployment of forces abroad. The military leadership has to accept and to implement the judgement of the civil authority. This does not prevent the military from influencing political decisions. On the contrary: In modern democratic societies it is expected that military expertise be taken into consideration in security and defence policy matters.

A prerequisite for applying the state monopoly of force is civilian control over the armed forces as one of the central instruments of the state. Such control must be legitimized by law. At the same time, this instrument of force must be given the resources to function effectively. This is the core of the problematic of civil–military relations.

A characteristic of civil–military relations in democracies is the implementation of democratically legitimized power over organized state violence. Democratic rule is more than civilian primacy or dominance of the military since the military could also be, and has often been, misused by civilian politicians. Anglo-Saxon political analysts have studied the complicated and often controversial civil–military relations most intensively. Their research concentrated mainly on their home countries and on developing countries, while today another focus is the development of civil–military relations in the transformation societies of the former Eastern block. The centre of attention in the past was the control held by civilian institutions rather than the democratic norms and rules which have been taken up in the debate of security sector reform or security sector governance under the label of accountability and oversight (Ball *et al.* 2003, Brzoska 2003, Wulf 2004a). The terms 'Innere Führung' (internal leadership) and 'citizens in uniform' arose in the German debate demonstrating particular concern about the integration of the German armed forces, re-established in the mid-1950s in a democratic society.

The debate in the Anglo-Saxon literature illustrates how important the regulation of civil–military relations is. But despite the gradually increasing trend of armed forces' internationalization, civil–military relations in the international arena are regulated on an ad hoc basis; their implementation is very much by accident. The challenges of civilian and democratic control are the following:

- to prevent praetorianism, that is a direct intervention by the armed forces into politics, and to avoid too strong a military influence or the pressures of their self-interest,
- to avoid the misuse of the military by civilian authorities,
- to institute democratic principles and norms and to establish rules and politically binding decision-making processes.

The unconditional acceptance of civilian primacy over the military, democratic control and the existence of the necessary civilian defence expertise are preconditions for a legitimate authority over the armed forces (Heinemann-Grüder 2003, 26).

The Anglo-Saxon literature in no way questions the need for civilian rule over the armed forces. However, the ways and means of practicing this control are controversial. One can distinguish between two main schools of thought, the 'separatists' and the 'fusionists'. The separatists expect the military to stick to its profession and its military ethos and to remain politically neutral. The separatist school warns against the potential militarization of foreign and security policy. Fusionists, in contrast, expect a direct participation of the armed forces and want to make use of their expertise in security policy. While the separatists emphasize the differences between the military and civilian society, the fusionists plead for partnership and co-operation, even concordance on the basis of common values (Schiff 1995). Neither of the two schools questions the final authority of civilian decision-making, but both underestimate the importance of the self-interest of the military in security policy – the officers' career ambitions, the military's social status, the desire to procure modern equipment and so on.

Huntington (1957), who is till today an important representative of the model to separate military and civilian spheres, on the one hand emphasized in his seminal publication, *The Soldier and the State*, the uniqueness of the armed forces and underlined the significance of their professionalism that he considered a necessity to fight and win wars. On the other hand he wanted to reconcile the gap between the armed forces and politics in a society that was traditionally critical of the military. Huntington noted an ideological divide between a generally conservative officer corps and a liberal and individualistic civilian society (Feaver, Kohn and Cohn 2001, 2). An additional factor that is not in the focus of this debate is the question as to whether the divide between the military and civilian society is a result of a disinterested public which no longer feels threatened by strong military adversaries (Born 2004, 214).

Huntington distinguished between 'objective control' of the military, which is established through the professionalism of soldiers as managers of violence, the autonomous nature of the military profession, the apolitical attitude and the uniqueness of military tasks, and 'subjective control', which is established through maximizing civilian control and taming the military by joining civilian and military elites (Heinemann-Grüder 2003, 29, Cohen 2001, 434). Huntington's key to civilian control of the armed forces was the clear separation of military and civilian tasks and a systematic division of labour between military and politics. He emphasized that the profession of the military could be compared to other professions such as medicine or law. All of them do their job on the basis of expertise. The patient decides on the basis of information from his doctor if an operation should be performed, but he does not interfere with how the operation *is* performed. The soldier, as the manager of violence, has the expertise of how to apply force but does not decide if force *is* applied (Cohen 2001, 433).

Janowitz (1960) criticized how definitively Huntington juxtaposed military and political spheres, and claimed that the armed forces were well integrated into society and that a civil–military gap or ideological divide did not exist. If a large gap between the different professionalisms in the military and civil society did emerge, and the military became unresponsive to civilian control, the civilians would withdraw their support for the military (Feaver, Kohn and Cohn 2001, 3). Janowitz rejected the separatist school of thought and appealed for pragmatic professionalism and co-operation. Instead of separations he and his school propagated a fusion or partnership model (Bland 1999), since military and civilian spheres in society were not antagonistic. The co-operative relations and concordance between military and civilian cultures were important, and not so much which institution had the responsibility for security and defence policy (Schiff 1995).

There is no doubt that the military is characterized by a number of specifics. Differences do exist between the military and civilian sectors, including in those areas that are of importance for civilian and democratic control. Former soldiers who became political leaders, such as De Gaulle and Eisenhower, have emphasized the specifics of the military profession. Even a liberal, democratic society has these differences. They are manifest in the military hierarchy that includes a systematic dominance by superiors who have a whole catalogue of sanctions at their disposal. The traditional masculine military service offers another example as it is still not a mirror image of the gender roles in democratic societies, even though the service is now open to women. Military service is still male dominated (Feaver, Kohn and Cohn 2000, 1, Heinemann-Grüder 2003, 31). A US military journal writes about the 'functional imperative that prizes success in war above all else' which 'implies behaviours and values markedly different from those predominant in civil society' (Hooker 2003/4, 5–6). Subordination and obedience are fundamentals in military hierarchy and stand in contrast to liberal and individualistic values in the non-military sphere. Moskos, Williams and Segal (2000b, 6), however, identify an erosion of traditional military values in post-modern armed forces through the interpenetrability of civilian and military arenas in society.

The drastic changes since the 1990s have revitalized the debate about the civil–military gap, especially in the United States. Moreover, the experiences in the wars in Iraq and in Afghanistan have re-posed the question – in a similar way as occurred during the Vietnam War – as to whether the armed forces have drifted away from the core values of society. The proponents of the fusionist school, who believe that the armed forces must be integrated into society, maintain that this is no longer the case. The abolition of conscription has exacerbated the split between the military and society. According to this position the military has a different ideology following the recent Afghan and Iraqi wars and following the ending of conscription and is possibly hostile towards civil society. In addition, the military seem to be resisting changes in society, as the debate about homosexuality in the armed forces illustrates. Of course, such differences combined with a lack of civilian control lead not only to frictions between the military and politics but also to military inefficiency.

Huntington's heirs reject the claim of an ideological divide. Some proponents of this school believe the political elite to be ignorant, hostile and not respectful of the military. The political leadership, so they claim, is trying to micro-manage the military. In any case, they argue that the alleged gap in different values is not of relevance, since public opinion in the United States is rock-solid behind the military. The central problem, accordingly, is not one of the military but of the political elite (Feaver, Kohn und Cohn 2001, 4–5).

Strong criticism against the assertion that the military and politics are drifting apart is raised within the armed forces and the question is asked on what empirical proof this allegation is made. The existing tensions are exaggerated, it is said, and there is no disagreement between the military and society about basic values (Hooker 2003/4, 7–10). This is not a superfluous academic debate because the type and form of civil–military relations affects directly the way the military intervenes abroad. The military leadership has complained before, during the administration of President Johnson, about political interference into military matters and micromanagement style, when Johnson himself selected bombing targets in Vietnam. Conversely, the military had the opposite experience during the Gulf War at the beginning of the 1990s. In contrast to the Vietnam War, the relations between the military and political elite were based on trust and mutual respect. The government was convinced that the military would pursue the best strategy and battlefield tactics, resulting in a military victory. The story of civil–military relations in the Gulf War, however, is not one of harmony and clearly defined military and political roles. According to other observers, it was 'one of blurring and muddle, culminating in a remarkable collapse of civilian oversight' (Cohn 2001, 455). The conclusion of Lloyd J. Matthews, the editor of the journal of the US Army War College, illustrates how tense and hostile these divergences were. He warned his colleagues in 1996 that 'there will be instances where civilian officials with Napoleon complexes and micromanaging mentalities are prompted to seize the reins of operational control' (quoted in Cohn 2001, 436).

This debate presumes that high intensive civilian control will be detrimental to military efficiency and will lead to inflexibility or might unnecessarily delay military intervention. Such doubts surfaced, for example, in the debate of the German Bundestag (parliament) when parliamentary authorization for deployment of German troops was discussed in 2004. The defence ministry requested to have advance authorization for deployment, up to a certain level of personnel strength, in parts of Afghanistan outside Kabul, if this would be required. The forces did not want to wait for a lengthy parliamentary debate in order to be able to react quickly and flexibly when needed. But parliamentary authorization and oversight should not be discussed exclusively with a military efficiency view in mind. Parliamentary participation in the political debate and decision-making process is a necessary condition, according to Damrosch (2003, 58 and 60), for the parliament to serve a constructive function in building public support for military engagements.

This explanation of civil–military relations indicates how complex the situation is at the national level in democratic countries. In countries with weakly legitimated or illegitimate governments, democratic control is usually completely lacking and there is a danger of the militarization of political processes. Governments not only run the risk of being toppled by the military, the military is also threatened of being manipulated by politics. A coup d'état by the military is but the most extreme form of interference in politics. Even in democratic societies, faced with the threat of war and other threatening situations, civil rights are restricted and liberal values endangered. In addition, the armed forces are being tasked with missions outside civil and democratic control. The US 'war against terror', with the Patriot Act, points in this direction.

The engagement of private military companies and their growing activities in recent years is an additional complication to upholding the delicate civil-military balance. The relationship between the military and private military firms is not without a certain degree of tension that affects the operations of the armed forces. But more important is the fact that neither the executive government nor parliament has effective control over these new actors on the battlefield (as explained in Chapter 2).

The obviously insufficient democratic controls of the armed forces and of private military companies at the national level are even more visible and distinct on the international plane. Moskos, Williams and Segal (2000b, 11) conclude in their analysis that 'we can, for now, confidently state that the dominant trend is a blurring of the lines between the military and civilian entities, both in structure and in culture. This permeability between military and civilian structures is a major new historical phenomenon'. If this conclusion is valid, then the evolution of new types of civil–military relations at the national and more so at the international level is both a challenge and a chance. However, as I discuss earlier, the international community is far from establishing the accepted national democratic practices of civil–military relations with regard to international interventions.

In general, state institutions are accountable to those who are affected by their decisions. Democratic norms imply that decision-makers are accountable and responsible to the elected representatives of the voters. Usually the executive government takes the decision to deploy troops abroad; in several countries the executive requires parliamentary authorization for the deployment decision and the government is accountable, in addition, for its implementation. Thus parliament might have a say over the whole life cycle of an intervention, from the start until the troops are brought home (Hänggi 2004, 4).

Born and Hänggi (2004) correctly point at a democratic deficit not only in international and regional organizations but also in the national context. Decisions in foreign and security policy, despite noticeable constitutional differences in many democracies, seem to be one of the least democratic policy areas, and the control and oversight rights of parliaments are not very advanced. They speak about a 'double democratic deficit' in decisions about war and peace – nationally and internationally. My own conclusion, explained in more detail later, is that there is a qualitative difference in the democratic deficit at the two levels. Rules and regulations do exist nationally in many countries, even though they are often insufficient to comply with democratic norms. However, decisions in most international organizations are not taken democratically and rules and regulations are but rudimentary or non-existent.[8]

The democratic deficit in international interventions

Lack of democratic controls

Democracy, in its purest form, implies the rule of law (accepted norms which are applied in politics including mechanisms for sanctions against the violators of such norms) and secondly majority decisions based on elections (as the principle for political decision-making). Both principles are inadequately developed for security and peace policy at the national level and underdeveloped or completely lacking at the various international levels. This problem is common in the decision-making processes concerning war and peace, but not absent in numerous other internal fields either.

Democracy theory differentiates between four different types of democratic legitimacy: First, result-oriented legitimacy, expecting a majority acceptance of political actions (*government for the people*). Second, inter-governmental legitimacy based on peoples' participation in decision-making. Elections are the mechanism in this form of legitimacy (*government by the people*). Third, supra-national legitimacy, also based on peoples' participation but beyond the national plane, as is partly emerging in the EU (*government by the people*). Fourth, legitimacy through international law accepted not only in democratic societies but also instituted as a global norm. Concurring to international norms can give legitimacy to international decisions, even if they are not democratic (*government for the people*) (Wagner 2004).

The mandate to deploy UN troops through a UN Security Council resolution has the highest authority and legitimacy internationally, despite the fact that such resolutions are not democratically decided. Critique can be raised at several levels:

First: international norms are often not only interpreted differently, which, though being a normal reaction, can itself lead to controversial conclusions, but in addition some governments have the power to deploy their military or threaten its deployment even in cases beyond the realm of self-defence. This is a clear violation of international norms, yet nevertheless common practice.

Second: the permanent members of the Security Council can veto majority decisions. Although this is grounded in the UN charter, it is all the same not democratic. Furthermore, the veto-wielding powers of the Security Council and their allies are not interested in an enhanced role for all UN members in resolutions on peace operations. Decisions taken by the General Assembly, such as the 'uniting-for-peace' resolution in the case of the Korean War, are not normal procedures according to the UN Charter, but have recently not even been considered in critical cases (such as, for example, in the Kosovo War), even though this would have been possible, given the precedent of the decision during the Korean War. A strengthened role combined with wider participation of other UN member states would challenge the dominance of the veto powers and might restrict their room for manoeuvre.

Third: the work in the UN and in most regional organizations takes place as inter-governmental processes, based on co-operation between governments. Democratic control is exercised, if at all, only at the national level, in as far as parliaments hold the executive accountable for their policy in the UN. An international parliament or inter-parliamentary bodies do not exist.

Finally: the democratic deficit is manifest in international organizations since non-elected and non-democratic governments have full rights in the decision-making bodies – among them, many governments that are opposed to the establishment of democratic norms in their own country. Democracy has spread among the UN members and more members can today be classified as democracies than ever before. But 35 per cent of the world's population live in countries classified as not free, 21 per cent in partly free countries and only 44 per cent in free countries (Freedom House 2004).

The hiatus between the growing power of international organizations and the deficit of democratic norms and rules is a great challenge for democracy (UNDP 2002, 101–122). The global norm is the deficit in democratic norms (Hänggi 2004, 5). The division of power, as it is known in democracies, is absent in international organizations. The UN has neither a legislature, nor an executive, but a Secretariat with a Secretary General at the helm. It is executive governments that make decisions in the UN and in the relevant regional organizations too. The UN is accountable only to its members' governments, and not to those who they represent, the *demos*, despite the opening sentence in the UN Charter, 'we the peoples'.

That this state of affairs will soon be changed is more than doubtful, even though the foreign ministers of more than 100 democratic states declared in the World Forum on Democracy in Warsaw in the year 2000 to respect and to uphold two key democratic principles: that the legislatures be duly elected and transparent and accountable to the people and, in addition, that civilian, democratic control over the military be established (Ku and Jacobson 2003b, 8).

Democratic goals have been mainly pursued (with a few exceptions such as to some extent in the EU) in national or sub-national territories. Yet, more and more nation state functions are being delegated to international organizations without, however, fully transferring the democratic principles for example of the representation of citizens, transparency, and the accountability of the executive. But the legitimacy of international decisions and their acceptance by the public depends largely on the application of democratic principles. The same standard that is applied in national laws, that individual and institutional or state actions have to be in accord with the law, should also be applied at the international level. In both systems laws are broken, but violations of the law do not imply that the law does not exist (Ku and Jacobson 2003b, 9). The undemocratic character of international relations and international law throughout history makes the process of democratizing this system extremely difficult. Without doubt, Keohane's (1998) conclusion of a democratic deficit in international organizations is still valid.

Decisions to deploy armed forces

To deploy armed forces abroad is a momentous decision. An important aspect is accountability, both for the initial deployment decision and to be continued throughout the period of deployment. The question of if and why international deployments should be democratically governed is easily and very principally to be answered thus: 'In representative democracies, all essential matters should be subject to democratic decision-making processes, that is representatives of the people have the opportunity to influence government policy' (Born 2004, 212). Why should – and actually can – a life-and-death question as war and peace in the world be excluded from this democratic decision-making process? In democratic societies such rules are applied, although often differently and at times controversially. Parliaments usually have a lesser or bigger part in the decision-making process (Born und Hänggi 2004). Yet a similar pattern is completely absent internationally and comparable modalities are not negotiated, even less agreed upon. I describe in Chapter 3 that UN resolutions for peace operations are normally preceded by intensive debates and, in addition, that criticism is raised because often the efficiency is lacking in these deployments. These debates concentrate primarily on military and technical reasoning aiming at more flexible and successful operations. The democratic control of the armed forces that is exercised to some degree in democratic countries plays absolutely no role in these debates or the reform reports. Even in research publications this is not a topical issue, though exceptions are Ku and Jacobson (2003a) as well as Born and Hänggi (2004).

The decision to deploy forces and to intervene with military power must be based on legitimacy. The increasing intensity of UN peace operations makes accountability more urgent each time a new operation begins. The international community introduced during the twentieth century a system to regulate conflicts peacefully, first through the League of Nations and then through the United Nations. This arrangement is a system of collective security. The reasons usually given for legitimizing today's interventions are: the protection of human rights and humanitarian concerns. But criteria for when or when not to intervene have not been codified. Today's structures are certainly more differentiated than during the beginnings of the establishment of the conflict regulatory systems, as the failures of the League of Nations were taken into account in the UN Charter. Nevertheless, due to the non-existence of the United Nations' own troops, it is up to the member states to decide how resolutions for peace operations are implemented. Not even the promoters of a peace operation are required to participate in the operation by providing resources (troops, materiel or funding), although occasionally arm twisting by major countries takes place to 'encourage' member states to contribute troops.

Regional responsibilities

The Charter of the UN allows for the possibility of tasking regional organizations. It is no surprise that regional organizations have in recent years been requested more often to implement UN peace operations. This is largely due to increasing expectations to intervene on humanitarian grounds, and also because of the negative experiences of UN-led military interventions as well as reluctance on the part of a number of governments to engage their own troops. Most regional organizations face similar problems in their regions as does the UN globally. Political differences, scarce resources and the lack of a willingness to engage one's own troops have resulted in inflexibility and inefficiency in the regions too. But the regional approach promises new opportunities for success because regional actors have a more intimate knowledge of the root causes and background of the conflicts. But as mentioned earlier, democratic control is usually lacking in the regional organizations too.

Furthermore, regional initiatives or actions by ad hoc coalitions of UN members are themselves not uncontroversial. Some members are troubled that such coalitions are also carried out to serve parochial, regional or even great power interests and not primarily to establish peace. The visible engagement and interference of former colonial powers in regions of their former colonies raises suspicion and revitalizes old memories (Smith 2003, 97) even if governments are committed to peace operations in a genuine desire to serve humanitarian purposes. Peace operations in addition are perceived as the stabilization of the present world order, which serves the interests and privileges of the rich and militarily dominant powers who are not abashed to defend their positions by interfering into the sovereignty of other countries (Pugh 2004). Humanitarian concern or the promotion of democratic values could also serve other purposes – a situation not new in history at all. Gunboat diplomacy and military occupation has a long tradition and was usually also legitimized by pretending to pursue noble aims.

'Nothing in the present Charter precludes the existence of regional arrangements or agencies for dealing with such matters relating to the maintenance of international peace and security' (article 52). Article 53 of Chapter VIII of the UN Charter gives the Security Council the right, under its authority, to utilize regional organizations for enforcement action where appropriate. The main responsibility remains, however, with the Security Council. The new emphasis on regional solutions and peace operations is promoted to compensate for the lack of UN resources and to be able to intervene more effectively. But the problem of the democratic deficit and lack of democratic rules in implementation is not solved.

NATO's engagement in the former Yugoslavia from 1995 to 1999 illustrates that regional arrangements within a universal security system are not unambiguously codified, especially since NATO with its new claim for global reach is not, strictly speaking, a regional organization. Shawcross (2000, 324) emphasizes the uniqueness of NATO's action which, nonetheless, can now be looked at as a precedent: 'This was the first sustained use of force by NATO in its fifty-year history; the first time force was used to implement Security Council resolutions without specific authorization from the council; the first time a major bombing campaign was launched against a sovereign country to stop crimes against humanity within that country; and the first time that a bombing campaign alone, without assistance of ground troops, appeared to succeed in its aim.' However, it proved to be questionable subsequent to the escalation of the conflict if the proclaimed aim, namely to stop the flow of refugees, succeeded. In addition, heavy political collateral damage resulted from this campaign. Several NATO member countries experienced substantial internal emotional, political controversies, and hostile reactions were publicly displayed internationally both within and outside the UN. Thus, regional actions are no magic bullet or a cure-all concept.

Parliamentary oversight is glaringly lacking globally and in most regional organizations. On the one hand this is surprising, since the co-operation is inter-governmental on the basis of relations between various executive branches of government that should be democratically controlled. On the other hand this is no surprise at all. Hardly any regionally oriented parliaments or inter-parliamentary bodies exist. The few existing bodies, such as the European Parliament or the ECOWAS parliamentary process, have only a marginal say in peace, security and defence policy. (I address this issue with regard to the European Parliament in Chapter 5). Inter-parliamentary arrangements, and the co-operation of the various national parliamentarians, are an exception in this area. One of these exceptions is NATO.

Tension, especially in democratic societies, has resulted from the increase in international military interventions and the internationalization of the armed forces. Although often the aim is the promotion, establishment and upholding of democratic values, at the same time the main decisions to act are taken democratically only in national – but not in the relevant international – forums. In the final chapter I take this issue up again and try to answer the question as to whether democratic principles and norms have a chance to be more appropriately applied in future decisions.

2
Privatizing Power: The 'Lean' State and the Armed Forces

Outsourcing threatening to undermine the monopoly of violence

Privatization of military and security services embraces a wide variety of different concepts and developments. Privatization, occasionally also called commercialization or outsourcing, includes – willingly or unwillingly – giving up state authority in the exercise of the monopoly of violence. As already mentioned in the introduction I differentiate between two principally different types of privatization of power or violence. The first type, bottom-up privatization, describes activities of non-state actors, who use violence for their own political or economic gain. Usually, these actors operate without the authorization of state authorities or even against their explicit wishes, though occasionally representatives of the state system are also accomplices. These non-state actors, who can also be classified as violence entrepreneurs, such as militias, warlords, organized criminals, rebels, insurgents, secessionist movements and gangs, create a situation of insidious insecurity.[9]

The second type of privatization, top-down privatization, which is the focus of this book, is purposely planned and implemented by governments. The aim is to outsource traditional military and state functions to private companies.[10] These companies offer a wide range of services: they work for armed forces not only in war, but also for non-state institutions such as international agencies and humanitarian organizations in post-conflict societies, for governments in their fight against rebels or insurgents, as well as for multinational companies.

The present discussion about the activities of these private military firms, for example in the conflicts in Africa or the Middle East, sometimes creates the impression that this is an entirely new phenomenon – rather than a trend that has developed with ups and downs over centuries. The state monopoly of violence however, as it is ideally defined in theory, has never been fully accomplished, and governments have long entrusted companies or other private actors with diverse military tasks.

The most prominent example is weapons manufacturing. Monarchies and republics in Europe, facilitated by industrialization, established state arsenals to equip the armed forces with modern weapons during the period of nation state formation. Before this period the demands of the armed forces were met by private suppliers. Large private companies again took over the arsenals of the armed forces at the end of the nineteenth century, especially in the United States (Howard 1976, Kaldor 1981, Markusen 2003). In many European countries renouncing state military arsenals, which supplied the armed forces with weapons, munitions and other military equipment, seemed impossible for a long period of time. Today, however, most of these state-managed organizations have been privatized. This process was largely completed during the 1980s and 1990s in those Western European countries in which the defence industry had previously been organized in public enterprises (France, Italy and the United Kingdom). In other countries (e.g. in Germany and Japan) defence production has been privately organized since the rearmament after the end of the Second World War. In the countries of the former socialist block in Eastern Europe, the privatization of defence production is also proceeding and has been accomplished to a large extent. Exceptions to this trend are countries such as China and partly also India, as well as a few countries with smaller weapons production capacities; in these cases weapons are still largely produced in public enterprises or military arsenals.

Today, some defence ministries privatize not only logistical services, training or military planning but increasingly sectors of the infrastructure of the armed forces as well. Companies have been entrusted with the management of military installations, especially military bases, including the servicing of living quarters for soldiers and their families, the management of their fleet of cars, the purchase and stocking of uniforms, the running of canteens and so on. This type of outsourcing is mainly the result of economic reasoning: according to the dominant economic theory the market is better qualified to handle these functions more efficiently than the armed forces themselves. Yet this privatization policy is controversial within the military and is contested by soldiers. In addition, the private sector still needs to produce the empirical evidence that it can contribute to solving some of the budgetary difficulties of the defence sector. Markusen (2003) has presented an analysis of the economic results of privatization of defence production that puts a damper on the enthusiasm for privatization. The anecdotal evidence of the experience with private military companies needs further substantiation for a final judgement. However, the data is interesting enough both for finance and defence ministers to pursue the outsourcing practices.

It is difficult to come to a definitive conclusion as to what kind of privatization in the armed forces goes beyond a certain threshold whereby the monopoly of violence is endangered. The recent wave of privatization however, most markedly developed and implemented in the United States and the United Kingdom (as I detail in Chapter 8) also concerns military functions that are clearly linked to the monopoly of violence, most directly so in combat.

Causes and motives

The causes and motives that lead to the demand for services from private military companies are manifold and sometimes overlapping. The following section attempts to summarize the main reasons. At least eight military, economic, political and ideological reasons for commercialization or privatization can be identified:[11]

First, the availability of qualified military personnel: On the supply side, there are vast quantities of highly qualified military experts who are no longer used in the armed forces. Many countries cut their military budgets and demobilized soldiers after the end of the Cold War. The number of soldiers worldwide declined between 1988 and 2002 from 29 to 20 million (BICC 1996 and 2004). Disarmament during the first half of the 1990s did not only produce a surplus of weapons but one of ex-combatants too. They are now looking for new jobs and can find them in private military companies. Company profiles, presented in their annual reports, in media interviews or on company web sites, indicate that their contract personnel are mainly ex-combatants.[12] Special Forces with fighting experience from a host of countries, as well as Gurkha troops from Nepal and soldiers from Fiji, from the countries of the former Soviet Union, Eastern Europe, Israel, South Africa, and Chile are commonly hired.

Second, reductions in the military sector: The other side of the development mentioned above is the consequence of today's reduced personnel levels despite the fact that some armed forces are over-burdened by the increasing number of military interventions abroad. Outsourcing of military missions is a reaction to bottlenecks in the availability of specialized troops. In the early 1990s, private military companies developed counter-cyclical: while military budgets decreased, their turnover grew. Economic and personnel constraints in the military as well as disarmament facilitated privatization. The reduction of the number of weapons deployed in the armed forces created new business areas for such companies. Many armed forces, for example, no longer procure trainer aircraft but have their pilots trained by private companies who have such equipment at their disposal; these are usually the manufacturers of such aircraft (Aviation Week and Space Technology, 4 August 2003, 44–50 and 13 January 2003, 32).

Third, changes in war fighting: Armed forces tend to use ever more modern equipment. The concepts of 'Revolution in Military Affairs' and 'Network Centric Warfare', aimed at a systematic electronic network of the battlefield with a commander being able to base his commands on the availability of real time data of the fighting, are the most vivid expressions of this general trend. The armed forces themselves, however, are no longer in a position to use and maintain all the systems of this modern equipment; they depend on the logistical services of companies. This is not an entirely new development; but the trend has become omnipresent. An 'army' of engineers and technicians, IT and logistical specialists, pilots and trainers, care for the functioning of the complex weapons systems. Modern armed forces – led first and foremost by US forces – have tried to speed up the modernization of weapons and strategies; it is a process prevalent in many armed forces.

Fourth, demand by weak or besieged governments: Several governments, such as those in Papua New Guinea, Sierra Leone and Zaire, hired private military firms with fighting capabilities when they feared being overrun by rebels. Such war and fighting services, similar to mercenary activities, were offered and carried out mainly in African countries (Musah and Fayemi 2000, Lilly and von Tangen Page 2002). Instead of the deployment of the state armed forces to defend the country or the government, governments contracted private specialized companies either because the military was not capable of carrying out the mission or the government did not trust them. Some companies have established themselves as a serious alternative to insufficiently trained or equipped, or not trustworthy, state armed forces (Mair 2004). The deployment of Executive Outcomes personnel in Angola contributed to forcing UNITA to the negotiating table, and the same company facilitated the end of fighting in Sierra Leone, at least temporarily.

Fifth, the intensified demand for international interventions and emergency aid: The increasing number of war refugees, ethnic cleansing and genocide, and the fact that civilians are becoming primary targets has intensified the perception in the international community of the need to intervene in conflicts, even with the use of military power. The United Nations considers this a moral obligation. Even if these decisions for UN mandated peace operations are not new, they have been drastically intensified in number. The demand for UN peace missions was always larger than the offer of member states to make their troops and other resources available. This situation strengthened the demand for the services of private security and military companies to support or even replace the state troops. Today it has become the common practice of emergency aid organizations to hire such companies for protection. They are engaged in building or protecting refugee camps and speeding up the logistical support for UN blue-helmets.

Sixth, the intensified demand for armed forces in various deployments related to the 'war against terror':   Threat perceptions have completely changed since 9/11. This has affected the armed forces as they are tasked with new and additional missions. The United States deployed in 2004, 400,000 soldiers abroad, with a presence in over 120 countries and military bases outside the United States. The deployment in Afghanistan reached 25,000 and 150,000 in Iraq (IISS 2004, US Department of State 2004b). Increasingly the armed forces seem over-stretched. On the one hand more money is going into the military budget for these various battlefields, and more and more reservists are being called upon. On the other hand, however, the troop's strength has not been substantially enlarged. During the Gulf War in 1991, 711,000 active soldiers served in the US Army. This number had gone down to 487,000 – one third less – at the time of the Iraq War in 2003. This reduction is supposed to be partly closed by private companies. More than 15,000 contract personnel – other sources mention 20,000 – served as employees of private military and security companies in 2004 in Iraq (Associated Press 25 April 2004). They are the second largest armed contingent after the US forces and larger than all other coalition forces combined. This gives the ratio of one employee of private contractors to about seven to eight US soldiers.

Seventh, public opinion: Political leaders who recognize the importance of civil society and the unacceptability of human suffering have had an impact on military thinking. There is an increasing readiness to use military means to stop violence and end wars. For some governments it is more attractive to task military firms with this job rather than the armed forces. Public awareness and the criticism when 'body bags' return home – for example as in the United States during the Vietnam War – has an effect on government decision-making. It is less eye-catching to send contractors than uniformed soldiers.

Eighth, the concept of 'lean state': Singer (2003, 66) calls it the 'power of privatization and the privatization of power'. The relatively new and quickly growing market for privately supplied security has developed into a subset of a systematic scheme of the privatization of state functions. The concept of a lean state is central to this development. Many state functions – civilian as well as military – are outsourced in order to find market solutions that are more cost effective. The neo-liberal concept of the lean state is dominant and hardly contested. It is propagated globally as the cure-all remedy. Thus, privatization has not stopped at the gates of military bases and even sensitive military functions are privatized – not only telecommunications, railways and utilities. Deployment of private military companies is seen as an effective free market method of meeting the military demands of governments and international agencies. Outsourcing and public–private partnership are no longer alien terms in the military.

Privatizing military missions is the reversal of the dominant trend of the 1960s and 1970s in developing countries when often the military staged coup d'etats to take over politics and engage in an active role in running the economy. Privatization and outsourcing of military activities is not only taking place in a few industrial countries but also in many developing countries – although the context is usually different. Several of the above mentioned motives are the cause for privatization in industrial countries. In underdeveloped countries or failing states, private services are generally demanded to protect or defend the government, to stabilize a society or to re-establish law and order. In cases, military companies can certainly deliver some of these services efficiently. Privately organized security can contribute to avoiding anarchy or chaos or other local security problems (Mandel 2001). They are seen as an alternative in keeping public order if the state has insufficient security forces at its disposal. In addition, private actors are attractive to the government since they are only paid for the services they deliver; a standing regular army always costs resources that might be scarce.

Types of private military companies

Privatization in the armed forces or the police is no clearly defined term. It is often used with an indistinct notion of what it really means. The services offered cover: protection of personal property as well as factories or mines of globally operating companies; management of military bases or airports; air, sea and land transport for UN peace missions; armed and unarmed protection of convoys of humanitarian organizations; as well as the recruitment and training of soldiers in specialized street fighting or intelligence gathering, logistics or combat. The services include technically complex as well as 'dirty' tasks such as the defence of privileged and corrupt elites.

The customers that purchase such services from the private military vary widely too. NATO, the EU, the UN, the African Union (AU) and the Organization for Security and Co-operation in Europe (OSCE) are among them. Their main customer, however, is the US armed forces, who demand a wide variety of different services.

The order books of the companies are full and still growing now that military budgets are increasing and many international interventions have resulted in serious personnel bottlenecks in the armed forces. Private contractors are booming as a consequence of the Iraq War and its aftermath. Many of them face serious recruiting problems today. This affects the quality and training of contract personnel. To profit from the growing market, companies regularly hire personnel who are not up to the task or who have a dubious service history, such as officers from Augusto Pinochet's Chilean army, the South African Apartheid forces or the French Foreign Legion (*The Guardian* 5 March 2004).

Ex-soldiers of the former Soviet army work as contractors next to the regular Russian forces in Chechnya, Azerbaijan, Armenia and Kazakhstan. Russians and Ukrainians were deployed in the war between Ethiopia and Eritrea. The government of Sri Lanka hired pilots from private companies to fly fighter helicopters, and in Brunei there are Nepalese Ghurkas – former members of the British forces – fighting in defence of the country. Specialists from Levdan, an Israeli company, assisted the president of Congo-Brazzaville in establishing a new armed force to enable him to dissolve troops which still seemed loyal to the former president (Schreier and Caparini 2005, 19, 64).

Examining at the type of services being offered (and their connection to the actual fighting), three types of different company profiles have been identified which Singer (2003, 93) calls the 'Tip of the Spear Typology'. He groups the companies into (1) military support firms (implementation/ command) (2) military consultant firms (advisory and training) and (3) military provider firms (non-lethal aid and assistance). Participation in combat is not just with the finger at the trigger. Often technical services for combat are more decisive than the soldier with the machine gun in his hands. A computer expert who, for example, transfers data on troop movements to the computer of the commander plays a central role on the 'automatic battlefield'. The categories of combatant and non-combatant are increasingly blurred. Mandel (2001, 137) differentiates privatization according to its scope (foreign assistance versus domestic substitution, bottom-up versus top-down), its form (direct combat or military advice) and its purpose (defensive versus offensive). The UK government (UK Government 2002, 8) distinguishes between advice, training, logistical support, supply of personnel for monitoring roles and demining. The categories within these various different definitions overlap.

Based on data from press and company reports it can be assessed that the strongest growth in private military company activities is presently in the areas of technical services and in training, while most companies refrain from engaging directly in combat. Few companies indeed have done so: Executive Outcomes from South Africa, Sandline International from the United Kingdom and Levadan from Israel have carried out fighting operations through offering their know-how to besieged governments. The following taxonomy (Table 2.1) is meant to elucidate the different types of private services offered by companies and other private actors and to indicate their relevance to the state monopoly of violence.

Table 2.1 Private military actors

Type of activity	Legal and social status	Main users	Main areas of activity
I. Private security companies			
Property protection			
Protection and surveillance	Legal, often not regulated	Private citizens and companies	Urban centres in many parts of the world
Guarding factories, mines, and so on	Legal, often not regulated	Multinational companies	Many countries
Neighbourhood patrol	Legal, unregulated	Private citizens	Urban centres in many parts of the world
Law and order in public places (subways, malls, and so on)	Legal, semi-regulated	Local governments, shop owners, and so on	Many countries
Crime prevention and correctional services			
Kidnap response	Legal, not regulated, often undesired by police	Private citizens and companies	Countries with high kidnapping rates
Management of prisons	Legal, mainly regulated	Governments, armed forces	Industrial countries, post-war societies

Continued

Table 2.1 Continued

Type of activity	Legal and social status	Main users	Main areas of activity
Investigation and intelligence gathering	Legal, not regulated	Companies, governments, armed forces	Many countries
II. Defence producers *Weapons production*			
Research and development	Mainly licensed by governments	Military procurement agencies	Industrialized countries
Production	Mainly licensed by governments	Military procurement agencies	Industrialized countries
Military assistance			
Military training	Licensed by governments, occasionally illegal	Governments in developing countries, rebel groups	Developing countries, transformation countries, crisis areas
Export of weapons and components	Licensed by governments, occasionally illegal	Governments in developing countries, rebel groups	Developing countries, transformation countries, crisis areas
III. Service providers *Management of military installations*			
Management of car fleet	Legal	Armed forces	Industrialized countries
Management of canteens	Legal	Armed forces	Industrialized countries
Construction and management of military bases	Legal	Armed forces	Few Western governments domestically and abroad
Financing			
Major military projects and weapons procurement	Legal	Defence ministries and procurement agencies	Industrialized countries

Continued

Table 2.1 Continued

Type of activity	Legal and social status	Main users	Main areas of activity
IV. Private military companies *Consulting and planning*			
Threat analysis, strategy development,advice for armed forces	Regulated, occasionally illegal	Official planning authorities, armed forces	Global
Logistics and support Logistics in emergencies and war	Legal	Defence ministries, humanitarian organizations	Many countries
Mine clearing, refugee camps, infrastructure demobilization, reintegration of soldiers and refugees	Legal	Humanitarian organizations, UN-agencies, governments	Post-conflict areas
Construction and management of refugee camps, reintegration of refugees	Legal	Humanitarian organizations, UN-agencies, governments	Crisis and war areas, post-conflict areas
Technical services and repairs Technical services, air control, intelligence gathering, IT-services	Licensed by governments	Armed forces	Many countries
Weapon repair	Licensed by governments	Armed forces	Many countries
Training Military training, weapons and special forces training, language training and psychological warfare	Licensed by governments, occasionally illegal	Armed forces, rebel groups and insurgents	Industrialized and developing countries, conflict areas

Continued

Table 2.1 Continued

Type of activity	Legal and social status	Main users	Main areas of activity
Peacekeeping and humanitarian assistance			
Logistics for peacekeeping	Regulated	UN and regional organizations	In crises, conflict and post-conflict areas
Disarmament, mine clearing, weapons collection and destruction	UN mandate	UN and regional organizations	In crises, conflict and post-conflict areas
Logistics in complex emergencies and nation-building programmes	Legal, unregulated	UN agencies, humanitarian organizations	In complex emergencies, refugee camps, conflict and post-conflict areas
Protection of convoys, refugees and humanitarians	Legal, unregulated	UN agencies, humanitarian organizations	In complex emergencies, refugee camps, conflict and post-conflict areas
Combat forces			
Combat	Mainly illegal, occasionally government-requested	Besieged governments, rebel groups and insurgents, governments seeking a low profile, multinational companies	War-torn societies, developing countries
V. Non-statutory forces			
Rebels			
Combat, terror	Illegal	Self-employed, employed by governments	Civil wars, failed states, crisis areas
Warlords			
Combat, terror, violence markets	Illegal	Self-employed, employed by governments	Civil wars, failed states, crisis areas

Continued

Table 2.1 Continued

Type of activity	Legal and social status	Main users	Main areas of activity
Organized crime Criminal acts for economic gain	Illegal	Self-employed, employed by governments	Countries with high crime rates
VI. Mercenaries *Combat troops* Combat	Illegal, occasionally government- requested	Besieged governments, rebel groups and insurgents, multinational companies	War-torn societies, developing countries

Source: Based on Wulf (2002, 97–98, revised and updated).

As can be gathered from the earlier table, many different kinds of actors are engaged in the business of security (Vines 2000). I distinguish six different forms of privatization and outsourcing of military and police missions. The first two types (private security companies and defence producers) are not the focus of this book.

First, private security companies: In a number of countries, a vast range of sectors of society are covered by security services provided by companies and private initiatives. Certain functions, such as the provision of security, law and order in subways and other public places, are outsourced from state authorities to private companies. Because of high crime rates, usually in urban centres, it is not just the state authorities, but also private business, that contracts security companies. This form of outsourcing is most advanced in the United States; security company employees outnumber police by three to one (Eppler 2002). This type of privatization is not concentrated in industrialized countries alone but urban centres in the developing world demand such services too. In this respect cities like Los Angeles are not different from Manila, Nairobi or Sao Paulo. It is a fast growing market with an annual growth rate of 9 percent (www. freedoniagroup.com, quoted in *Financial Times* 10 November 2000, 11). Some of these business activities take place in a legal grey zone – for example the contracting of armed security guards for the protection of companies in crises areas. The recruitment practices of companies are not always transparent and the background of employees might be doubtful. Often personnel are not properly trained for the job, although many former police are also hired.

Second, defence producers: Usually, defence producers are not mentioned when discussing privatization in the military – probably because the public is used to the fact that the armed forces procure their weapons and equipment from private companies, which are normally large enterprises. Since armed forces depend increasingly on complex technologies, defence producers are directly or indirectly involved in the combat operations of the military. In some areas of activity, especially in technical services and the maintenance and repair of weapons and other equipment, the distinction between defence producers and military companies is blurred. In contrast to security or military companies, the different work of the defence producers (development, production and export of arms) is usually strictly regulated by law and production or export licenses – despite the fact that scandals in arms trafficking are regularly reported. Defence producers are moving progressively beyond their classical production lines as the outsourcing of military missions has opened up an additional interesting business avenue. Some defence producers are moving into the area of privatized military missions or are taking over smaller private military companies (as described below).

Third, service providers: It is first of all an economic consideration that has led defence ministries to outsource the management of military bases or living quarters, the provision of uniforms, financing procurement and running the expenditures of major weapons systems. Such programmes are operated under the assumption that the private sector can deliver these services more cost effectively than the armed forces themselves. Some companies have been newly established; often with a government share of their capital (e.g. Gesellschaft für Entwicklung, Beschaffung und Betrieb, the Company for Development, Procurement and Maintenance, *GEBB* in Germany), or else services are contracted to entirely private companies who specialize in providing such services.

Fourth, private military companies: Ever more services that were traditionally considered to be typically military in nature are outsourced to the private sector. The list of private military companies in the Annex illustrates how manifold this new business sector is. It is a result of the 2003 Iraq War and its aftermath that both the contract volume as well as the number of such companies has grown considerably. Halliburton, one of these companies, received contracts from the Pentagon in 2003 that grew from US$900 million to US$3.9 billion. Contracts for private military companies in the United Kingdom tripled from US$800 million to US$2.5 billion from 2002 to 2003 (Schreier and Caparini 2005, 22). The companies are working for the armed forces on pre-war, war and post-war jobs. Instead of tasking the state forces, governments contract these specialized firms. Combat operations, however, are usually not contracted and most companies reject getting directly involved in fighting. The legal basis of the different types of jobs is not always clear, as I detail later, since international norms are almost completely absent. Often the contracting governments provide weapons for the contractors. In exceptional cases, such as the contract signed by Sandline International with the government of Papua New Guinea, the company agreed to supply 'weapons, ammunition and equipment, including helicopters and aircraft (serviceable for up to 50 hours flying time per machine per month), and electronic warfare equipment and communications systems' (Sandline contract, paragraph (c), quoted in Singer 2003, 247). The distinction from mercenaries is hazy in such cases.

Fifth, non-statutory forces: These, as mentioned earlier, are the groups of militias, rebels, insurgents, warlords, organized criminals and similar groupings, which – for their own political or economic gain – exert violence, engage in civil wars, topple governments or create an atmosphere of insecurity for large parts of the population. They are one of the main causes for the emergence of severe crises and inner-state war. These groups, with the exception of organized crime, are usually structured as paramilitary units. It should be noted that included within this group of non-statutory forces there are rebels and insurgents who sometimes fight an illegitimate government. To classify them as 'illegal' (as in Table 2.1) is therefore somewhat problematic and can only be done in the formal sense that they do not possess a government authorized legality.

Sixth, mercenaries: Mercenaries are soldiers who are usually hired by governments or rebel groups to fight. This classical category of fighters, known throughout history, still exists. They are contracted, as individuals or in groups, purely against payment. Mercenaries moved back and forth from one warring party to its enemies in the seventeenth century, during the 30-year war in Europe, if they got better pay. They do not engage in combat to defend their 'fatherland' or for 'honour' but for those who pay them dearest (Thomson 1994). Mercenaries were mainly engaged on the African continent during the period of decolonization in the last century. Often, their deployment was intended to destabilize or topple weak or besieged governments. Their main area of deployment till today remains

Africa. They are recruited in former war zones, where many ex-soldiers with fighting experience are demobilized and find it difficult or impossible to reintegrate into civilian life again. The UN General Assembly instituted in 1979, as a reaction to mercenary activities, an ad hoc committee to establish a convention against 'Recruitment, Use, Financing and Training of Mercenaries', which calls for the prohibition of mercenary activities. The Special Rapporteur of the UN on mercenaries reports to the UN every year. Occasionally he also criticizes private military companies in his report (UN ECOSOC 2002). Similarly, a Green Paper of the British government to parliament lists the activities of private military companies under the heading "Mercenaries: Africa's Experience 1950s–1990s" (UK Government 2002, 28–38, Annex A).

In Chapter 8 I give details for each one of the private military companies and the six different types of services they offer (consulting, logistics, technical services, training, peacekeeping and combat), and, in addition, I address the function of outsourcing to service providers in the UK.

Private limited companies

Lacking or insufficient international norms and controls

Mercenaries engage, as a rule, in combat for a contractor; they are, as Singer (2001/2002) describes them, 'guns for hire'. Although private military companies also have their roots in wars they are distinct from mercenaries in their typical hierarchical company structure. In this sense they are more akin to defence producers and security companies, for indeed defence producers and private military companies too do not operate as individuals or in small ad hoc groups but rather as enterprises. Private military companies openly recruit their specialists; they offer a wide range of services and products and usually work for several governments or institutions at the same time. They compete for contracts in the world market and, to the contrary of mercenaries, they do not try to hide their existence, as the former prefer to do.

Yet dissimilar to defence producers, private military firms are more like virtual enterprises, and in this way similar to internet firms. Among the military firms there are large undertakings as well as small and medium sized companies. Many of them were newly founded when this market began to emerge, and some of them disappeared after only short periods of time. They need comparatively small amounts of capital since they need not invest in large production facilities. They hire small numbers of personnel on a permanent basis but usually have a database of ready-to-go specialists for short-term assignments. The US company, Military Professional Resources Incorporated (MPRI), for example, employed in 2003 – according to their web site – 700 people full-time yet additionally 12,000 were ready to be called upon. During the Iraq War their full-time employment jumped to 1500. The company claims willingness to take over any kind of military job, except for combat (www. mpri.com). The companies try to hire experienced personnel, often ex-combatants, to save the cost of training and to be able to deploy them quickly (Avant 2000).

Private military companies are often called modern mercenaries (Musah and Fayemi 2000, 1, Vines 2000), but the companies hate this comparison. In contrast to the mercenaries most of them are properly registered as companies, they pay taxes and do not want to violate international law. Further, and crucially for how they view themselves: They claim that their service can contribute to conflict resolution, and, indeed, the experience noted from some company engagements was that they contributed to the ending of violent conflicts. This, however, is contested, as for example in Sierra Leone in the mid-1990s where private military deployment of companies like Executive Outcomes and Sandline International was not seen in so positive a light by observers as the companies claim it to have been (Musah and Fayemi 2000). But the reasoning of 'combat companies' in reaching their own positive conclusions of their involvement leaves aside certain opportunity costs. For example, scarce resources in developing countries need to be reallocated to hire companies, which in turn weakens the state armed forces even more and thus further limits their capability to uphold law and order. Furthermore, the deployment of companies is usually restricted to brief periods of time, and not only is the success of their assistance short-term too, but it does not affect the root causes of conflicts. In response to this, the argument of the military companies is that addressing the root causes of conflicts is not what they are normally hired for. The rapporteur of the United Nations concluded: 'The presence of the private company which was partly responsible for the security of Sierra Leone created an illusion of governability, but left untouched some substantive problems which could never be solved by a service company' (quoted in the British Green Paper, in UK Government 2002, 17). Military companies do not want to be compared to arms dealers either. The now defunct UK company Sandline International, which was involved in combat in Sierra Leone, published a paper that stated that private military companies provide not just arms but also training, assistance and weapons for their customers: 'Therfore, PMCs [private military companies] are not "arms dealers" but are more packaged service providers' (Sandline International 1998).

The concept pursued by several governments emphasizes their desire and political will to outsource military services to private military companies; usually the selected companies work with a government licence. But such a licence does not necessarily constitute the legality of the companies' practices according to international law and norms. They operate in a grey zone, and, although they are different from mercenaries, some companies even take on illegal jobs. Since the definition of their activities is neither clear nor uniform and since the international norms against mercenary activities do not apply to formally registered and government-licensed companies, their operations are largely unregulated according to international standards. Even the distinction between combatants who are deployed by governments and contract personnel of companies is distorted. The relevant international treaties (see Box 2.1 later) define a mercenary as one who is recruited to fight in armed conflict for private gain, who is not a national of the parties to the conflict and who has not been sent by a state that is not a party to the conflict. The mercenary is not recognized under international law as a combatant with certain rights, as for example is a prisoner of war or a regular soldier; on the contrary: mercenary activities are a criminal offence. Some actors in wars have a primary economic interest and a number of wars are prolonged because of the economic assistance and interest of groups and companies. But in contrast to mercenaries – who still fight in Africa for payment, or in contrast to the troops that marauded and pillaged Europe in the seventeenth century and moved from one site of the front to another if the pay was better; or the Condottieri of the sixteenth century that Machiavelli criticized – private military companies pay attention to being properly registered and to act as 'normal' enterprises. They make sure that their contract personnel do not violate all of the six criteria constituting mercenarism.

Companies are sensitive about scandals or public criticism since this could damage or even ruin their business. The US company DynCorp was publicly criticized when seven of its employees became involved in prostituting 12-year-old girls in Bosnia. The company fired the implicated employees, certainly on the grounds of the resultant bad public image (Schwartz 2003). But they were never prosecuted. The only court cases to result involved the two whistleblowers who had made the scandal public and were sacked (Schreier and Caparini 2005, 11). More recently, many scandals were reported from Iraq. The torturing of prisoners in the Abu Ghraib prison, involving private contractors, is but the publicly discussed tip of the iceberg. Companies do react to bad publicity: Sandline International of the UK, that was itself the centre of public debate, started a campaign to counter allegations by emphasizing on its web site its competencies and claimed to abide strictly by international humanitarian law and to observe human rights. The US company MPRI informs visitors to its web site that they operate in a number of countries under US government licence.[13]

During the last two decades, the UN General Assembly, the Security Council, and the UN Economic and Social Council (UN ECOSC) as well as the UN Commission on Human Rights have passed over 100 resolutions stigmatizing mercenary activities. But it is not only mercenaries who exert military or police power beyond the control of public scrutiny and accepted laws – more often it is personnel of military and security companies. The law of the market reigns. Companies offer their services to everybody – states, multinational companies, UN-agencies, humanitarian organizations, rebels or drug barons. International norms are so far of relevance only to these activities when companies violate the right of the sovereignty of states enshrined in the UN Charter (i.e. if they are involved in the internal matters of a state) or if they are directly caught up in conflict. Occasionally this has been the case, as for example the British company Sandline in 1996 in Sierra Leone and in 1997 in Papua New Guinea. Normally however, companies do shy away from stepping over this sensitive legal borderline. But their activities, potentially decisive in combat, are not covered by international norms. The Organization for African Unity (OAU) agreed on a Convention for the Elimination of Mercenarism in Africa in 1977. The emphasis was particularly on mercenary activities directed against governments and freedom fighters (Gaultier *et al.* 2001).[14] The most important provisions of the OAU Convention were accepted during the same year as a First Additional Protocol of the Geneva Convention of 1949, an international treaty that contains the most important rules limiting the barbarity of war (see Box 2.1). This Additional Protocol took away the status of combatant from mercenaries, and the UN International Convention Against the Recruitment, Use, Financing, and Training of Mercenaries agreed by the UN General Assembly in 1989 forbids, as the title suggest, certain mercenary related activities.[15] But it was not before 20 October 2001 that 22 UN member states had signed and ratified the treaty, the minimum quorum for the treaty to enter into force.[16] The UN Human Rights Commission established the permanent office of a Special Rapporteur in order to encourage more members to ratify the treaty and to report regularly on mercenary activities. Detailed reports have been published annually since 1988.

The narrow definition of the different conventions is problematic since to be classified as a mercenary all six criteria must be met. It has

Box 2.1   Protocol Additional to the Geneva Conventions of 12 August 1949, and relating to the Protection of Victims of International Armed Conflicts (Protocol I), 8 June 1977

Art. 47 Mercenaries

(2) A mercenary is any person who:
  (a) is specially recruited locally or abroad in order to fight in an armed conflict;
  (b) does, in fact, take a direct part in the hostilities;
  (c) is motivated to take part in the hostilities essentially by the desire for private gain and, in fact, is promised, by or on behalf of a Party to the conflict, material compensation substantially in excess of that promised or paid to combatants of similar ranks and functions in the armed forces of that Party;
  (d) is neither a national of a Party to the conflict nor a resident of territory controlled by a Party to the conflict;
  (e) is not a member of the armed forces of a Party to the conflict; and
  (f) has not been sent by a State which is not a Party to the conflict on official duty as a member of its armed forces.

Source ICRC:
http://www.icrc.org/ihl.nsf/7c4d08d9b287a42141256739003e636b/
f6c8b9fee14a77fdc125641e0052b079

On committing an offence see the International Convention against the Recruitment, Use, Financing and Training of Mercenaries, adopted on 4 December 1989. The text of the convention is reprinted in UNHCR (2002, Annex I, 25–32).

seldom been the case that mercenaries have been prosecuted under this convention. The criteria are as loose as they are because governments wanted to be able to make use of mercenaries in certain cases; for example, foreign advisors are excluded. According to the UN Special Rapporteur, the different conventions cannot be applied, or at least not easily, to the increasing activities of non-state actors, private security groups, militias, combat volunteers, or private military companies. Many governments did not ratify the treaty, for example the UK government, because they 'regard the definition as unworkable for practical purposes. In particular it would be difficult to prove the motivations of someone accused of mercenary activities' (UK Government 2002, 7). The Special Rapporteur concludes with regard to private military firms that mercenary activities have survived the end of the Cold War, but their methods have changed: There are still individual mercenaries who enlist to fight in armed conflicts, 'just as there are mercenaries within today's international military security companies' (UN ECOSOC 2002, 16). He calls for a revision of the definition and emphasizes that military protection is a core function of the state and the international community that cannot be handed over to private actors who are not accountable to international law. An international group of experts has made detailed proposals aiming at a tight control of private military and security companies in order to close some of the existing legal gaps (UN ECOSOC 2001a).

Only a limited number of countries have passed laws to prohibit or have introduced license systems to regulate military companies. South Africa passed such a law in 1998, the Foreign Military Assistance Act. Nobody carrying a South African passport is allowed to recruit, train, deploy or finance mercenaries, or engage himself as a mercenary. This law regulates but does not prohibit all types of non-state military assistance. Nonetheless, private military companies are covered by this law, and this was the reason for Executive Outcomes to close its business in South Africa after its adoption.

In the United States – where private military companies have flourished more than anywhere else – companies are required to register with the Department of State; it is mandatory for them to acquire a government license in order to be active abroad, for example as a military consultancy company. All contracts above US$50 million must, in a manner similar to the regulation of arms exports, be submitted to the Congress before signing. As Table 2.2 illustrates, a number of countries have passed laws

Table 2.2 Legal regulations to control private military companies in selected countries

Country	Regulation or law
Australia	It is an offence to recruit mercenaries within Australia or for Australians to fight abroad in non-governmental forces.
Austria	It is prohibited to form military associations; no regulations regarding mercenaries.
Belgium	Planned prohibition of Belgians serving in foreign armies and foreign countries, but not passed as law.
Canada	Prosecution for enlisting in an army actively engaged in warfare against a country allied to Canada.
Denmark	Prohibited to recruit in Denmark for foreign war services.
Finland	Punishment for recruiting Finnish citizens to the armed forces of another state.
France	No regulation.
Germany	No regulation, mercenary activities are not prohibited.
Greece	Recruitment of mercenaries is illegal.
Italy	All mercenary activity is prohibited.

Continued

Table 2.2 Continued

Country	Regulation or law
Japan	No relevant legislation.
Netherlands	Illegal to enter military service for a nation with which the Netherlands is at war.
New Zealand	No relevant legislation.
Norway	It is a criminal act to recruit, without permission, troops for foreign military service or support private organizations of a military character.
Portugal	Prohibited to engage in mercenary activities, such as combat, but not to give advice or technical assistance.
Russia	Recruitment, training or financing of mercenary activities, and participation by a mercenary in armed conflict, are punishable by imprisonment.
Spain	Prohibited to work as a mercenary only for members of the armed forces.
South Africa	No person within South Africa or elsewhere may recruit or train persons for, or finance or engage in, mercenary activity that is defined as 'direct participation as a combatant in armed conflict for private gain'.
Sweden	Recruitment for foreign military service only by permission.
Switzerland	Prohibited to join forces for fighting abroad, except Vatican Swiss Guards.
Ukraine	Prohibition of mercenary activities, imprisonment up to ten years.
United Kingdom	No regulation.
United States	Companies offering military advice to foreign nationals are required to register with and obtain a licence from the State Department under the International Transfer of Arms Regulations. Congressional notification is required before the US Government approves export of defence services worth in excess of US$50 million.

Source: UK Government (2002. Annex B., S. 39–43).

to regulate mercenary activities but private military firms remain largely unregulated and uncontrolled.

Companies on the battlefield

Privatization is controversial among soldiers. A good number of them are concerned about their future role with regard to the privatization of military functions. In contrast, others promote this trend and stress that – thanks to the support of contract personal – the armed forces can concentrate on their core tasks. The proponents of wide-ranging utilization of contractors emphasize that defence ministries have mostly cut in the 'tail' (the support structure) and only minimally in the 'tooth' (the combat structure) of the armed forces, thus using the contractors as force multipliers (Garcia-Perez 1999, 40). Besides the alledged benefits of saving resources the following advantages of outsourcing from a military perspective are mentioned: an enhanced deployment capability of the forces by making contract support available within a theatre; offsets and gains in operational tempo; the possibility to maintain high-tech; increasing combat power in force constrained circumstances – for example when a host nation is limiting the presence of state uniformed strength; a focus on combat operations; and the provision of capabilities that the armed forces do not have (Schreier and Caparini 2005, 45).

However, the privatization process also bears some inherent risks. The professional journal of the US logistics forces lists in 2004 – on the basis of substantial experience with contract firms in the Balkans, Afghanistan and Iraq – the following bottlenecks: (1) a significant gap in operational doctrine on who is responsible for the lines of communication; (2) loss of visibility of assets on the battlefield; (3) loss of control of contractor personnel and equipment; (4) increased responsibility of the armed forces for the contractors security; (5) need for additional manpower, materiel, and funding resources to support contractor personnel; (6) concern about the availability of commercial supplies in a hostile environment; and (7) gaps in logistic support if commercial supply lines become disrupted (McPeak and Ellis 2004, 7).

There are a few fundamental differences between private companies and the armed forces. The military is geared to defence, war, armed conflict, questions of life and death and to win a war; the private companies are on the battlefield for economic gain. Private companies want to make a profit and try to economize on personnel and other inputs. They will deliver only what is written explicitly in the contract. Like other businesses and enterprises they deliver their services on the just-in-time method, and hence prefer typically a minimal stock of material. The military in contrast plans for the worst-case scenario and typically tries to plan for maximum requirements. This is the primary reason why the logisticians of the armed forces doubt the reliability of private firms in critical situations (Orsini and Bulitz 1999).

The economic motives of private companies can negatively affect military flexibility in crucial situations. Although increased flexibility is one of the main reasons to contract companies in the first place – because the military should be able to profit from the private sector's flexibility – the concrete result on the battlefield might just be the opposite since the companies try to minimize their inputs and may create bottlenecks. The commander on the battlefield has no complete overview of his resources and no command over the contractors; the different lines of command increase the risk for both the military and the contractors in dangerous situations.

Will companies be there when the military needs them? The exclusively monetary motivation of companies and their personnel and their inflexibility raises the question as to whether companies will behave dependably according to the armed forces' requirements? Can the company management really guarantee that their staff will move close to the frontline when the battle begins and when it gets dangerous? Employees cannot be commanded, but can leave their job by simply cancelling their contract.

A small number of large enterprises have been contracted by the US government with multi billion dollar agreements. The work is implemented in large parts by newly hired employees, but also through a lot of subcontractors. The subcontractors have sub-subcontracted jobs. Thus, a long line of contracts has been created which is no longer neither transparent to the Pentagon in Washington and the commander in the war theatre nor is it clear how dependable and responsible the different contractors are. Apparently, the Pentagon is not in a position to state how many contract personnel are working for them in Iraq. The contractors are not part of the military line of communication and cases have been reported where contractors failed to deliver food and water to the soldiers in the desert because the contractors refused to drive into the fighting zone (Hartung 2004). Difficulties are exacerbated by the fact that the commander is responsible for the security of the contract personnel in his geographic region.

The more services are bought by the military from the private sector, the less practical training the soldiers will have in that particular area. Private companies have become more and more the principal supplier of certain critical services and logistics. The typical military support functions are no longer carried out by the military themselves. Contract firms keep their stocks until the military calls for them. The military is about to lose, and in fact to an extent they have already lost within just a brief period of time, important know-how and competencies; they will become dependent on private suppliers, a dependence which cannot easily be reversed (Avant 2000, Orsini and Bublitz 1999, 131). The dependence of the armed forces is increasing permanently in areas such as the maintenance and repair of modern weapons systems, information technology and training of forces for the protection of assets and people.

Minimum economic conditions for effective privatization

Increasing the privatization and delegation of public missions to the private sector has certainly been of great economic benefit in a number of areas. Examples and empirical proof have been plentifully presented in published literature. According to these studies, the economic success of privatization – independent of the various fields of the public sector – depends on at least three minimum conditions (Markusen 2003, 472–78):

First: the service to be contracted by the public sector must be open to true and sustained competition. Real competition is essential to prevent companies from maximizing their profit-seeking strategies. Companies are, first of all, responsible to their shareholders and not to the government or the taxpayer. As long as there is no serious competitor, the contractor will increase his price and suppress innovation and quality and hide information about the true cost of the products and services supplied. Economic benefits will only be gained when several bidders bid for the demanded services, but not through privatization per se. Often, merely the potential of a competition (between the private and the public sector or within the private sector) can itself facilitate the realization of less costly services.

Second: the client himself must have a clear understanding of what kind of services are expected and he must be able to articulate his demand. If the definition of the contract is vague, the supply of the services can be expected to be inadequate.

Third: the client must be in a position to control and verify the services delivered. Success in outsourcing requires management and control by the public sector authorities. But the promoters of a far-reaching privatization policy dislike regulation and state controls and, in addition, the state often lacks the required resources for proper monitoring. Two contradictory principles create a dilemma here: The advocates of privatization want to free the private sector from bureaucracy, red tape and tight regulations, but to guarantee the proper delivery of the contracted services there is a need for monitoring.

Based on these three criteria I analyse in Chapter 8 the extent to which privatization in the military sector has been successful and when these three minimum conditions have failed to be met.

The public good 'security' and the democratic control of the monopoly of violence

The policy of outsourcing military functions is an effort to create more efficient armed forces. But this notion also has an inherent danger since a central function of the state, the monopoly of violence, could be damaged or endangered. Privatization is not by definition a total renunciation of state functions or their controls, but rather the *delegation* of public services to non-state organizations. In many developing countries a proper and efficient state monopoly of force has never existed. And the long-term historical trend shows that exercising the monopoly of force in the nation state is actually an exception. Exercising the state monopoly of force historically was seldom the rule; whilst even today it is implemented and accepted as the norm, although not always appropriately practiced, primarily in Europe. Furthermore, despite the fact that this norm is not principally questioned in practice, it is still being restricted or undermined in actuality.

The key to public security is the focus on the question of who exercises force in practice and who should be entrusted with the legitimate authority over the control of this force (Mandel 2001, 135). At the global level the monopoly of violence is a completely open question. A generally accepted, globally practiced monopoly of violence does not exist and the weakness and impotence of the UN Security Council in the case of the current Iraq invasion is demoralizing evidence of this fact. Security and peace are public goods (Mendez 1999); this fact is not contested. According to the dominant economic theory a public good can be enjoyed by everybody and its consumption by one individual does not reduce the consumption of others. Both the society as a whole and its members, the individuals in that society, profit from increasing security. However, supplying the public goods of peace and security by the state efficiently is not so easy. There is no possibility of decentralizing this responsibility by collecting a fee for such security services. Too many free riders would have plenty of incentives to avoid the payment of this fee (Sandler and Hartley 1995). Co-operation of the actors involved is necessary and competition among them increases insecurity. This is the main reason for the public sector to remain the principal guarantor of security.

Deployment of private military companies is not without tension, because – as stated above – pursuing at least two partially competing principal concepts creates friction; namely the concept of delegating the state's guarantee of security to contractors versus the contractors prime motive of economic gain of their company. The public good 'security' and the private good 'economic gain' can be in competition with each other or even be contradictory. As a result of this, privatizing public goods has certain limitations that need to be observed. Private military firms are specialized and offer professional services that are used in wars and violent conflicts – to prevent them or to fight them. But companies might be reluctant to engage in providing security or preventing war by military means if too high a risk exists of losing the companies' assets in such conflicts; the example of the Russian and Ukrainian aircraft companies in the Eritrea–Ethiopia War mentioned in the preface exemplifies this (*The Times* 19 February 1999, www.newsint-archive.co.uk, Adams 1999, 103). But the opposite can be the case as well. These services are the companies' business; they might not thus be interested in a quick and efficient settlement of conflicts since that might reduce their turnover and profit.[17]

Deployment of private companies has a deep impact on how the state monopoly of violence is exercised and controlled. An important consideration must be that these companies are presently not accountable to parliament or the public. A few critical voices can be heard, even in the United States where privatization is pushing ahead at a considerable pace. Congressman Jan Schakowsky concludes that 'there's a great lack of transparency when you contract out, yet if something happens, we're supposed to use our military to go in and rescue them and get involved in other conflicts' (quoted in Schwartz 2003). And Senator Tom Daschle wrote to the Secretary of Defense: 'It would be a dangerous precedent if the United States allowed the presence of private armies outside the control of a governmental authority and beholden only to those who pay them' (quoted in *Washington Post* 27 April 2004).

While the government is held accountable by parliament, private companies are responsible only to the shareholder and client. This is precisely the reason why some governments want to make use of private companies. In the United States, for example, since controls held by Congress have limited the government's room for manoeuvre in arms exports and military assistance related to anti-drug programmes, the government has been happy to rely more on private military companies. Another example underlines this point. The Congress had limited the US troop strength in Bosnia to 20,000; the government compensated for this limitation by contracting about 2000 private personnel (Schreier and Caparini 2005, 68). Furthermore, governments have often been publicly criticized when the casualty rates of their own soldiers go up in wars. When this happens to private contractors the government is less directly in the limelight. After all, contract personnel have not been commanded to the battlefield but have chosen out of their own free will or out of economic necessity to sign these high-risk contracts.

Governments in developing countries who hire privately organized combat troops when they are weak or beleaguered are often, at the same time, the kind of governments that are short of resources. To find the funds to pay such private companies' troops they might have to mortgage their own economic and political future. Companies or supporting troops have been paid for their military services by receiving mining rights for oil or diamonds, tropical wood and so on. This results in mutual dependencies between client and contractor, and conflicts might be extended in the bilateral interest of such contracts. In such a situation it is not clear which state tasks can be implemented, who decides upon them, and if decisions are taken as to the way in which the monopoly of violence (that strictly speaking is no longer a monopoly) is carried out. The contractors seem to create their own demand or at least have an influence on the demand for security services, if security is purchased commercially.

There are presently no indicators that the privatization trend is being reversed or that countervailing forces are in the making – even though some of the more dubious firms, such as Executive Outcomes and Sandline International, have closed down. The people who ran the companies simply continue to operate under a different name. If the publicly available, though still far from complete, evidence does not mislead us, then privatization is going to increase. The originally ad hoc engagement of private military firms in Angola, Sierra Leone, the DRC, the Balkans and the Middle East has turned into a visible phenomenon in all inter and intra state wars as well as in post-conflict societies. Iraq is today's culmination of this long-term trend. Consequently, it seems essential to design and apply rules in international law for the engagement of these private military firms.

Numerous legal and practical questions are still unanswered. Why are contract personnel allowed to bear arms? To what extent is the Geneva Convention on combatants, prisoners of wars and civilians on the battlefield of relevance, when contract personnel fight side-by-side with Special Forces? Can the company employees be classified as deserters when they leave their 'job' in critical situations? Since armies in principle have come under the full control of the nation state, the state becomes responsible and is to be held accountable for violence done by its citizens beyond its state borders. Is this principle called into question now? These are not only conceptually important questions but they are very concrete and practical, because often soldiers and employees of companies can no

Table 2.3 Arguments pro and contra deployment of private military companies

Area	Pro	Contra
Economics	• Companies work more cost effectively	• Evidence for their cost effectiveness is rather weak • Business practices of the companies are not very transparent • Real cost of military missions are blurred through outsourcing
Military	• Troops can concentrate on their core missions • Companies are more flexible and are quicker to deploy people • Synergies between companies and the armed forces are created	• Dependency of the military on firms • Companies are unreliable on the battlefield • The *just-in-time* method is not suitable for wars • Additional tasks of the military to protect contractors
Peacekeeping and humanitarian intervention	• Quick reactions of companies in crises • Quality of UN-missions increases • Protection of humanitarians • Cautiousness of deploying national troops	• Responsibility of the international community for protection is delegated • Dubious firms are legitimized by the UN
International crises	• Stabilization of collapsing states • Engaging the private sector in post-conflict reconstruction	• Continuation of conflict in the interest of companies • Companies might damage the foreign policy of their home country • Distinction between civilians and military disappears • Companies act as proxies of their government
Technology	• Better know-how of companies	• Technology is not available in critical situations
Policy	• Governments can reduce the presence of their forces by hiring companies	• No democratic control of companies • States should have to guarantee security

Continued

Table 2.3 Continued

Area	Pro	Contra
		• Complicated civil–military balance is disturbed
Law	• Companies operate under government licence • Codes of conduct regulate business practices	• Lacking legal regulation of company deployment • Hard to prosecute companies and employees for criminal acts or violations of human rights • Geneva Convention (combatants/non-combatants) is undermined

longer be distinguished from each other. The confusion about who is who demonstrates, as a spokesperson of the US Army concluded, 'that in many situations soldiers and civilian contractors have become virtually indistinguishable – and interchangeable' (quoted in *Washington Post* 13 May 2004). Employees of the US company Aviation Development who were working on aerial surveillance operations for the US Central Intelligence Agency (CIA) in Peru directed the shooting down of a small private passenger plane by mistake; a US missionary family on their way home died in the attack (Singer 2001/2002, S. 218). The casualty rate of contract personnel has steeply risen in Iraq (Isenberg 2004). But this is only one side of the coin: the casualty rate of Iranians who die through the actions of private contract personnel or who are tortured or mistreated in prisons is probably rising too, although there are no systematic statistics to validate this point. Can a government, who has signed these contracts, not also be held accountable for these situations?

Table 2.3 summarizes the arguments pro and contra the privatization of military tasks presented in research and the media and by the companies themselves. In the case study concerning outsourcing in the United States and the United Kingdom in Chapter 8 I analyze the validity of these arguments and draw conclusions in the final chapter of this book.

Part II

International Interventions and Privatizing Military Functions

3
With the Highest Authority: UN-Peacekeeping Missions

Traditionally the United Nations (UN) was reluctant to deploy troops with a mandate authorizing the intent to use of force. The first aim was to ensure peace or to end conflict by peaceful means alone, and in most of its peace operations the UN did not employ force. The four most important exceptions were the Congo mission of 1960–64, Bosnia and Herzegovina 1992–95, Somalia 1993–95 and the special case of the Korean War 1950–53 that was not mandated by the Security Council but by the General Assembly. The troops in the latter conflict were not under UN but rather US command. All of these armed deployments ended with traumatic results (Findlay 2002). The traditional image of the lightly armed blue-helmets of the UN that engage in violent conflicts and wars solely as moderators or mediators has drastically changed since the end of the Cold War. So-called robust peace operations and peace enforcement operations that assign to UN troops the task of keeping warring groups apart or to become involved as a party to the conflict have become the rule in recent years.

In addition, the number of international military interventions has grown significantly. I have mentioned in the introduction the principal political and military reasons for this development. An additional cause rests within the organization of the UN itself (and especially within the Security Council). Whereas during the Cold War the UN Security Council often lacked the necessary consensus or was hindered by a veto of one of its permanent members in mandating for peacekeeping missions, present day calls by the international community for timely military interventions have become louder and more frequent (Eisele 2000; UNGA 2001a). These calls share an underlying reasoning, namely to prevent, mitigate, or end humanitarian catastrophes. Another explanation is that the more willing and ready the UN is to engage powerful military forces the less likely it is to have to use them (Findlay 2002, 3). Robust peacekeeping thus prevents the escalation of conflicts. The Human Security Report (2005) presents empirical data proving that the number of direct deaths in wars has gone down over the last six decades and hypothesizes that this is a result of UN peace missions. Further, the UN High-level Panel on Threats, Challenges and Change states: 'In the last 15 years, more civil wars were ended through negotiations than in the previous two centuries in large part because the United Nations provided leadership, strategic co-ordination, and the resources needed for implementation' (UNHLPT 2004, 33). The statistics clearly show a declining curve in the number of civil wars and an increasing curve in the number of UN peacekeeping and peace building operations (ibid.).

When UN or other international or regional organizations deploy troops under their command, the question of the democratic control of these armed forces and the legitimacy of the decision arises. The public debate has primarily been concerned with the authorization of such operations. In Germany, for example, this has taken place against the background of its militant history and the changing position of the executive government and parliament in the second half of the 1990s. NATO's air war in Kosovo was a particularly catalytic development in raising public emotions. The need for democratic control, described in Chapter 1 of this book, is not only of relevance for the authorization of troop deployment but for its implementation and eventual withdrawal as well. Even though decisions to deploy troops are often controversial and problematic, the authorization is clearly regulated in most countries. Most UN member states have entrusted their executive government with the decision-making; in a few countries parliament plays a role too. With regard to the practicalities of the implementation of troop deployments, the questions are: who is responsible, to whom do the troops report, how is the line of command arranged in these multinational assignments and how is the completion of an operation and the withdrawal of troops organized? Authorization by the Security Council is, of course, based on international law but this does not automatically imply that it has been democratically decided upon.

My assumption, based on empirical observation, is that accountability and democratic control of internationally implemented interventions is – as a rule – more complex and complicated than national deployments. When conducting international interventions the desire of democratic decision-makers for efficient control is stronger, because the risk for the troops is larger, the missions last longer, and the success of a military action is less likely. This can be illustrated with recent examples: It is easier for the executive and legislature to decide on the use of troops for short-term tasks in natural disasters, as for example in 2000 during the floods in Mozambique, than in a long-term and unstable post-conflict situation as in Afghanistan or a war-torn society such as in the Democratic Republic of Congo (DRC). The question is, whether the exclusively nationally oriented democratic control of the armed forces – conceptually as well as practically – serves the purpose of multinational missions or if this control is no longer sufficient and needs to be reformed? Are agreed multinational procedures for democratic control required and even possible for multinational troop deployments? Furthermore, can the concept of global governance contribute to the finding of solutions to these new challenges?

The next part of this chapter addresses the transformation in the conditions of UN peacekeeping and the changes in the reasoning for military interventions. More precisely: What has led to the often used argument of *humanitarian* necessity for peace enforcement missions of the UN, while in the past the principle of non-interference in internal affairs of states was more dominant?

Peace operations by the United Nations

When the UN was founded, shortly before the end of the Second World War, the international community looked upon classic warfare between states as the pre-eminent threat to world peace. The removal of war and violence from international relations was seen as the main purpose of the UN, something deemed possible by creating a system of collective security through the institution of the UN. In this sense, the UN remained influenced by the ideas of the former US President Woodrow Wilson and the concept of the League of Nations. In its simplest and purest version, a system of collective security requests that those states committed to it intervene more or less automatically in defined situations without recourse to domestic debate over these issues (Ku and Jacobson 2001, 27). Yet such an automatism is neither stipulated in the statutes of the League of Nations nor in the UN Charter.

Chapter VII of the UN Charter empowers the Security Council to 'take such action by air, sea, or land forces as may be necessary to maintain or restore international peace and security' (Art. 42). Therefore, under the UN Charter, responsibility and control over international military missions is referred to an international institution. Formally, this might be interpreted as the transferral of the international monopoly of force to the UN. However, a closer look at the practice of international relations shows that the UN was often denied the means to fulfil this supposed monopoly. Although the UN ranks as the highest international authority on questions of war and peace, one cannot attest democratic control of UN-authorised military forces given the composition and the lasting blockade against reform of the Security Council. In the final chapter I address the possibilities for and barriers against the implementation of democratic rules in international organizations.

On the other hand, the UN Charter stipulates under Art. 2(4) that 'all Members shall refrain in their international relations from the threat or use of force against the territorial integrity or political independence of any state'. Provision is made for the peaceful settlement of disputes as an instrument of the UN before any military power can be used. To guarantee the effective performance of this task, the Charter (Art. 45–47) provides for a Military Staff Committee composed of the Chiefs of Staff of the permanent members of the Security Council as well as its associated members.

In theory, the Military Staff Committee is responsible under the Security Council for the strategic direction of any armed forces placed at the disposal of the Security Council. However, the provisions of Art. 45–47 have, as of yet, not been implemented. A Military Staff Committee does not exist and the Security Council has never had UN forces at its disposal, despite the fact that the enforcement action has been used 60 times (as on May 2005) since the UN was founded (UN Department of Peacekeeping, http://www.un.org/Depts/dpko/dpko/index.asp, accessed 26 May 2005).

The 'stand-by forces' requested by the former UN Secretary General Boutros Boutros-Ghali served as a compromise between the constant ad hoc decisions in crisis situations and the UN forces as originally foreseen. In his Agenda for Peace, Boutros-Ghali laments the fact that only very few member states have kept ready contingents of this kind for UN use (Boutros-Ghali 1992). This initiative to reform the UN to become a more independent actor was resisted and quickly stopped by drastic cuts in the organization's resources. The UN was prevented from becoming flexible and independent and it thus remains an instrument of the most powerful member states (Debiel 2003, 13).

The UN's peace operations consist of (1) monitoring and observing missions; (2) classical missions in which the blue-helmets create a buffer zone between the conflicting parties; (3) a newer type of peacekeeping, in which the UN forces receive a more robust mandate and become involved in post-conflict reconstruction programmes; and (4) peace enforcement missions conducted by forces mandated to use force beyond the scope of self-protection.[18]

The classical peacekeeping missions by UN blue-helmets are not based upon force but are impartial in character and initiated only with the explicit consent of all parties to the conflict. The normally light armament carried by the blue-helmets is designated only for self-defence, in contrast to the troops operating under a peace enforcement mandate. The blue-helmet missions are authorized under Chapter VI of the UN Charter and the troops are under the political and operative patronage of the UN Secretary General. Notwithstanding this provision, it is the countries that contribute the troops who themselves remain legally responsible for military and civilian personnel deployed during these missions (Gareis 2002, 21).

During the four decades from the founding of the UN until the end of the Cold War, the UN conducted 17 classical peace operations, some of which still continue today (such as in Palestine and Cyprus). Only in two of these operations, in addition to the special case of Korea, did the UN resort to military power to enforce stability. Over 70 per cent of all blue-helmet missions have taken place since 1988, the year in which the UN blue-helmets were awarded the Nobel Peace Prize. Along with this dramatic increase in the number of peace operations came the widening of their scope, and a growing number of troops was deployed. Yet disillusionment surfaced in the mid-1990s after a period of enthusiasm about the possible results of peacekeeping for world peace, and the number of troops deployed was substantially reduced. Figure 3.1 illustrates that since 1999, and particularly during the last few years, this trend has reversed yet again. More peacekeepers are presently deployed and at the end of 2004 the number of the peacekeepers rose to over 60,000 once more as it had been a decade before. Missions have changed along with their growing numbers. The UN no longer only functions as a buffer between conflicting parties but has taken on more and more tasks such as the consolidation of peace and state-building, the demobilization, disarmament and reintegration of armies and paramilitary units, and the repatriation of refugees as well as creating transitional administrations. The most extensive operations have taken or, as the case may be, are taking place in Cambodia, the former Republic of Yugoslavia (Bosnia and Herzegovina as well as Kosovo) and in West Africa (DRC, Sierra Leone, Liberia and Burundi).

Furthermore, missions in which the UN has no longer operated with the explicit consent of the conflicting parties but rather included enforcement action have also grown in numbers. The first mission of this newer kind occurred in 1993 in Somalia (UNOSOM II) where the mandate referred to Chapter VII instead of Chapter VI and which thus meant the inclusion of enforcement action. This was followed by operations in Kosovo and East Timor. Prior to this, the conception and practice of UN intervention was based upon the informal 'Chapter Six and a half', situated in between the

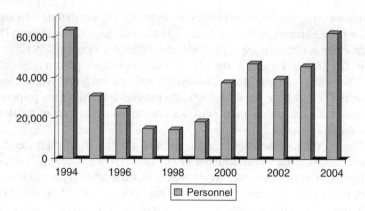

Figure 3.1 Personnel in UN peace missions

Notes: Data gives figure for end of year except 1994 = January 1995; 1998 = November; 2004 = September.

Source: UN Department of Peacekeeping (http://www.un.org/Depts/dpko/dpko/contributors/ 2004/September2004_1.pdf, accessed 25 October 2004).

consensus orientated Chapter VI and the enforcement Chapter VII and envisioning robust armament of the blue-helmets (Kühne 1993).

The contributions of the member states have varied greatly during the last decade as well. At the heyday of peace operations in 1991, one could only find 2 developing countries among the 10 biggest troop-contributing countries; today it is the reverse. In 2004, 14 developing countries formed the apex of those countries that provided military and police forces. Among the first 15 top troop-contributing countries only Ukraine is from outside this group of developing countries. In total 54,000 soldiers, almost 6000 police officers and 2000 military observers were operating in the fall of 2004. Out of these, 8936 came from Pakistan, 8219 from Bangladesh, 3588 from Nigeria, 3445 from Ethiopia, 3320 from Ghana and 3044 from India. The five permanent members of the Security Council together contributed 2775 peacekeepers (http://www.un.org/Depts/dpko/dpko/ contributors/2004/ September2004_1.pdf, accessed 25 October 2004).

The end of the Cold War led to an increased readiness for more extensive peace operations. Jakobsen (2002) notes that 'demand and supply' conditioned causes for the increase in numbers of peace operations. The demand for peace operations grew with the victory of the free market economy and the general trend towards globalization – a trend that not only brought about economic growth but also resulted in destabilization in many countries. The expectations of liberal democracies towards further strengthening of democracy and human rights, the political conditionality in aid programmes towards the creation of good governance, as well as economic reform and infrastructure adjustment programmes – these were not always met. In some countries this led to the breakdown of traditional structures as well as to economic, social and political destabilization. The demand for additional peace operations tends to be greatest in so-called failed states, that is, those states where one can no longer identify a sovereign and where no efficiently functioning state authorities exist.

The demand for military supported UN peace operations has always been greater than the amount of troops and other resources available to it. This is partly because the end of the Cold War dissolved both the blockage in the Security Council due to ideological wrangles as well as the 'southern dimension' of the East–West conflict with its spheres of interests and proxy states. The shortage remained despite the fact that the end of the Cold War did provide an increasing availability of some additional forces that could be used to promote the augmentation of operations. Europe's standing armies possessed spare capacities that were offered for peace operations. New tasks were sought after and the scope of actions of these forces widened (Wulf 2002, 93). What is more, a classic principal of UN peace operations was abandoned, namely, that of not deploying troops from the permanent members of the Security Council and not from countries involved in the conflict region. This new practice increased the potential for further peace operations. In addition, candidates for EU and or NATO enlargement offered their services for peace operations as a means to underline their qualification for membership. Despite all these changes the acute shortage of resources remained. Of course, other factors played a role too in intensifying the requests for UN interventions, such as the so-called CNN effect, that is the fact that war and conflict scenes are increasingly being broadcasted 'live' into the living rooms of Western democracies with the resultant knock-on public demand for action.

From unilateral to multilateral (humanitarian) intervention – and vice versa?

Priority for sovereignty

Intervention signifies an intrusion into the inner dealings of a nation. This is done with the intention to change or retain the political power structures in that nation. To exert this influence, the interventionist powers resort to political and economic, as well as military, means. That said, in both political and political science parlance, intervention connotes primarily military engagements.

There exists a strong tension between the principles of state sovereignty and equality among nations expressed in the UN Charter on the one hand and the special protection of individual and collective human rights on the other. Art. 2(7) of the UN Charter stipulates that 'nothing contained in the present Charter shall authorize the United Nations to intervene in matters which are essentially within the domestic jurisdiction of any state'. Yet, the UN Charter also demands the protection of human rights in accordance with the Universal Declaration of Human Rights. The primacy of political sovereignty and the principle of non-interference were given the highest status at the UN. The prevailing opinion was based on the assumption that the consensus gained through the Peace of Westphalia in 1648 concerning the absolute sovereignty and equality of states served as the basis for international order. A dissolution of this consensus, it was believed, would have resulted in anarchic power struggles.

However, already during the Cold War, and much more so after its termination, the tendency to acknowledge the status of human rights as an international rather than an inner-societal topic gained force. Implicitly this led to the querying of the absoluteness traditionally accepted under the principle of non-interference. Gradually (and often reluctantly) governments accepted certain limitations on their conduct out of a growing respect for human rights (MacFarlane 2002, 34). This should not be seen as a linear or one-sided development as the principle of non-intervention continues to be regarded as a cardinal principal, most notably by regional organizations and in the judgements of the International Court of Justice. Military interventions have been carried out by the great powers and their regional counterparts since the foundation of the UN – primary among them is the United States, though the former colonial powers as well as the Soviet Union were also involved. The right to intervene was defended even amongst socialist countries. Sometimes the great powers intervened directly, and sometimes indirectly, by using their proxies. Further, it was not only the great powers who intervened in support of their own national and security interests. Regional powers acted for the same reasons when they interfered in their neighbouring countries, as was demonstrated by Egypt in 1962 with regard to Yemen, or India in 1971 in West-Pakistan or Bangladesh respectively. In addition, South Africa did so several times in the 1970s and 1980s with regard to its neighbouring countries, also Vietnam in 1978 in Cambodia, and Tanzania in 1979 in Uganda (MacFarlane 2002, 411). As stated earlier, the United Nations conducted its own interventions during this time, albeit to a far lesser scale than it did after the end of the Cold War. The reasons behind these earlier UN missions were, characteristically, to be found in the keeping of the peace and the prevention or ending of wars.

In summary, MacFarlane (2002, 45) comes to the following conclusion: 'the practice of intervention during the Cold War was largely unilateral, statist and motivated by the pursuit of power and other egoistic interests in an anarchical bipolar system. Multilateral organisations played a minor role in the practice of intervention but a more important one in strengthening of norms of sovereignty and non-intervention. Although human rights questions took on a more prominent place in international law during this period, this had little effect on the politics of intervention, which was weakly constrained by normative considerations. Several interventions of the period had significant and positive humanitarian consequences. But these were incidental to the political logic underlying the operations.'

Accent on humanitarian interventions

The number of unilateral interventions decreased notably with the end of the Cold War, whereas multilateral Security Council authorized interventions have risen. An increased level of UN activities became possible owing to a more offensive interpretation of the threats to peace and security by the Security Council. The publication of the Agenda for Peace in 1992 in which preventive diplomacy, peace building, and peacekeeping measures and peace efforts in post-conflict situations were underlined, expresses well the enhanced self-confidence of the UN (Boutros-Ghali 1992). Western governments, having promoted democratization and human rights protection as official goals of their foreign policies, were hesitant to reject interventions when tabled in the name of democracy and human rights. The high number of deaths inflicted by wars coupled with an increasing number of refugees as well as changes in the nature of warfare and its consequences, led to the promotion of humanitarian aspects including requests for 'humanitarian intervention'. The reasoning increasingly came to be that the international community should not only be allowed to intervene in case of gross violations of human rights such as genocide and ethnic cleansing but should in fact be obliged to do so. The advocates of NATO's air campaign in Kosovo in 1999 referred to this argument in particular.

Since then, a plethora of documents and reports by the United Nations have dealt with the question of humanitarian intervention, crisis prevention and the necessary resources for these missions (examples are the Brahimi report: UNGA 2001a, and the report of the UN Secretary General to the UN General Assembly focusing on the prevention of armed conflict: 2001b). Referring to Rwanda and Yugoslavia in his report on the prevention of armed conflicts, the secretary general requests 'a moral responsibility [by the UN] that vulnerable people are protected and that genocide will never happen again' (UNGA 2001b, 35). He places emphasis on the well-timed usage of Chapter VI of the Charter (namely prevention through peaceful means) but recalls that Chapter VII (that is enforced prevention) can have a deterring effect (UNGA 2001b, 36). Prior to this, in 1999, the UN Secretary General Kofi Annan had maintained in an article featured in the British weekly *The Economist* that humanitarian concerns had not been accepted as providing a legitimate basis for the usage of military force. He called for a reinforcement 'of the international norm of intervention for the protection of civilians' (Annan 1999, 82).

The principle of the primacy of the political sovereignty of states in international relations has also been called into question. In the so-called Millennium Report, the secretary general emphasizes that the UN Charter speaks of the sovereignty of peoples, not of states, and therefore by no means allows governments to grossly disrespect human rights (UNSG 2000). The justification from both a political and international law perspective is that human rights violations and humanitarian crises threaten the peace and stability in neighbouring countries and the wider region. Therefore, it is the duty of the Security Council to attend to these problems and possibly to resort to the deployment of military force.

At the beginning of this new development, Security Council resolutions highlighted the exceptional character and the uniqueness of specific situations (humanitarian necessity in the intervention in Somalia, and the saving of democracy in Haiti were emphasized) in order to avoid creating a binding precedent for future interventions. However, more and more frequently the Security Council justifies resorting to military means by stating the necessary protection of human rights, the preservation of democracy, the ending of civil wars, or safeguarding the survival of refugees – thus referring to humanitarian reasons. Some governments of developing countries challenge the lawfulness of 'humanitarian interventions' to this day.

The International Commission on Intervention and State Sovereignty established by the Canadian government addressed the problematic balance of these two mutually exclusive principles of non-interference and intervention on behalf of defending human rights. The commission presented its report at the end of 2001 and wanted to change the terms of the debate by arguing and concluding that it was not a question of a 'right to intervene' but of the 'responsibility to protect' people (International Commission on Intervention and State Sovereignty 2001). This exact wording is also used by the United Nations High-level Panel on Threats, Challenges and Change (UNHLPT 2004, 65). These are attempts to defuse the dilemma of the principles of non-intervention into internal state matters and intervention in the name of human rights for the purpose of protecting people at risk within a state. Such interventions should include political, economic or judicial measures, and in extreme cases – but only in extreme cases – military coercive means (International Commission on Intervention and State Sovereignty 2001, and the Co-President of the Commission Evans 2002). The commission suggested that military actions needed to be based on the following six threshold criteria:

1. *Just cause*: There must be serious and irreparable harm occurring to human beings, or imminently likely to occur, of the following kind: large-scale loss of life, actual or expected, with genocidal intent or not; state inability to act or a failed state situation; or large-scale ethnic cleansing.
2. *Right intention*: The primary purpose must be to halt or avert human suffering, preferably on a collective or multilateral rather than single-country basis.
3. *Last resort*: Military intervention can only be justified when every non-military option for the prevention or peaceful resolution of the crisis has been explored. This does not mean that all options have been tried and have failed.
4. *Proportional means*: The scale, duration and intensity of the planned military intervention should be the minimum necessary to secure the defined human protection objective.
5. *Reasonable prospects*: There must be a reasonable chance of success in halting or averting the suffering.
6. *Right authorization*: The United Nations Security Council is the foremost authority to mandate military intervention for human protection purposes.

The United Nations High-level Panel on Threats, Challenges and Change offers a similar catalogue of decision-making criteria (UNHLPT 2004, 67). Yet these reports are no final and unequivocal basis for intervention. Indeed, by these criteria it is indisputably clear that one can classify the reasons for the Iraq War as insufficient, though it is doubtful whether the controversies surrounding the decision for the air war in Kosovo would have been different had the reports already been published at that time. Today 'the emerging norm' is widely accepted 'that there is a collective international responsibility to protect, exercisable by the Security Council authorizing military intervention as a last resort, in the event of genocide and other large-scale killing, ethnic cleansing or serious violations of international humanitarian law' (UNHLPT 2004, 66). But the tension between the two justifiable principles of non-interference and protection of people remains.

The enforcement of liberal and democratically motivated humanitarian interventions within the scope of the UN is confronted with a series of problems. *First*, the UN has turned to these interventions selectively. Why did the UN intervene in Somalia but not in Rwanda? Why was the UN's engagement in the conflict in Sudan, which has already dragged on for several decades and long before the Darfur crisis, limited for such a long time to aid donations and the sending of a UN Secretary General Special Envoy endowed solely with diplomatic means, whereas East Timor was subject to rapid and effective military intervention in 1999? Large and powerful countries do not have to fear UN interventions at all as the protracted conflict in Chechnya suggests. *Second*, the phenomenon of unilateral interventions conducted without a UN mandate has by no means come to an end, as the NATO intervention in Kosovo, Russian involvement in Georgia and Tajikistan (Tuzmukhamedov 2000), Indian and Pakistani encroachments at the border in Kashmir and cross-border conflicts in Africa and the Iraq War sufficiently document. When governments feel that a situation calls for intervention then they continue to intervene without a UN mandate in order to enforce their own interests. *Third*, the UN member states do not provide enough financial and human resources to enable the UN to perform all of the peace building and peacekeeping tasks that they are called upon to fulfil. Grievance concerning this matter is expressed eloquently in numerous UN documents (UNGA 2001a).

USA: en route towards unilateral interventions?

In the United States, the pendulum of the notion of military interventions has swung back and forth. With the end of the Cold War, the number of American interventions decreased notably. At the same time, the United States pushed for many UN mandated interventions in the Security Council and abandoned their veto with which they could have prevented UN blue-helmet missions, though the scope of their own engagement in these UN missions was limited due to conditions set by the US Congress.

Then, towards the end of 1992, the former Chief of Staff of the US forces and later Secretary of State, General Colin Powell, surprised the US National Security Council with the statement that the US forces would be capable of conducting a successful intervention in Somalia, if required. Previously, he had rejected all similar requests. On 9 December 1992, 1300 US marines landed in Mogadishu and within weeks the US government increased their numbers to 25,000 soldiers (Western 2002, 112). The decision to engage in this mission came as a surprise given that General Powell had sounded a note of caution with regard to the collapse of Yugoslavia in the early 1990s and had formulated the so-called Powell-Doctrine. In essence, Powell's position was: (1) to intervene only when massive means are at one's disposal; (2) when political and military means have been precisely defined; (3) when the mission is of a character that can be successfully conducted; (4) and when the mission bears broad public and parliamentary support. General Powell was not a great friend of 'surgical bombing' or 'limited attacks'. He took advantage of the aversion held by most military planners against imprudent military actions and warned expressively against experts who recommended using this kind of strategy. According to him, this policy had quite literally led the United States into a quagmire many times (Western 2002, 120). His critics maintained that his reservations were of such a dimension that, in practice, no intervention could take place without an overwhelming military force that rendered the mission devoid of any risks altogether. Yet after the US operation in Somalia ended in a complete fiasco and the US forces withdrew after suffering casualties, the Powell reservation became the dominant line of thought. The United States did not want to get entangled in peacekeeping missions again.

This attitude still held true at the beginning of the Clinton administration. Yet the 'never again' mindset turned rapidly into a renewed engagement vis-à-vis multilateral interventions. With Powell resigning from office, the US position with regard to military interventions changed under the new Chief of Staff Shalikashvili (Goldstein 2000) – a policy change that was taken up during the presidential campaign by the republican candidate, Senator Dole, who accused US President Clinton in 1996 of initiating an unprecedented number of military interventions compared to previous administrations. President Clinton justified the US engagement in various war and conflict scenes in the former Yugoslavia by stating that in the new world order, national sovereignty should rank below human rights protection. According to him, the universality of human rights was to be a core concept when considering ethnic and religious conflicts, something that he hoped would be applied both within and outside of national state borders in the future. Although the Republican-dominated Congress prevented the Clinton administration's international engagement at times, it generally adhered to the liberal principle of responsibility for humanitarian questions. In 1999, Clinton said in a speech that: 'It's easy ... to say that we really have no interests in who lives in this or that valley in Bosnia, or who owns a strip of brush land in the Horn of Africa, or some piece of parched earth by the Jordan River. But the true measure of our interests lies in not how small or distant these places are, or in whether we have trouble pronouncing their names. The question we must ask is, what are the consequences to our security of letting conflicts fester and spread' (quoted in Jablonsky 2001, 52)?

With regard to Kosovo, the Clinton administration shifted from diplomacy, reinforced by the threat to use military power, to a policy that used military means supported by diplomatic efforts. In contrast, early in the presidential campaign of 2000, George Bush (junior) pronounced his intention to turn away from this policy. In his opinion, the armed forces exist to win wars rather than to keep peace (Hassner 2002, 37). The president's then National Security Advisor, Condoleezza Rice (2000, 54), argued against both the deployment of US blue-helmets as a worldwide police emergency task force and the concept of 'limited sovereignty in the name of humanity'.

It does not come as much of a surprise that the Powell-Doctrine (calling for restraint on the one hand and overwhelming military force on the other) is only partially in use today. We can no longer speak of constraint. The Bush administration went far beyond this doctrine with regard to its policy towards Iraq and in its position taken in the 'US National Security Strategy Document' (US Government 2002a) of 17 September 2002. Due to the new preparedness to engage the military following the terrorist attacks of 9/11, the US government turned the founding principle of the Powell-Doctrine, namely to exercise constraint upside down.

This new strategy of the Bush administration amounts to nothing less than the implicit and general denunciation of the principle of sovereignty and the equality of peoples. The security of other countries becomes secondary to the security of the American people. However, the United States of America does not replace the principle of sovereignty and equality of peoples with a new liberal, universally recognized principle, but reserves the right to ensure American security if necessary by recourse to 'preemptive strikes' against potential threats – as in the case of Iraq – even through militarily enforced regime change. This concept is justified by the so-called Webster formula of 1856 stating that a country can use force in self-defence from such a time as when an aggression is imminent and when no other means are available. International law experts criticize this 150-year-old interpretation as no longer relevant (Nolte 2003, 131 and Tomuschat 2003).

Thus, the central dilemma (or even contradiction) between the primacy of sovereignty and the primacy of humanitarian intervention is solved by the US government resisting any encroachment of their own sovereignty but justifying intervention against others, if they deem it necessary. The accentuation of military strength, the indifference of the Bush administration towards arms control negotiations, the denunciation and withdrawal from international contracts and the exemption of American citizens from the jurisdiction of the International Criminal Court are consistent with the logic of this administration and perfectly match the 2002 National Security Strategy of the United States.

From a political perspective, this stands for nothing less than a radically new orientation of the entire international relations system, in which unilateral military interventions are of vital importance for American interests and which is propagated from a position influenced by fundamentalist concepts. The politics of the 'war on terror', easy to understand and effectively presented to the public, can be said to have a similar ideological function as the containment of communism throughout the Cold War – namely to conduct politics in a 'friend-foe' scheme. 'We have found our mission' Bush declared (quoted in Hassner 2002, 38). In terms of military strategy, the position of the US government has shifted from a deterrence orientation towards 'pre-emptive' military strikes whenever they are deemed necessary. According to this strategy, pre-emptive strikes should not be considered as exclusive means but should be confined only to certain cases. In practice, however, this strategy has not been universally applied as is suggested by contrasting the Iraq War to the negotiations about the North Korean nuclear programme and the agreement with Libya about the complete abandonment of their weapons of mass destruction programme.

Democratic control of armed forces

The notion of war and peace based on the internal state monopoly of force and the right to fight an external war in order to defend attacks (Aron 1986) has been called into question by the recent developments previously described. Such developments jeopardize the state orientated monopoly of force inasmuch as globalization leads to denationalization and promotes the relocation of authority, that is to say from the nation state to supranational actors in political, commercial and civil societal domains. The United States resists the relocation of authority, although in the economic sphere they pursue their interest through globalization. The latter has not only changed the conditions for the model of the nation state, but the consequences of globalization and the reaction to international military interventions has another long-term effect, namely, it calls into question the concept of nationally organized and orientated armies. Does global governance – a responsible, globally orientated world domestic policy or world order policy (Messner and Nuscheler 1997; Nuscheler 2000a,b) – have an answer to this? Undoubtedly it is right to assume 'when problems globalize, politics needs to globalize accordingly. It is not sufficient to rely solely on an ad-hoc and reactive crises management but new structures of global order need to be created' (Nuscheler 2000a, 474).

Global governance depends on the enhancement of international norms and a new world order in which nation state sovereignty is limited due to the existence of a higher-level executive authority and globally accepted legal norms. A tendency towards global governance manifests itself in civil society in a number of ways. Does this development take place with regard to the military too? Precisely because the military possesses the instruments of ultimate power, it is highly important to regulate its legitimacy, civilian control and accountability. Yet it is exactly owing to military requirements that the military is the least democratically structured organization in most countries; the conduct of the military in situations of armed conflict and its command chain structure collide directly with the concepts of liberty and individuality (Kohn 1997, 141). These differences are intentional and essential, because otherwise there would be no need to have civil-political control over the military (Feaver, Kohn and Cohn 2001, 1).

Expert studies offer a plethora of systematic analyses on the institutionalization of democracy in nation states. Likewise, the literature on global governance hosts many future-orientated publications. Yet, the democratic control of the armed forces and the question of responsibility in international operations are poorly researched.

It has already been mentioned that the provisions of the UN Charter have never been implemented in totality. Questions remain over how (1) authorization of military operations; (2) civilian control over military personnel and military operations; (3) civilian responsibility for the security of the armed forces; and (4) responsibility for norm compliance of the military in international operations, are to be regulated.

The authorization aspect is fairly straightforward. The UN Security Council (and in exceptional cases the General Assembly, such as with the Korean mission) decides over the deployment of UN troops. Thereafter, the implementation of this decision is transferred to the national level. Generally, the national executive (and in exceptional cases, the national legislature) decides routinely as to whether and to what extent their own troops should contribute to an international military operation. Only very few parliaments (out of 17 NATO-member states examined only Denmark, Germany, The Netherlands and the Czech Republic) are involved in the decision over the deployment of UN blue-helmets (Born and Urscheler 2004).

Whereas nation states possess elaborate and systematic doctrines for military operations containing clear delimitations of competences and responsibilities, similar regimes at the international level are almost completely lacking for UN peacekeeping missions concerning the civilian control of military operations and responsibilities for norm compliance (Ku and Jacobson 2001, 35). For military operations conducted under the auspices of the UN (and NATO) the requirement prevails that military commanders are responsible to civilian authorities – mostly the UN Secretary General. The UN operation in Kuwait was an exception to this rule inasmuch as it did not possess a UN command structure. The Security Council authorized this mission, yet the armed forces were responsible to their respective national civilian authority. Moreover, it has become common practice that those units operating under UN command touch base regularly with their national superiors. Ku and Jacobson (2001, 45) conclude: 'It is highly unlikely that these commanders have ever followed an order given in the international chain of command to which their national authorities have not at least acquiesced, if not given their approval'. It is fair to assume that international military operations have been altered by national instructions with respect to both planning and conduct. In this game of mixed competences and responsibilities, questions regarding who has the final say and what are the clear delimitations of competence are not answered. Nuscheler (2000a, 482) correctly addresses the non-military aspect when he states: 'The "holy cow" of the by now already anachronistic concept of sovereignty and traditional thought in terms of national power politics constitutes mighty and hard to come by hurdles towards more global thought and practice'.

But what exactly does that mean for UN peacekeeping missions? Without question it is unwise to abandon political control functions within the national framework before international control mechanisms have been created. So far, this has not happened. In most cases, not even the national parliaments possess sufficient control mechanisms. Were the UN a democratically structured organization, problems would be easier to solve. Yet neither does the UN Security Council reflect the global political structures in its present formation nor can the UN General Assembly perform parliamentary functions being a non-elected intergovernmental institution.

The dilemma vis-à-vis mixed responsibilities and competences reoccurs with respect to the safety of UN forces. When the Security Council decides to initiate a peace mission and assigns the implementation to the secretary general or the Department for Peacekeeping Operations, and the member states do not provide sufficient resources (as has occurred in previous peace operations), who will bear the responsibility for efficient and effective operations and the safety of the armed forces? Will it be the Security Council, the secretary general, the national authorities who decide upon the deployment of national forces, or the commander in chief on the ground? The example of the Dutch armed forces, who were supposed to protect the people in Srebrenica, albeit with insufficient means and an unclear mandate, illustrates well the inherent problem with mixed competences (UNGA 1999). The national command and competence structures usually at work at the national level do not apply here. The problem becomes worse due to the fact that Security Council decisions are neither democratic nor transparent at all times. Given that functions of competence and accountability are difficult to establish between the international institutions and the respective national executives, it is not surprising that parliamentary control is even more difficult.

At the national level especially, many norms with respect to the conduct of soldiers in war and conflict situations have been developed. However, not until 1999 was it decided that armed forces under the command of the UN are subject to the Geneva Conventions. The crimes committed by Canadian peacekeeping forces in Somalia are publicly known. These soldiers were tried by their national courts, but not by the UN. Even in these cases national responsibilities were never assigned to the international authorities. This issue only became regulated with the establishment of the International Criminal Court (with important exceptions, particularly that of the self-imposed exclusion of the United States).

On the one hand, increasing internationalization and globalization demands an abdication of sovereignty and requires co-operation among nations. On the other hand, the lack of legitimacy and the democratic deficit becomes more and more evident. The more decisions are transferred from the national to the international sphere the more difficult the situation will be for the elected national parliaments. This is true not only with respect to the UN; the EU, at present creating an EU Rapid Reaction Force, has equally not arrived at a clear-cut, non-ambiguous solution concerning all aspects of control and responsibility either (Assembly of Western European Union 2001, Bono and Mawdsley 2002, Hummel 2003). The tendency towards privatization of security exacerbates the problem of insufficient parliamentarian control over the armed forces.

4

South Africa: From Pariah to Regional Cop

African solutions for African problems?

Reservations in South Africa

South African peace missions, either within Africa or to any other part of the world, were not on the agenda in 1994 at the end of Apartheid when the Mandela government took office. The main focus, understandably, was on internal change and the task was to promote and implement the transformation of society towards becoming a democracy and to reform the armed forces and police after the long isolation of the country during the Apartheid era. The government facilitated the restructuring of the armed forces by integrating the various forces – the regular army and several groups of freedom fighters – that had previously fought each other and uniting them into one unit, the South African National Defence Forces (SANDF). The government made sure that it had the support of a majority of the population for this reform process (Cawthra 2003 and 2004).

When in 1996 the United Nations asked the South African government to send troops on a peace mission to Burundi, Nelson Mandela said publicly: 'We have been approached by the UN but we have to be very cautious about our background where our Army destabilized the neighbouring countries ... We are prepared to supply humanitarian assistance ... but the military, I will resist that' (quoted in *Mail* and *Guardian* 19 July 1996). Nevertheless, the public debate pro and contra South African involvement in peace missions had begun.

Although the acceptance of the White Paper 'Defence in a Democracy, White Paper on National Defence for the Republic of South Africa' (Republic of South Africa 1996) in May 1996 by parliament did not complete the reform process it was a major milestone, firmly establishing the civil and democratic control of the armed forces. Despite the government's reluctance to engage in African conflicts it was difficult from the beginning to abstain completely from these conflicts. Even before the Mandela government was installed in power Western and other African governments had requested the African National Congress (ANC) to take over regional responsibility for future economic and social development and especially also for security in the region. Another, and possibly decisive, reason for South Africa to eventually change its policy of reluctance or even abstention was the intensified conflicts in the Great Lakes' region – in Zaire and in Rwanda (Williams 2000, 84). The White Paper of 1996 itself contains in Chapter 5 a brief mention and a few defining conditions concerning 'international peace support operations'. Listed as conditions for participation, the Paper especially values parliamentary approval and public support, a clear mandate, mission and objectives, realistic criteria for terminating the operation, and authorization by the United Nations Security Council. Further, operations in Southern Africa were to be undertaken together with other South African Development Community (SADC) member states rather than conducted unilaterally, and in wider Africa with the sanctioning of the Organisation for African Unity (Republic of South Africa 1996, Chapter 5, Art. 19–26). These qualifications in the White Paper illustrate the South African caution and reluctance. The document, in addition, refers to the fact that the government does not necessarily mean by 'international peace support operations' the deployment of military power but first and foremost peace efforts based on the agreement of the warring parties.

Western withdrawal and pressures on Africa

The trend of military backed South African peace missions correlates to the global development. After the euphoria of the early 1990s concerning the possibilities of creating a world free of wars had subsided and was replaced by disillusionment, many governments no longer wanted to contribute their own troops to United Nations peace operations in the same scale as previously. The US experience in Somalia and the inactivity of the UN in Rwanda (and originally in the Balkans too) resulted in reservations among countries such as the United States, France and Great Britain and a drastic reduction in their UN troop contributions. Ironically this happened at a time when the demand for blue-helmets continued to rise to a point larger than ever before. This had particular relevance in the African continent (Bermann and Sams 2000, 379, Kent and Malan 2003, 9), where the Western permanent members of the UN Security Council (France, the United Kingdom and the United States) assisted with a number of measures to facilitate peacekeeping initiatives in Africa *by* African countries under the headline 'African solutions for African problems'. This included support for the Organization of African Unity (OAU), technical assistance for military training in selected countries, support for training operations and the suggestion of the creation of an African Crisis Response Force (ACRF), later renamed the African Crisis Reaction Initiative (ACRI) (Cleaver and May 1998, 32, and Malan 2004, 200). The basic premise of looking for solutions in Africa itself coupled with various support measures by Western countries was positively received in most countries of Africa. But, at first, tangible peace operations of a regional character were initiated and implemented only in West Africa by the Economic Community of West African States (ECOWAS). This situation led to expectations regarding South Africa as a regional power in Southern Africa (as with Nigeria in West Africa) (Shaw and Cilliers 1995).

White Paper on South African Participation in International Peace Missions

The cabinet of the South African government drafted a 'White Paper on South African Participation in International Peace Missions' and submitted it to parliament (Republic of South Africa 1999). The acceptance in February 1999 in parliament was the culmination of a two-year process of public debate. In a similar manner to the Defence White Paper of 1996, a lengthy public consultation process preceded the final acceptance of the 1999 White Paper on peace missions. Not only were the various concerned ministries of the government and the armed forces consulted, but numerous non-governmental experts and civil society too were expected to contribute to the debate. The original government draft from 1997, which was primarily directed at the procedures and processes of the armed forces and reflected the professional predisposition of the drafters, was thoroughly revised and expanded and includes in its final version clear political criteria. Conflict resolution that includes economic, social, cultural and personal security requires, according to the White Paper, multidisciplinary approaches based on good governance, a robust democracy and economic and social orientation (Republic of South Africa 1999).

Williams (2000, 88–95) characterizes five decisive pillars of the White Paper: (1) a definition of the concept of peace missions; (2) prioritization of conflict management; (3) a definition of the relationship between peace missions and South Africa's emerging national interests; (4) the likely contribution South Africa could make; and (5) a definition of the overarching principles and procedures that would govern involvement in peace missions. These five strategic pillars are described below:

First, defining peace missions: During the consultations about the White Paper the government decided to use the term 'peace missions', which is intended to include the whole spectrum of possible interventions: political-diplomatic initiatives, military-based initiatives and development and humanitarian-inclined initiatives. This term was felt to be less militaristic and underlines the premise that the original concept of 'peace support operations' is reserved for military operations.

Second, South Africa's approach to conflict: The White Paper presupposes that sustainable peace and stability can only be achieved if the root causes of conflict are addressed. This emphasis is based on the concept of Nathan (2001, 4), at the time Director of the Centre for Conflict Resolution of the University of Cape Town, who described Africa's problems with the image of the 'the four horsemen of the Apocalypse'. He concluded that Africa's troubles stem from authoritarian rule and the exclusion of minorities from governance, combined with inequity and weak states that lack the institutional capacity to manage normal political and social conflict. To address the root causes of conflicts and to invest in sustainable peace processes it is necessary – according to the government White Paper – to involve government as well as non-governmental organizations and not just troops.

Third, peace missions and national interests: The process leading to the publication of the White Paper also showed that South Africa is not guided only by altruistic motives to contribute to the resolution of African conflicts. The document clearly states that South Africa's own evolving national interests must be considered, namely the security of the country and its people, social and economic development, and global and regional peace and stability. This notion of national interest is more explicitly described as the promotion of human rights, of democracy and international law, of international peace and conflict resolution mechanisms, and South Africa's interest in world politics and regional co-operation (Republic of South Africa 1999, 16–17).

Fourth, South Africa's likely contribution to peace missions: Without giving up the unambiguous preference for such peace missions that address the root causes of conflicts and not just the symptoms, it was understood in South Africa that the international community was expecting practical and concrete assistance in crises. When the aim is to prevent violence, it could also be necessary to apply military power. An obvious commitment in this regard is South Africa's willingness to contribute to a UN Standby Force. The White Paper authorizes the relevant ministries to prepare for the participation of military, police and civil capacities (Williams 2002, 92).

Fifth, functions and procedures of peacekeeping missions: The White Paper underlines the importance of a clear and unequivocal international mandate from the UN, preferably in accordance with agreement of OAU and SADC and of the public in South Africa. The White Paper elaborates in detail the entry and exit strategies: Peacekeeping personnel can be deployed only on a voluntary basis and – if possible – only in co-operation with South Africa's neighbours or other African countries.

Theory and practice: peace missions in Lesotho, DRC, Burundi and ...

Lesotho: intervention almost single-handedly

The prime minister of Lesotho asked the governments of South Africa, Mozambique, Zimbabwe and Botswana in September 1998, shortly before South Africa's publication of its White Paper on peace missions, to intervene in Lesotho to restore law and order. Internal unrest, palace intrigues and several attempted coups were the background to this request. SADC had already authorized, four years previously in 1994, a troika of South Africa, Botswana and Zimbabwe to quell uprisings in Lesotho. Several agreements had finally led to elections in 1998, but the results of that election were contested by the opposition which had won only 1 out of 80 parliamentary seats. The result was again unrest in the country with young officers of the Royal Lesotho Defence Force trying to topple their commander and refusing to restore law and order; instability in the region followed. When the opposition refused to accept investigations by a SADC committee, South Africa's acting President Chief Buthelezi decided after consultations with the governments in Zimbabwe, Botswana and Mozambique to intervene. Six hundred South African troops invaded Lesotho on 22 September 1998 in Operation *Boleas*; a small contingent of troops from Botswana followed one day later. Their aim was to protect the Katse dam, to isolate the military base in Mkonyane, in which the rebelling officers had wielded power, and to protect the Royal Palace as well as other government buildings in the capital Maseru (Williams 2000, 97; Berman and Sams 2000, 184; Kent and Malan 2003). Despite this limited mission South Africa suffered 9 casualties and the Losotho forces 60 as resistance was stronger than had been expected by South Africa.

SADC had not explicitly authorized this intervention. Although the SANDF claimed otherwise, that the operation was mandated by SADC, in reality this was not the case and the military action was controversial even within South Africa's government. Indeed, some high-ranking officials of the Pretoria Foreign Ministry criticized the fact that they had not even been consulted in the planning process (Bermann and Sams 2000, 185–86). Despite the few telephone contacts between several heads of government of the region in which the operation was called a SADC Force, the international legal basis was rather dubious. Militarily the operation was eventually a success, but only the protection of the Katse dam, which is important as a water reservoir for South Africa, could possibly be loosely defined as protection of South Africa's national interest (Kent and Malan 2003, 4).

At a time when the White Paper on peace missions was about to be submitted by the government and authorized by parliament, several of the highly claimed principles for participation in peace missions were grossly violated by the Lesotho intervention. It is surprising not only to what extent important government units were excluded from the decision, but also that it was taken without consultation of parliament and without an African or a UN mandate. Given the scarcity of information a public debate did take place, but only after the fact. Although the constitution does allow the president to decide on troop deployment and neither parliament nor the public need to be formally consulted, nevertheless, given the definition of the criteria in the White Paper of 1999 there was a glaring gap between theory and practice in the Lesotho intervention. Williams (2000, 101) concludes: 'For a government committed to a peace-building agenda, Lesotho was a poor example of implementation'.

Democratic Republic of Congo: participation based on a UN mandate

South Africa had its initial experience of participation in internationally authorized peace missions in 2000 with a small contingent of four military observers and troops in the UN Eritrea and Ethiopia peace operation (UNMEE). A larger contingent of SANDF forces was first in operation as of April 2001 when the government contributed 150 soldiers, primarily technical support personnel, to the UN operation (MONUC) in the DRC (Kent and Malan 2003, 7; http://www.un.org/Depts/dpko/dpko/contributors/, accessed 30 December 2004). The decision was preceded by complex negotiations and controversial public discussions within South Africa.

As a result of the protracted and in 1998 renewed eruption of large-scale fighting in Zaire (now respectively the DRC) the Security Council of the UN decided to engage in its peace operation MONUC. The UN has had peacekeepers in the DRC since November 1999, and their number has increased to 10,570 soldiers, 155 police officers and 505 military observers, as well as 707 international civil personnel and 1135 local civil personnel (http://www.un.org/Depts/dpko/missions/monuc/facts.html, accessed 30 December 2004). On 8 August 1998 Zimbabwe's President Mugabe invited the heads of state from Angola, the DRC, Namibia, Rwanda, Tanzania, Uganda and Zambia for a meeting in Victoria Falls to co-ordinate the Southern African military engagement in the DRC. South Africa was not invited because of an ongoing disagreement between Presidents Mandela and Mugabe about the chairmanship of the SADC Organ on Politics, Defence and Security. While Mandela, in his function as Chairman of SADC, did not want to deploy SADC troops in the DRC but rather emphasized the need for negotiations and a peaceful settlement to the conflict, Mugabe immediately deployed Zimbabwean troops to assist the rebel leader, and later President of Zaire, Kabila. Zimbabwe claimed that their military engagement was based on the agreement in Victoria Falls, which Mugabe considered a SADC decision. When Mandela protested, Mugabe countered by proclaiming: 'No one is compelled within SADC to go into a campaign of assisting a country beset by conflict. Those who want to keep out, fine. Let them keep out, but let them be silent about those who want to help' (quoted in Nathan 2004, 18). Angola had already stationed troops in the DRC to fight their Angolan rebels; while Namibia soon followed Zimbabwe's example. The reactions in Southern Africa, which were supposed to be co-ordinated according to SADC rules, were thus completely contradictory.

Eventually, in 2000, the government of South Africa concurred to the insistence of the UN, which was always short of peacekeepers in the DRC, and made – reluctantly – a sizable contingent of South African peacekeepers available for the MONUC mission. The South African troop strength was gradually increased to 1400 soldiers in 2004, more than 12 per cent of the total MONUC personnel. This decision in South Africa was based on a lengthy consultation process within the government and an intensive public debate. The government orientated its policy, in contrast to the Lesotho intervention, on the concept of the 1999 White Paper on peace missions.

Burundi: mandated by the African Union[19]

Only half a year after the first deployment of troops in the DRC, South Africa, mandated by the AU, took over the task – with a limited number of troops – to protect and guarantee the security of high-ranking government officials and parliamentarians in Burundi's capital Bujumbura. This commitment was, and is, pursued in conformity with the wishes of the UN to place more responsibility on the shoulders of regional powers for the peace process in Burundi. South Africa pledged to take on the task of the lead nation in the AU's African Mission in Burundi (AMIB). Originally however, South Africa did not want to send any troops to Burundi. Nelson Mandela declared his willingness to act as a mediator in the peace process and began his work at the end of 1999. Prior to this engagement numerous attempts by the UN to pacify the internal unrest and stop the violence had failed. (In more recent years South Africa's Vice President Zuma has taken over the role of mediator while President Mbeki made an effort until recently in his role as Chairman of the AU to facilitate the peace process.) A number of neighbouring countries as well as UN experts had suggested deploying peacekeepers in Burundi during the mid-1990s, though the Burundian government had protested energetically against the stationing of a full-scale battle group as had been suggested by Boutros-Ghali. NATO countries meanwhile were disinterested in participation given their commitment in the Balkans (Furley 1998, 256). As Undersecretary General responsible for peacekeeping at the time Kofi Annan had planned a troop contingent of 20,000 soldiers, but only 6 African countries – Ethiopia, Malawi, Tanzania, Chad, Uganda and Zambia – were willing to contribute troops; in addition the United States and Belgium offered financial and logistical assistance. This process failed however, both because of the refusal of the then Burundi government to have UN peacekeepers stationed in the country as well as the lack of troop contributions. The UN Security Council, therefore, did not pass the necessary resolution.

By the end of 2002, Tanzania's former President Julius Nyerere was successful in mediating a ceasefire between various rebel groups and the Burundian government. The treaty was signed on 2 December 2002 in Arusha, Tanzania. The AU decided, with some delay, upon a peace mission in April 2003 and South Africa agreed to lead the mission and send 1600 soldiers (1 battalion and 2 companies). Ethiopia, under the condition of financial reimbursement, pledged 1600 soldiers (1 battalion and 2 companies) and Mozambique 280 soldiers (an expanded company). The total personnel strength was mandated for up to 3500 peacekeepers, including military observers and civilian experts. The mandate – limited originally to one year, with an option for extension or handing over to the UN – focused on the mediation between the warring parties, monitoring the ceasefire, protection of safe transport for demobilized soldiers and rebels, technical assistance for demobilization and disarmament, and the protection of the leaders of the various groups (Boshoff 2003).

South Africa's contingent gradually grew to over 1500 soldiers in spring 2004, a little less than originally pledged, and had at the end of 2004 scaled back to about 1000. The UN took over the AU mission in May 2004, and as at the end of 2004, 859 troops from Ethiopia, 995 from Kenya, 940 from Nepal and 1198 from Pakistan serve in the UN mission in Burundi, in addition to the South African peacekeepers (http://www.un.org/Depts/dpko/dpko/contributors/2004/November2004_ 5.pdf, accessed 30 December 2004).

South Africa was willing to accept this responsibility to assist to avoid a further spill-over of the Hutu–Tutsi conflict into Eastern DRC. The Pretoria government was well aware of the risk of deploying troops in the region without either a functioning peace agreement or precise and agreed plans for demobilization measures. The main burden of the AU-commitment rested on South Africa's shoulders, being required to con-tribute the largest contingent of troops, and it was due to the lack of willingness of other countries that South Africa felt pressured into taking and accepting this responsibility to lead the peace mission.

The AU resolution stipulated that troop-contributing countries would finance the first two months of the mission themselves. The AU estab-lished a peace fund that was intended to collect contributions worth € 200 million, but the resolution did not give details as to where the funds should come from. In the meantime the European Union (EU) has allocated into an African Peace Facility financial means from its devel-opment budget of € 250 million for the peace missions in crises regions of the AU (Keane 2004). The UN budget for the Burundi mission alone amounts to US$330 million for the 2004/2005 mandate. South Africa budgeted Rand 496 million (around € 60 million) for 2004 alone, amount-ing to a doubling of the previous year's budget (*Mail* and *Guardian* 23 February 2004). Yet it was not expected in South Africa that they would be reimbursed as originally indicated in the AU resolution, since neither the AU peace fund nor the AU general budget had financial means of that magnitude available.

Given the criteria of the 1999 White Paper on peace missions, the deployment of troops in Burundi can be classified as a well-co-ordinated action of the South African government (Kent and Malan 2003, 5). Both the parliament (in its right to authorize the budget) as well as the public (through a lively debate in the media) were involved in the decision-making process.

Regional organizations: fit for peace missions?

The United Nations, both the Security Council and the secretary general, have continued to emphasize since the 1990s the special importance of regional organizations in promoting and facilitating peace and stability within their respective regions. Regional organizations can contribute to conflict prevention in a number of specific ways. These organizations build trust among states through the frequency of their interaction, and have an intimate knowledge of the history of a conflict. Because of their proximity regional organizations can function as a local forum to de-escalate tensions, pacify conflicts and promote a comprehensive regional approach to cross-border issues (UNGA 2001b, 31). In reality, however, the two regional organizations with South African membership, the AU and SADC, have no convincing record of peace missions to justify such expectations.

The South African government has made its participation in peace missions contingent upon a mandate from the UN or the AU, or on the co-operation among the members of SADC. This policy decision was made with the full knowledge that enormous political differences exist between the member countries in both regional organizations and that only insufficient peace mission resources are at these organizations' disposal. Despite this understanding and experience South Africa's government has nevertheless always stressed in its political declarations concerning peace missions the need for regional co-operation.

African Union: old wine in new bottles?

The AU policy of international peace missions is strongly influenced by the OAU heritage of non-intervention into the internal matters of its members. This is understandable given the colonial and post-colonial history of most African states as well as the tensions within the UN with the same problem of non-intervention versus intervention to prevent or stop violence. The principle of sovereignty and non-interference in internal matters is firmly rooted in the OAU and AU and has repeatedly led to their inactivity. Yet having said this, article 4(h) of the AU Charter does authorize the Union to intervene in a member state 'pursuant to a decision of the Assembly in respect of grave circumstances, namely: war crimes, genocide and crimes against humanity' (African Union http:// www.africa-union.org/home/Welcome.htm, accessed 28 December 2004).

The OAU General Assembly after three decades since its foundation passed the so-called Cairo declaration in 1993 regarding a 'Mechanism on Conflict Prevention Management' (Nhara 1998, 33). The heads of state of the OAU member countries declared their willingness to interfere in international conflicts, but would leave the leading role to the UN. In its time the OAU intervened in at least 13 different conflicts, mainly through applying diplomatic and other political means, as in such conflicts as Rwanda, Somalia, Central African Republic, Sierra Leone, Western Sahara and others. Only five of these interventions can be categorized as peace missions (Nieuwkerk 2004, 57).

The AU emphasized its desire to promote peace and stability in Africa with the transfer from the OAU to the AU, the declaration of the AU constitution in July 2000 and the establishment of the AU Peace and Security Council within the AU one year later. This policy is meant to underline the ambition of finding African solutions for African problems, but it is also a reaction to the many long-drawn-out and intensified conflicts in the African continent. The AU took over the previously existing peace fund of the OAU to achieve this goal and aims at expanding it with additional financial resources. At the same time the AU decided to create a Standby Force and five African regional organizations pledged to contribute to its realization (Keane 2004). But this realization is not imminent, and sceptics doubt if the AU really has 'new tools in the box' (Malan 2004). In addition, the potential tension of the contradictory principles of non-interference in internal matters and intervention to stop war or prevent conflict and violence has not been solved in the AU either.

The OAU was forced into inactivity in numerous violent conflicts because of internal quarrels, its limited mandate and, probably most importantly, because of the lingering political differences among the members in an organization that lacked or had insufficient resources of its own. Furthermore, the organization had only limited experience in international crisis management. The political will to find solutions for African problems has been strengthened with the foundation of the AU, but the institutional prerequisites needed to implement this newly evolved political will are still not fully functional. Additional assistance (financial resources and training) has been offered by the United States and several Western European countries, but this is by far inadequate to enable Africa to wield a credible military force for peace missions. Weapons and other military equipment for African peacekeepers have scarcely been supplied so far since reservations exist – for example in the EU – of using development funds for arms deliveries; the EU's African Peace Facility excludes these deliveries explicitly (Keane 2004). Therefore, AU peace missions still depend on assistance from the UN, sub-regional organizations (such as ECOWAS in West Africa) or ad hoc coalitions. It is possible that an experiment practiced in Liberia, could be repeated elsewhere in Africa. Two private military companies, Pacific Architects and Engineers (PAE) and ICI-Oregon, assisted with the logistical requirements of the UN mandated ECOWAS troops; the invoice was picked up by the United States (O'Hanlon and Singer 2004, 86).

Southern African Development Community (SADC): conflict among neighbours

A number of the difficulties to effectively carry out peace missions diagnosed for the AU are similar or indeed the same for SADC too. The conflict within SADC concerning the procedures of the military intervention in the DRC has not been principally resolved even to this day, thus indicating the limited room for manoeuvre of this regional organization (Berman and Sams 2000, 175).

As the name of SADC suggests, the original purpose of the organization was economic development in the region. But the creation of a common security architecture has been added and is now of great importance too. In article 21(h) the members agree to cooperate in 'politics, diplomacy, international relations, peace and security' and article 22 requests members to establish 'institutional mechanisms for co-operation and integration' (http://www.sadc.int/index.php?action = a1001&page_id = amended_declaration_and_treaty_of_sadc, accessed 29 December 2004.) The official SADC policy does not define the term 'security' uniformly: Security policy is meant to address the stability in member countries, the security of the countries and their citizens, and cross-border conflicts. This policy is orientated to the term 'common security' that was developed over two decades ago by the Palme Commission in the context of the East–West antagonism addressing inter-dependency of relations. Common security suggests that countries need to co-operate with their neighbours even when they disagree on controversial issues or when they antagonize each other. The common (in)security in the East–West relations was grounded in the threat of mutually assured destruction through nuclear weapons. Such a Damocles sword does not terrorize Southern Africa. This might be one of the reasons for the predominance of internal conflicts in the region as they have not been marginalized by the threat of a nuclear catastrophe.

SADC decided as early as 1994 to establish an Organ for Politics, Defence and Security and implemented it in 1996, primarily because cross-border conflicts endangered the peace process in the region. These conflicts were quite frequent in Southern Africa, as the following examples illustrate: the long-lasting war in Angola which ended in 2002, the war in the DRC, the various unrests in Lesotho and the 1998 intervention, the failed secession in Namibia in 1998/1999, unrest in Malawi after elections in 1999, the constitutional crisis in Tanzania in 2001 and the government-organized repression in Zimbabwe since 2000. Yet despite all these menacing conflicts affecting the whole region the Organ of Politics, Defence and Security was unable to actively mediate or intervene – partly, but not exclusively, because of the unsettled dispute about the function of this organ between South Africa and Zimbabwe. One can distinguish between 2 groups in the 14 member countries comprising SADC. The first group emphasizes the political aspects of foreign and security policy; within this group among others are South Africa, Botswana, Mozambique and Tanzania. The second group stresses defence policy and wants to strengthen the organization's military arm; this group includes Angola, the DRC, Namibia and Zimbabwe, who formed a military alliance in 1999. Nathan (2004) classifies the two groups as the 'pacific' and 'militarist'.

The potentially vital role of regional organizations in peace missions is one of the firm general expectations of such organizations (Berman 2002). The experiences in Europe and Asia have facilitated the prospects for a more active and expanded responsibility of regional organizations (Hirsh 2000). Therefore, it is surprising that the so-called Brahimi Report, the central reform proposal for UN peace missions, widely ignores this issue (UNGA 2001a). The balance sheets of the two regional organizations AU and SADC are no reason for optimism. In practice they have proven that regional organizations are as awkward and inflexible as the UN themselves; practical measures often fail or are forgone because of a lack of political agreement. Old traditional and historical antagonisms, contrasts and differing attitudes continue to exist, as the Anglophone and Francophone disagreements graphically underline in West Africa (Cleaver and May 1998, 37). This is the main reason for the formation of ad hoc coalitions at the global and regional level in order not to be doomed to total inactivity when regional groupings or the UN are not able to come to a decision (Wilson 2003). Ad hoc coalitions can bridge or circumvent the gap when a lack of agreement within regional organizations appears. This was the case – with South African participation – in the peace missions in the DRC and in Burundi. It is an established wisdom when initiating peace missions that only those countries can join forces that are willing and able to exert the necessary political will and have the necessary military and civil capacities.

Three fundamental problems prevent closer co-operation in peace missions and other relevant security areas within SADC today (Nathan 2004): first, SADC lacks common and fundamental values fully accepted by all members. In contrast to the EU, for example, not all SADC member countries are democratic. The index of Freedom House (2004) categorizes Botswana, Lesotho, Mauritius, Namibia and South Africa as free countries. Malawi, Mozambique, Seychelles, Tanzania and Zambia are classified as partly free; and Angola, the DRC, Swaziland and Zimbabwe as not free. The second reason is the unwillingness to give up certain sovereignty rights on behalf of the regional organizations. This is partly due to internal political reasons since a number of SADC countries can be considered as weak states. The third reason is the lack of sufficient economic and human resources to establish and institutionalize SADC sufficiently. It is therefore not surprising that the peacekeeping record of SADC is miserable.

Military capacities and the new role of South Africa

At the end of 2004 South Africa had deployed about 2500 peacekeepers in African peace missions. This is quite a sizeable force, given the total military strength of 60,000 soldiers in South Africa and the fact that the armed forces were not reformed in 1994 with the intention to serve in future peace missions. An end of South African deployment in peace missions is not expected but these missions are a heavy burden on the armed forces as the different contingents need to be rotated regularly, and it is discussed within the armed forces if the threshold of capacity has already been passed. The UN has stationed almost 49,000 of its 64,000 military, police and civilian personnel in African peace missions. Within these UN peace missions, African countries have contributed large peacekeeping contingents as the following Table 4.1 underlines.

Table 4.1 The largest contingents of African UN peacekeepers*

	United Nations
Nigeria	3,735
Ethiopia	3,432**
Ghana	3,357
South Africa	2,398**
Kenya	2,210
Morocco	1,704
Senegal	1,575
Namibia	889
Tunisia	523
Niger	466

Notes: * including police and military observers; ** including personnel of the original AU mission in Burundi which was transferred to the UN 21 May 2004 according to UN resolution 1545, UN operation in Burundi (ONUB).

Sources: UN Department of Peacekeeping Operations (http://www.un.org/Depts/dpko/dpko/contributors/, accessed 30 December 2004)

About one third of the total strength of the 64,000 peacekeepers in UN peace missions is from Africa.

South Africa's original refusal to participate in peace missions has now been replaced by a cautious willingness to engage, even militarily. Reasons for continued caution are primarily of a political nature and a result of risk assessment; the government does not want to be drawn into non-resolvable African conflicts. Promoters of peacekeeping argue that South Africa cannot prosper in a sea of insecurity but needs to press for stability on the continent. Acceptance of this responsibility is seen at the same time as an entry point for international recognition (Neethling 2002). With regard to Burundi, Nelson Mandela said: 'This tiny African country would strike a blow for multilateralism and dialogue if it could prove that talks can lead to peaceful coexistence' (quoted in *Mail* and *Guardian* 24 November 2003). Pierre Steyn said as South Africa's Minister of Defence in 1998: South Africa must sail between 'the Scylla of national interest and humanitarian concern, and the Charybdis of financial and military prudence' (Steyn 1998, 32). This dilemma still plays an important role in South Africa's decisions to expand its role in Africa. Presently, the willingness to intervene internationally is the predominant motive.

South Africa is – together with Nigeria in West Africa and considerably ahead of Kenya in East Africa – a military and economic dominant regional power as illustrated in the following Table 4.2. Despite this impressive concentration of economic and military resources in South Africa and Nigeria these figures need to be seen in a global perspective in order to come to a conclusion on the countries' peacekeeping capabilities. The Gross National Product (GNP) of the Sub-Saharan African continent is approximately 1 per cent of the world and lower than that of the Netherlands. Similar relationships apply for military expenditures. South Africa's military expenditure amounts to 0.3 per cent of the world's total, or to approximately 6.6 per cent of Britain's. Only in the area of the number of military personnel is the difference less significant.

Table 4.2   Economic and military indicators

	South Africa	Nigeria	Sub-Saharan Africa
GNP in b. US$	113.3	41.4	300.9
GNP per capita US$ (PPP)	11,290	850	1,831
Number of military personnel	60,000	79,000	1,340,000
Defence budget in million US$	2,460	770	8,100

Sources: BICC 2004; UNDP 2003.

To effectively engage in peace operations and to deploy troops quickly into crises regions additional transport capabilities (transport aircraft, helicopters) and logistics are needed. Even South Africa will depend on assistance from abroad for these services if the present commitment is not reduced but expanded as expected. The armed forces have requested improved equipment capabilities and experts call for structural reform; some of these proposals have gone right to the nuts and bolts of such reforms (Heitman 2002). Today both Nigeria and South Africa have taken on a leading role in several areas, including peace missions. This claim for leadership has led to an informal bilateral and strengthened alliance between the two countries. President Olesugun Obesanjo of Nigeria declared passionately concerning the emerging Abuja-Pretoria-axis: 'Our location, our destiny and the contemporary forces of globalization have thrust upon us the burden of turning around the fortunes of our continent. We must not and cannot shy away from this responsibility' (quoted in Adebajo and Landsberg 2003, 192). South Africa's President Thabo Mbeki is seen in this division of labour as the one to push the concepts, for example in the so-called African Renaissance and the New Economic Partnership for Africa's Development (NEPAD), while President Olesugun Obesanjo presses for institutional changes, for example the strengthening of the AU. The media in South Africa asks self- critically if this amounts to a new form of 'African imperialism' or if South Africa is emerging as a 'new colonial power' (*Mail* and *Guardian* 18 February 2004 and 5 March 2004). Yet Thabo Mbeki repeatedly stresses that South Africa will engage in the sub-region 'as a partner and ally, not as a regional superpower' (quoted in Adebajo and Landsberg 2003, 187).

South Africa has developed during the last years a clearly identifiable position of military participation in peace missions based on unambiguous political criteria. It has gradually given up its previous resistance, which was taken with regard to the countries' apartheid history and its role as an international Pariah. Since then, the country has engaged with caution and prudence in mediating African conflicts and trying to help stop wars. Conceptually, decisions for participation in peace missions are dependent on a broad national acceptance and regional, continental or global integration. As to whether this will continue to be the case in future or if the government will fall back into the heavily criticized policy of the Lesotho intervention is an open question. The present government is ready to commit its resources in the region because of, amongst other reasons, the inadequate capabilities of regional organizations. In contrast to the declared intentions in the 1999 White Paper on peace missions, the deployment of troops is the primary focus of South Africa's contributions. It can be expected that South Africa will continue to engage in other protracted conflict regions of the continent or will, in the case of newly erupting conflicts, intervene with peace operations.

5
European Union: Civil Power in Camouflage

The European Security and Defence Policy (ESDP) has experienced an unprecedented dynamic since the end of the 1990s. This was never the case in the numerous previous attempts at initiating such a policy during the last 50 years. The primary aim of the present effort is to create capabilities for the so-called 'Petersberg tasks' – military based humanitarian aid programmes, peace enforcement, interventions and crisis prevention. These are the type of military tasks referred to by the US armed forces as 'Military Actions other than War' (MAOW).

The functions of the West European Union (WEU) have mainly been transferred to the European Union (EU). Several committees dealing with defence, security and defence industry aspects have been formed under the umbrella of the European Council; in addition, crisis reaction forces are in the making and the EU Commission has been given certain authority in security relevant areas. This process began, however, by arranging a number of institutional changes without an agreed strategy of the EU. One could have expected the design and agreement upon a strategy first and then the establishment of the necessary political and military structures. The process in the EU however was the reverse.

Only recently, and for the first time in the history of the EU, has a security strategy been introduced. The European Union Council agreed on 12 December 2003 to a strategy entitled 'A secure Europe in a better world' (EU Council 2003b). The dynamic of formulating the foreign and security policy was extraordinary. The contradictory positions and policies of the EU member states regarding the Iraq War in spring 2003 showed, on the one hand, the rift within the EU's foreign and security policy and intensified, on the other hand, the pressure to do the utmost to agree upon a common strategy.

The presentation of a European strategy was facilitated not only by these attempts to reconcile internal EU disagreements in foreign and security policy but also by the different perspectives on global security of the Bush administration which contrasted starkly in fundamental questions to the EU's positions. Robert Kagan (2002) has called in a sharply contrasted form, but with an added pinch of salt, to stop pretending that Europeans and Americans share a common view on the world. '[O]n major strategic and international questions today' Kagan wrote, 'Americans are from Mars and Europeans are from Venus.' Whilst Europe is turning away from power and dreams about the realization of the 'perpetual peace' of Kant, the United States, meanwhile, exercises power in the anarchic Hobbesian world and depends on the possession and use of military means. Further, whereas the Americans are not afraid to threaten or use force to create their world order, the Europeans insist on negotiations and agreed international norms. This divergent view of the world is reflected in the different character of the US National Security Strategy 2002 (US Government, White House 2002a) as compared to the new EU strategy of 2003.

The breathtaking tempo of the formulation and official authorization of the European strategy, however, is no indicator that the differences and conflicting views of EU member countries about a Common Foreign and Security Policy (CFSP) have been removed. Neither has the complicated relationship between the EU and NATO, and more specifically that to NATO's lead nation the United States, been clarified, nor the question about the possible future civil–military mix of potential international interventions carried out by the EU in wars and crises.

A new European security strategy

Javier Solana, the EU High Representative for CFSP had presented a draft of the new strategy in June 2003; it was to be accepted with some changes as official policy half a year later, under the same title, 'A secure Europe in a better world' (Solana 2003). At the same time the EU published its own draft constitution with several new institutional arrangements in the CFSP and ESDP the latter part of which received a green light from the EU Defence Ministers in December 2003 and from the EU Council in October 2004.[20] In addition to the above mentioned rift within the EU and the divergent world views held in the United States and in Europe, both the experience of the EU in the Kosovo War and the terror attacks of 9/11 accelerated this creation of a European security strategy.

What does a European strategy mean?

The security strategy addresses, as the title suggests, global security questions as far as they are relevant for Europe.

Five conflict-prone aspects of a new security environment are delineated as 'new threats' (EU Council 2003b):

First, terrorism that endangers Europe is seen as a 'growing strategic threat to the whole of Europe'. Europe is both a target and a base for terrorists.

Second, the proliferation of weapons of mass destruction is 'the single most important threat to peace and security'. Both the possibility of an arms race with weapons of mass destruction, especially in the Middle East, and the frightening scenario in which terrorist acquire these weapons are of concern for Europe.

Third, regional conflicts such as those in Kashmir, the Great Lakes Region in Africa, the Korean peninsula and the Middle East are classified as 'key threats' and impact on European interests and bring conflicts closer home.

Fourth, state failure, characterized by civil conflict and bad governance such as corruption, abuse of power, weak institutions and lack of accountability, corrodes states from within. State failure undermines global governance and adds to regional instability.

Fifth, organized crime was seen in the original Solana draft within the context of failed states. In the final version it is seen as a key threat to Europe since it is a threat to the internal security of Europe and can have links with terrorism.

The definition of these five key threats in the document was intended as an implicit signal to the US government that the EU rates them as seriously as does the US and that Europe is willing to fight against these threats. At the same time the new strategy directs attention to the economic power of Europe that makes the EU 'inevitably a global player'. The EU 'should be ready to share in the responsibility for global security and building a better world', but not only with military but also economic means. The document presents a picture – in addition to the analysis of key threats – that is in accordance with the objectives of the UN Millennium Report and that is more differentiated and complex than the US National Security Strategy as it addresses global challenges such as poverty, hunger, disease, scarcity of resources, migration and so on. But the EU security strategy does not really link these 'key threats' and 'global challenges', nor does it differentiate between these two levels of analysis. They stand more or less unconnected next to each other. It is therefore of no surprise that the strategy document suggests rather abrupt and short-term measures of primarily a military nature to counter the five key threats, while the global challenges and future chances for change are only generally mentioned but not detailed in the operative part of the strategy.

On the one hand the EU sees itself as a global player; yet on the other hand the strategy is formulated euro-centrically. This strategy is not directed at the general security of people, as for example the concept of human security, but exclusively on the security of Europe. Security requirements are thus derived almost entirely from the threats to Europe. But even here the options for action are rather vague.

Security and development

To contribute to an international order based on effective multilateralism the EU document emphasizes the role of trade and development: 'Trade and development policies can be powerful tools for promoting reform. As the world's largest provider of official assistance and its largest trading entity, the European Union and its Member States are well placed to pursue these goals' (EU Council 2003b, 10). Crisis prevention and conflict resolution are to be facilitated by applying the full spectrum of instruments at the disposal of the EU, including political, diplomatic, military and civilian, and trade and development. This assumes that political and economic assistance can help conflict-prone societies to end conflicts.

According to the EU strategy 'security is the first condition for development'. This is but the most obvious conjecture and requirement; the other side of the same coin is that development is a condition for security. The term 'pre-emptive engagement' in the original Solana draft was cut from the final official strategy version, probably because of the close connotation to the National Security Strategy of the US. Instead, the final document speaks of the need for 'tackling the key threats' to defend European security and to promote European values globally. The conclusion that 'the first line of defence' against the new threats 'will often be abroad' could easily be interpreted as legitimization for a military response that would be closer to defending national interest in the classical imperialist style than to tailoring policies according to the interdependencies of the twenty-first century.

Some comments by European policy makers are even more direct than the EU strategy in emphasizing globally oriented power politics based on a division of labour between the United States and Europe. In this concept, the US forces are meant to act as the sword while Europe should function as the shield. Is this the new world order of unquestioned US leadership and a loyal and devoted EU? Or are the commitments of the West to take on the necessary 'responsibilities' a revitalization of the colonial concept of the white men's burden?

The right civil–military mix

The new strategy document envisions a perception of security that oscillates vaguely between global challenges and (militarily interpreted) threats. In its operative part, which deals with a coherent EU foreign policy, the conception is focused on improved military capabilities even though the civil capacities of the EU are meant to play the major role. Although the strategy suggests comprehensive, early, quick and if necessary robust reactions of crisis prevention and conflict management against external and internal security threats, it defines no criteria to decide whether civil or military measures should be used. Instead, combined civil–military actions are described in general terms as especially useful operations without, however, stating in which phase of a conflict or in what situation such interventions would be best suited. The question arises if the experiences of the last few years in the war and post-war situations in Afghanistan and in Iraq have been taken note of at all. There is enough evidence available from both cases that civil–military co-operation is rather complicated.

Military intervention in wars, post-war programmes and in nation building processes show that indeed military interventions might be needed to stop violence and to protect economic and social development in crisis regions but at the same time they can be counterproductive. Military dominated intervention policies are not only no defence against most threats and no solution for most conflicts but they can also stimulate protests and counter reactions amongst the very people that are intended to be protected. Iraq in 2004/05 is the most current and acute example. The EU strategy concludes that '[i]n almost every major intervention, military efficiency has been followed by civilian chaos' (EU Council 2003b, 12). The experiences in Iraq are proof of this observation. But this should not lead to the conclusion that military intervention is always useful, especially since nowhere is it mentioned what this kind of 'military efficiency' could be. The speedy advance of the US forces in Iraq and the swift occupation of the country as well as the toppling of the regime of Saddam Hussein might be interpreted as a military victory. But what is the value of such a victory if the world's strongest military power is not in a position to build a sustainable and liveable society but is bogged down and entangled in asymmetric combat. The EU strategy rightly stresses that 'none of the new threats is purely military; nor can any be tackled by purely military means' (ibid., 7). Nevertheless 'more resources for defence and more effective use of resources' (ibid., 12) are seen as a necessity and are requested as first priority in order to offer more options for the EU. The strategy document repeats and stresses that crisis prevention is never to be ignored, but the allocation of resources for civil measures is noticeably placed second to that of the military and is particularly geared to post-conflict reconstruction.

Disarmament only for others? The dilemma of military build-up and arms control

The European political elite calls for a strong and independent European military posture to enable them to react in crises and wars. The focus of attention has clearly been on an intensified European role in international conflicts and the need for European military capabilities. But the role of arms control and disarmament plays only a marginal role in these considerations. Numerous crises in the world could be better controlled if disarmament and arms control were pursued more energetically. The EU could take the lead here and would have, in addition to the two instruments mentioned in its new strategy – military intervention and civil measures – a third instrument in crisis prevention at its disposal. Today's arms control initiatives could make future interventions unnecessary. Arms control and disarmament does not stand in contrast to the military planners request for more resources. On the contrary: A decisive policy of arms control and disarmament could free resources and would make the EU's foreign and security policy more credible.

The following paragraphs, while illustrating that arms control is not a present EU priority, will point at possibilities for change.

Arms control policy: words and deeds

The reversal of the predominant trend towards disarmament of the post Cold War period has several major causes that stretch beyond Europe.[21] The main reason for the crisis in arms control is the emergence of the United States as the sole and absolutely dominant military superpower and the disinterest of the Bush administration in arms control negotiations. Instead of trying to reduce or control armaments by arms control and disarmament agreements the US government policy is geared to expanding its own military domination to be able to fight so called 'rogue states' and the 'axis of evil'. Among the countries classified in that manner are some that are evidently investing in weapons of mass destruction programmes. Pre-emptive military reactions by the US, including the use of weapons of mass destruction themselves, are no longer excluded in order to prevent the proliferation of these weapons (US Government, White House 2002a).

'September 11' has not changed this perception, even though the tragic events made it crystal clear that impregnable defence systems are an illusion. While this conclusion is not new in many parts of the world, for the United States it marked a fundamental change in its perception of risks. But the answer to counter these new vulnerabilities is yet another attempt at strengthening US military power. The US reaction is based on the assumption that these risks can be overcome, or at least largely contained, through strength, including increased military strength.

The other major players of the arms control community (mainly Russia, China, India as well as members of the EU) have not been able to maintain the momentum of arms control that characterized the first half of the 1990s. Today, after the terrorist attacks, the United States' NATO allies, as well as many other governments, are supporting this new assertiveness against those seen as the source, or supporters, of terrorism by increasing military spending, purchasing new equipment and by strengthening their special military forces.

On reading mainstream statements on European security plans and perspectives it would seem that the promoters of European Security and Defence Policy (ESDP), especially those who have called for a strong and independent European military posture, do not see a dilemma between the present European military build-up and current arms control policy. The focus of attention has clearly been on an intensified European role in international conflicts and the need for European military capabilities. Arms control is on the backburner. There seems to be a separation between the European arms control community and the promoters of European military capabilities. They form different epistemological groups and so the discussion remains compartmentalised – or even worse: When arms control is discussed and called for, usually the need for control is directed at others (terrorists, rogue states, or states proliferating military technology) and, at best, they refer to multilateral treaties, with or without a reminder of the fact that these negotiations are presently blocked. A truly European arms control or disarmament policy that has an impact on the build-up of European military capabilities is completely missing from the debate.

The US government is openly (and equally from behind closed doors) criticized in Europe for its arrogance in arms control policy, for its military muscle flexing exercises and its Iraq War policy. But what about

European arms control initiatives? The problematic issue of French and British nuclear weapons, for example, is completely avoided in the EU Action Plan Against Weapons of Mass Destruction (EU Commission 2003a). A serious European arms control policy or disarmament practice that takes the build-up of the EU's own forces into consideration does not exist.

Verbal and written statements of the EU arms control positions are however, in contrast to the Unites States, characterized by the emphasis of the need for multilateralism, for co-operation and international give and take. Military actions are described as the *ultima ratio* and not as the first priority in crises. While the present US government seems no longer interested in a number of multilateral agreements on weapons of mass destruction, EU members can boast of an impressive register of participation in arms control treaties. Table 5.1 illustrates that the present 25 members of the EU are almost fully represented in the 9 most important categories of arms control treaties or agreements, and that there is the impressive number of 214 memberships out of a possible 225. Thus, in a formal sense at least, EU members are the most ardent promoters of arms control.

What does the concrete practice of European arms control and disarmament look like? The problem of the lack of arms control is not just rooted in the present position of the United States but is partly homemade in the EU. The necessity for EU military forces are barely questioned – only its institutional set-up. The same cannot be said in the case of arms control. The need and potential for an independent European arms control policy can be illustrated in two areas:

First: Procurement planners in the defence ministries in most EU member states have long since, and increasingly successfully, stressed the need for new capabilities in order to carry out the new types of missions. Naturally, the defence industry assists this position in its own interest. However, the various different military postures of EU member states are far from being prepared for the tasks foreseen for them in 'humanitarian' intervention and peacekeeping. The concept of territorial defence has largely been given up as the central mission for the armed forces, but the practical restructuring that this understanding necessitates has yet to take place at the required speed and scale. Excessive and inflexible infrastructures, too many troops and the wrong equipment for the present crisis situations still remain in Europe. General James L. Jones, the Supreme Allied Commander Europe who is responsible for the creation of the NATO Response Force, concludes: 'We have too much capability for the past and not enough capacity for the future' (NATO 2003).

Table 5.1 Membership of EU members in important arms control treaties (2004)

Country	NPT	BTWC	Geneva Convent.	Inhumane weapons	Open skies	CWC	CTBT	Land mines	Vienna docum.	Total
Austria	x	x	x*	x		x	x	x	x	8
Belgium	x	x	x*	x	x	x	x	x	x	9
Cyprus	x	x	x	x*		x	x	x	x	8
Czech Republic	x	x	x	x	x	x	x	x	x	9
Denmark	x	x	x*	x	x	x	x	x	x	9
Estonia	x	x	x	x*		x	x		x	7
Finland	x	x	x*	x	x	x	x		x	8
France	x	x	x*	x*	x	x	x	x	x	9
Greece	x	x	x	x	x	x	x	x	x	9
Germany	x	x	x*	x	x	x	x	x	x	9
Hungary	x	x	x	x	x	x	x	x	x	9
Ireland	x	x	x	x		x	x	x	x	8
Italy	x	x	x*	x	x	x	x	x	x	9
Latvia	x	x	x	x	x	x	x		x	8
Lithuania	x	x	x	x*		x	x	x	x	8
Luxemburg	x	x	x	x	x	x	x	x	x	9
Malta	x	x	x*	x		x	x	x	x	8
Netherlands	x	x	x*	x*	x	x	x	x	x	9
Poland	x	x	x	x	x	x	x		x	8
Portugal	x	x	x	x	x	x	x	x	x	9
Slovak Republic	x	x	x	x	x	x	x	x	x	9
Slovenia	x	x	x	x		x	x	x	x	8
Spain	x	x	x*	x	x	x	x	x	x	9
Sweden	x	x	x*	x	x	x	x	x	x	9
United Kingdom	x	x	x	x	x	x	x	x	x	9
Total	25	25	25	25	18	25	25	21	25	214

Notes: NPT = Non-Proliferation Treaty (1970); BTWC = Biological and Toxin Weapons Convention (1975); Geneva Convent. = Protocol I and II: Additional to the 1949 Geneva Conventions Relating to the Protection of Victims in Conflicts; Inhumane Weapons = Convention on Prohibitions or Restrictions on the Use of Certain Conventional Weapons which may be Deemed to be Excessively Injurious or to have Indiscriminate Effects (1983); Opens Skies = Treaty on Open Skies (2002); CWC = Chemical Weapons Convention (1997); CTBT = Comprehensive Nuclear Test-Ban Treaty (not in force as of 1 Jan. 2005); Land Mines = APMC, Convention on the Prohibition of the Use, Stockpiling, Production and Transfer of Anti-Personnel Mines and on their Destruction (1999); Vienna Docum. = Vienna Document on Confidence- and Security-Building Measures (2000). In brackets = year of entry into force.
x = membership in important arms control treaties;
* = reservations and/or declaration.

Sources: SIPRI 2004; Deutscher Bundestag 2004.

The same can be said for the armed forces of the EU member states since these are largely identical to the NATO forces in Europe.

Second: The EU's ambitions for independent or even autarkic military capabilities and security instruments are usually seen as competition to the United States. There is no doubt that co-operation with the US has become more difficult due to the Bush administrations policies, and this has further increased the European desire for more independence in security policy. Consequent attempts have – despite the permanently repeated willingness for transatlantic co-operation – strong competitive features. European defence and security officials continue to emphasize the gap in military capabilities between the United States and Europe.

Lacking arms control initiatives

Compared to the EU's policy declarations however, the agenda of implementation measures for arms control and disarmament is conspicuously short. Arms control initiatives or unilateral national disarmament measures have been almost completely absent in recent years. If disarmament does take place or when new weapons programmes are cancelled or postponed it is not based on an arms control or disarmament policy but rather the result of sheer financial necessity. Thus, where are the deeds matching the words? Let us examine some hard facts and indicators of arms control and disarmament in Europe.

1. *Nuclear weapons*: The two European nuclear states, France and the United Kingdom, have gradually scaled down their nuclear deployment (SIPRI 2001, 469–74 and 2002, 545–57). France itself is currently considering a nuclear doctrinal review, which might include refocusing on 'difficult' states. Yet no initiative has been taken by the two governments to fulfil their obligation as signatories of the Non-Proliferation Treaty to seriously negotiate the complete disarmament of nuclear weapons. This inaction in responsibly complying with an internationally binding treaty occurs despite the fact that the division within the EU into nuclear 'haves' and 'have-nots' is a serious stumbling block on the way towards a truly *Common* Foreign and Security Policy (CFSP) and an European Security and Defence Policy (ESDP). The French and British nuclear issue is simply taboo in Europe. The weapons of other countries are apparently the problem. Mohamed El Baradei, Director General of the International Atomic Energy Agency (IAEA), criticizes these demands of nuclear states that other nations not possess nuclear weapons while arming themselves (he referred to US pressure on

North Korea): 'In truth there are no good or bad nuclear weapons. If we do not stop applying double standards we will end up with more nuclear weapons' (El Baradei 2003, 43). In this area there is plenty of scope for French, British and EU arms control initiatives.

2. *Military expenditures*: Even if US military technologies seem way ahead, EU military expenditures are nonetheless not marginal and attempts at a military build-up are substantial. The downward trend in global military expenditures – which saw expenditures fall from over US$1000 billion at the end of the 1980s to roughly US$725 billion in 1996 – slowed down considerably during the late 1990s.[22] This trend has given way to a predominant expansion of military spending, and the terrorist attacks of 11 September 2001 have led to another sizeable increase in defence spending in a number of countries. Forty percent of the global total can be attributed to the United States alone and about one fifth to the EU member states.

The question that needs to be answered is why the predominant debate in Europe focuses on the scarcity of resources in the military sector rather than on emphasizing the fact that a fifth of the world total is already being spent by the 25 EU members. During the Cold War, both the Soviet Union and France suggested, in the UN, that measures be taken to curb military expenditures. These proposals were always rejected due to the alleged lack of data. Yet surprisingly, they have not been taken up again in recent years despite the increased transparency of military expenditures.[23] Instead of using this new kind of openness for a disarmament or arms control initiative, discussions within the NATO alliance focus on the need for increased rather than decreased defence expenditures among NATO's European allies.

3. *Procurement*: The economic performance in many EU member states has not been too positive in recent years. As a result, governments have cut government spending, including on large weapons projects. In addition, pressures to reduce public debt have had an effect on military budgets, especially procurement budgets. However, despite these difficulties, military procurement budgets have been steadily increasing in Western Europe since 1998 (SIPRI 2004, 369). Looking both at the equipment wish list of the military and the procurement projects already in the making, it is easy to predict that this share of the military budget will further increase in the years ahead. The reversal of the predominant disarmament trend of the post Cold War period in Europe has three major causes: The armed forces in most EU countries have long maintained that they require more modern equipment and that they have been stretched thinly during the post Cold War period. Furthermore, this

argument seems to have gained momentum now that the EU has agreed to build-up a crisis reaction force, which requires equipment different from that purchased by the military during the Cold War. Lastly, military capabilities in Europe are viewed and assessed in a competitive light, invariably measured against the US armed forces and its dominant technology.

4. *Military manpower*: The number of soldiers in regular armies worldwide continued to decline in 2002 for the thirteenth year in a row, although the rate of decline was dwindling. The figure for the EU was down from a total of 2.9 million soldiers in 1989 to a still surprisingly large 1.9 million for the 25 EU members, representing almost 10 per cent of the world's armed forces (BICC 2004). This does not reflect a weakening of military capability, but rather a general trend among rich countries to create smaller forces armed with better equipment. At the same time, this large number of personnel is an indicator of the slow pace or lack of restructuring reforms. Some of the EU armed forces are still structured, for the most part, as they were at the end of the Cold War, lacking the capacity to confront the new tasks of crisis prevention.

5. *Small arms control*: One area of special interest in arms control has been small arms and light weapons. The EU member states have been active in promoting this issue within the UN and contributed greatly to the UN conference on small arms in July 2001 (SAS 2002, 203–33). Even earlier, an EU Joint Action – including a budget line – had been agreed upon among the member states to promote small arms control and assist developing countries, particularly in Africa, in their small arms control efforts. To what extent these important policies have also contributed to reducing the exports of small arms from EU countries is not known. Despite the newly introduced annual publication of an EU export report, it is still far from transparent with regard to actual decision-making on the possible refusal of export licenses. Furthermore, while small arms control is an important issue, since these types of weapons are the weapons used in many conflicts, the economic dimension is of marginal value for the EU – except for a very small number of specialised producer companies.

Parochial policies in Europe

European arms control policy plays an important role at the declaratory level; in practice it is less convincing. Looking at it, not from the EU–US angle, but from the perspective of the rest of the world, the 'gap' in military capabilities looks quite different. The US spends more than double the EU (or the European NATO countries) for their armed forces, amounting to a budget of over US$400 billion per year. In total NATO as a whole spends over 60 per cent of global military expenditures. All other 175 countries of the world (including Russia, China, Japan and India) share the remaining percentage. A similar distribution pattern is noted for the expenditure on the development of new military technologies. In two other sectors the quantitative gap between Europe and the United States does not exist: The United States has a military personnel strength of about 1.5 million while the EU musters 1.9 million. Similarly, the stock of major conventional weapons amounts to 37,800 pieces in the United States and 42,400 pieces in the EU (BICC 2004, 178). The reasons for the envious looks in the EU at US military capabilities are not for a matter of quantities. But why is the military's power so much behind in the EU's self-estimation? There are three principal reasons for this situation:

First, and most importantly: Military and security decisions are not made at the EU or NATO–Europe level but are national decisions. Despite all political statements and an abundance of reports on the need for enhanced and intensified European co-operation, parochial decision-making is still on the agenda today. This has not changed as a result of EU initiatives for ESDP and the formulation of an EU strategy and an EU constitution. Admittedly, some progress towards more co-operation has been made in recent years, but it is doubtful if nationally orientated solo policies will be stopped in the near future.

Second: Although the figure for holdings of major conventional weapons in the EU looks impressive, a number of items (long-range transport aircraft among others) are lacking. A lot of equipment in Europe is essentially the remnants of the Cold War. Nineteen working groups were formed in the so called Helsinki Progress Catalogue of 2003, all of which identified gaps in equipment, such as in information gathering technology, in Atomic Biological and Chemical weapons defence, in combat search and rescue, in the Special Forces and in several other areas. All of them concluded that there is a need to procure new equipment without, however, detailing where the financial resources should come from (EU Council 2003b, Schmitt 2004, 111). Some weapons systems (like major battle tanks) are abundantly available but not appropriate for the new type of international engagements. Hence, additional hard structural cuts are required.

Third: Although the cumulative strength of the EU's armed forces is about 1.9 million in terms of manpower, the EU is still not able to deploy as many troops as the governments desire. Germany, for example, had a

Bundeswehr strength of about 270,000 and 128,000 support civilians in 2003 but is not in a position to sustain an international deployment of more than 10,000 troops over an extended period of time. The 25 EU member countries had 127,000 soldiers deployed abroad in October 2003 (Schmidt 2004, 129). Although it is often declared that more personnel are required for missions abroad, given the need for rotation (1/3 on deployment, 1/3 training and 1/3 home-based), it appears that not more than about seven per cent of the troops are deployable at any given time.

The explanation for both the inappropriate equipment and the inadequate number of deployable troops is the insufficient restructuring of the armed forces following the end of the Cold War. A host of reasons are responsible for this slow and inefficient reform process: national prestige, unprofessional leadership, military-organizational self-interest, economic interest in procurement of major equipment, and so on. As a consequence, extensive resources are being inefficiently spent in EU countries on the military.

There is plenty of scope for both arms control and disarmament initiatives by the EU and individual member states. This ranges from the area of weapons of mass destruction to small arms and military expenditures. The stalemate in multilateral arms control forums is no reason for inactivity. The experience of the Ottawa Treaty on the prohibition of land mines has shown that selective initiatives can make a difference even if major players (such as the United States, Russia, China and India in that particular case) refuse to co-operate in such a treaty.

Particularly promising are efforts to impose cost control measures – even though the US government might not be ready to negotiate or compromise in this specific area. The EU and its member states should take the initiative in the UN to control and reverse the trend of rising military expenditures. The EU does not spend too little but too much on its armies. Only if military expenditures are cut – not increased – will military planners be forced to co-operate in Europe. As long as money is available, national procurement will prevail over collaborative procurement.

The military build-up – paper armies?

To state quite clearly at the outset of this paragraph: the efforts by EU members to promote and institutionalise ESDP and to build a credible European reaction force are no comparison, either in quantitative or qualitative terms, to what is happening in the US defence sector. US forces are in a league of their own. Nevertheless, compared to the history of half a century of discussions and proclamations about a European defence posture, the last few years have been a period of extraordinary dynamism and militarization. While the present debate is focused on military capabilities it is in reality a debate about Europe's ambition for an active role in international security (Hagman 2002).

Civilian capacities

The core argument for civilian capacities is the hiatus between the armed forces' robust capability to wage war and the need for softer capabilities to restore the rule of law in failed states and post-conflict societies. According to the EU Council, ESDP should strengthen both civil and military capabilities and create appropriate structures to manage them (EU Council 2001, 110). The commitments to the military sector are much larger than in the civil area. Civil capabilities for policing of up to 5000 officers (of which 1400 are deployable in 30 days), strengthening the administration of justice (282 law experts), and civilian administration and civil protection (up to 2000 experts) remain modest (The United Kingdom Parliament 2003, chapter 2; Dwan 2004). It is not just the numbers that are lower for civilian experts than for the armed forces. When civilian experts are deployed they will usually have to be withdrawn from tasks at home, leaving a deficiency there. Further, since they serve on a voluntary basis, they can also refuse their deployment. This results in the inflexibility of the civil instrument. At the beginning of 2004, only 650 police officers and other civilian personnel served in the two EU police missions in Bosnia-Herzegovina and Macedonia (Lindstrom 2004, 133 and 139).

The comparative advantage of the EU, according to the promoters of the combined military and civil crises management instrument, is that the EU has capabilities available in both areas. Dwan (2004, 13) concludes: 'In theory, this is true but in practice, i[t] has been avoided.' The present commitments of the EU in the civilian sector are not only insufficient in quantitative terms; the EU also lags behind conceptually in preparing for the requirements in conflict-prone societies. The EU follows, with a certain time lag, the concepts of the UN and Organisation for Security and Co-operation in Europe (OSCE) but has so far not given qualitatively new impulses to the international debate (Dwan 2004, 9).

The 'Helsinki' process

The project to develop a European defence policy has a long history, dating back to the 1950s. The various earlier efforts usually failed or ended in political declarations with no real substance in military terms. This has changed dramatically in recent years. There are a number of reasons, motives and interests that explain why this process is now being vigorously pursued.

The decisive factor probably was the experience of the Kosovo war. This gave European ambitions for more military independence a strong impetus. Obviously, European NATO allies had difficulties in contributing military muscle to NATO's air war. And – as important – the EU itself had rather little to offer and was dependent on NATO. This war was controversial in EU member countries, but a politically and strategically more independent Europe, with the capacity for autonomous action backed up by credible military force, slowly gained acceptance among the EU political elite.

Another, but closely related, reason was and still is the above-mentioned desire to bridge the capabilities gap between US and European forces. The European project of autonomous military capacities was also facilitated by the perception that the Bush administration tried to sideline NATO before it began to look for allies in the Iraq War. An additional reason for the push in ESDP came in the wake of the 11 September 2001 terrorist attacks. Europe not only saw a need – despite all US–European quarrels and disagreements – to be able to assist the US in their anti-terror campaign but also felt that terrorism is a serious threat to Europe too. In conclusion, more military capacities were deemed necessary. ESDP, including the establishment of crisis reaction forces, was facilitated further by the institutional changes in the EU, including its expansion and the development of a constitution.

Ironically, it was the two countries furthest apart on European defence, Britain (the most 'Atlanticist') and France (the most 'European' of the EU) who gave European security and defence co-operation policy a push with their December 1998 Saint-Malo agreement. ESDP is essentially a compromise between these two countries. It was made possible by a remarkable shift in British defence policy. The United Kingdom would no longer block an EU role in defence but promoted it without, however, giving up its special relationship to the United States. The road towards an EU military capacity had thus been mapped out although the institutional and operational set-up was and still is open (Bertram *et al.* 2002, 25).

This initiative eventually culminated in the Helsinki Headline Goals, agreed within the EU at the Helsinki European Council summit in December 1999. The Headline Goals were intended to create a relevant and meaningful EU military capacity that would make arrangements for up to 60,000 troops with naval and air support to be deployed within

60 days by 2003. Two years after the agreement the EU announced that 'voluntary contributions confirm the existence of a body of resources consisting of a pool of more than 100,000 men, around 400 combat aircraft and 100 ships, fully satisfying the requirements defined by the headline goal to conduct different types of crisis-management-operations' (EU Capability Improvement Conference 2001, 96). But the Helsinki Headline Goals, the European Capability Action Plan of 2002 – euphemistically called a 'bottom-up' approach (EU Capability Improvement 2001, 98) – and the follow-up Helsinki Force Catalogue of 2003, which constituted the resultant total sum of the various national commitments, is only a fraction of the EU's 1.9 million soldiers, 160 destroyers and frigates, 75 submarines and over 3300 combat aircraft (Hagman 2002, 21, BICC 2003). The Helsinki Progress Catalogue of 2003 was supposed to assess the progress made and also to identify existing capability shortfalls. The EU Council officially concluded the process begun in Helsinki with the publication of the EU security strategy. The CFSP and ESDP combined are now the basis for the formulation of a new Headline Goal 2010 (Schmitt 2004, 115–120).

Despite the two military missions of the EU in Macedonia (Concordia with 308 personnel) and in the Democratic Republic of Congo (Artemis with about 2000), the real litmus test of the EU's military crisis reaction capabilities is yet to come. Cynics sometimes question the real EU capabilities. At the NATO defence ministers meeting held in Colorado Springs (Colorado, United States) 8–9 October 2003, then NATO Secretary General Lord Robertson said that there is 'the need for real deployable soldiers and not paper armies' (quoted in Monaco 2003).

EU–NATO relations: co-operation or competition?

The ESDP and the policy to emphasize the development of military capabilities is, according to official statements, not about building a competitor to NATO but about improving European capabilities, thus strengthening the European pillar of NATO and contributing more effectively to NATO-led operations. EU officials try hard to stress this co-operative aspect (EU Council 2002, 135). Others don't take these efforts seriously. 'Where is the beef?' asked US Senator Helms, the EU 'could not fight its way out of a wet paper bag', and Margaret Thatcher called the Headline Goals a 'monumental folly' designed to 'satisfy political vanity' with 'no military sense at all' (quoted in Hagman 2002, 32). In reality and despite all political statements to the contrary, at present the relationship is more competitive than co-operative between NATO

Table 5.2   Major military planning and implementation activities

Year	EU	NATO
1998	Franco-British declaration of Saint-Malo on European military forces	Defence Capabilities Initiative
1999	Helsinki Headline Goals	
2000	Capability Commitment Conference	
2001	Capability Improvement Conference	
2002	Capabilities Action Plan	Prague Capabilities Commitment for new military capabilities for modern warfare
2002	Mini summit of Belgium, France, Germany and Luxembourg	Prague Commitment for NATO Response Force
2003	Berlin Plus	Berlin Plus
2003	Helsinki Force Catalogue, Progress Catalogue	Launch of NATO Response Force
2003	Headline Goal 2010	Expansion of NATO Response Force

and the EU. Table 5.2 illustrates the parallel and duplicating processes in the two organisations.

The NATO 1998 Defence Capabilities Initiative (DCI) was designed to address the growing technological gap between the US and NATO forces while the EU Helsinki Headline Goals of 1999 were intended to give the EU a military capacity. The DCI was noticeably analogous to the 'wish-list' of the EU. Similarly, the launch of NATO's Response Force (NRF) in 2003 mirrors the EU crisis reaction force. The military missions of these forces are surprisingly vague: NATO officially declares in an astonishingly open and revealing disclosure that 'the missions of the NATO NRF are yet to be determined; however the global reach is an important element' (NATO 2003). The first political priority in the EU and NATO should be an answer to the question: What for? What are the tasks of these armed forces; in which crises will they be deployed and in which ones will they not be? Instead, at present, the priority in both the EU and NATO is adding capabilities. An illustration of this is the fact that NATO entitled its entire Autumn 2002 issue of NATO Review: 'Capabilities, capabilities, capabilities'.

The US government has expressed two almost mutually exclusive reactions to the EU's military ambitions. On the one hand it takes the EU aspiration to be a warning that the EU is taken increasingly more seriously than NATO by the Europeans. Former US Secretary of State, Albright, set out, as early as 1998 in response to the French–British Saint-Malo agreement, three criteria for judgements on the need for European capabilities – criteria that instantly became known as the 'three Ds': avoiding *de-linking* ESDP[24] from NATO, avoiding *duplicating* existing efforts, and avoiding *discriminating* against non-EU members (quoted in Hunter 2002, 33–34). On the other side the United States is increasingly indifferent to NATO and has marginalised the alliance after September 11. It prefers ad hoc coalitions and turns to NATO only when its leaders find it convenient.

To reconcile these differences the so-called 'Berlin plus' agreement was signed. This is a comprehensive package of agreements between NATO and the EU that assures NATO planning capabilities and assets for EU-led crisis management operations. Despite this agreement the relationship is far from harmonious and the process far from complete. To resolve conflicts both NATO and the EU are following the line of least resistance and doing what Madeleine Albright called duplication. NATO's Response Force is planned to have a strength of 21,000, recruited from the pool of the European forces with the highest combat readiness. Considering also the three-tier rotation principle of deployment, training and home-based status, this size is almost exactly the same as that planned in the EU Helsinki Headline Goals (Haine 2004, 168). With the parallel development of rapid reaction forces there is a fear that their missions could be hindered by the different chains of command. Furthermore, the existence of de-linking and discrimination cannot be denied. The process remains controversial as the discussion in 2003 concerning the establishment of an EU military planning headquarters shows. The conflict is not just a transatlantic disagreement however, but shows intra EU-divergence too. The EU military planning headquarters were favoured by France, Germany and others but rather disliked, although not fully opposed, by Britain. It can be noted that there are different types of intra-EU conflicts: among member states, turf battles within the Commission, and civil–military incompatibilities and frictions in humanitarian interventions.

As has been amply and repetitively emphasized, additional capabilities will require additional resources. But hoping for significantly increased military budgets is unrealistic. The economic situation and public budget priorities do not allow for substantial increases. It is also questionable whether additional inputs would actually be the solution. It is more likely that additional funds would rejuvenate the parochial policies, which have characterized European co-operation thus far. It remains an open question as to whether the EU's ambition to coordinate military R&D, strengthen the technological and industrial base and enhance defence industrial co-operation will be more successful this time (EU Council 2003b, 9–12; Mawdsley 2004). When lucrative defence contracts are at stake governments, parliaments, the defence industry and their shop stewards react nationally.

The result of present policies is an impressive list of requirements of military capabilities, both in NATO and in the EU. But most of these forces are 'double-hatted' (a label that clearly is an understatement) since the same troops are allocated both as UN stand-by, EU crisis reaction, NATO crisis reaction and the various multinational corps in Europe. It is a question of not if, but when, the problem of deciding which organisation has first priority arises. This can safely be predicted as the troops allocated to the reaction forces of both NATO and the EU are also the ones with the highest combat readiness.

The double democratic deficit in the ESDP

Security and defence policy in Europe has in the past been executed by governments and controlled by national parliaments. These parliamentary controls are in some countries more developed than in others. The democratic control of security policy in the EU aims at a policy based on majority rule, accountability of the executive, transparency of political decisions, the creation of sound civil–military relations, and the unquestioned primacy of politics over the military.

This ideal has never been fully reached at the national level since defence and security policy is not one of the most transparent sectors of society. Even in democratic societies this political arena is often shielded from the public eye because of the alleged need for military secrecy requirements. Nonetheless, no matter how imperfect parliamentary control is at the national level, it is clearly better developed in most EU member countries than in the ESDP process of the EU.

Within the EU the authority over the political process, that has historically been nationally orientated, is now partly delegated to the supra-national level of the EU institutions and partly to smaller regional units. In other words, the nation state has renounced rights of authority essentially subordinating itself to other public institutions. This process is slow and controversial, and it is in the field of security policy that it is the least developed. The result-oriented legitimacy mentioned in Chapter 1 which is based on the decisions of the executive being accepted by the majority might have been achieved today in some countries with regard to the establishment of an EU military arm. This is however not the case in all EU member countries. Furthermore, such fundamentally important questions regarding the future of Europe should be grounded on a comprehensive and legitimate democratic process.

Lacking structures, political differences

The existing democratic deficit in ESDP can be measured by several factors. This policy area is formally part of the 'second pillar' in the EU and as such inter-governmentally organized. The EU parliament has no direct parliamentary rights since it is the national executives that take ESDP decisions at the EU level. Instead however, it is national parliaments that might control ESDP decisions. Although the EU Commission requests ever more competencies in this area, member states are generally not willing to give up their sovereignty in security and defence matters. Often they guard their traditional rights jealously. Yet it is the Commission that is responsible for the implementation of decisions, for example in international crisis management. This activity is then based on the 'first pillar' of the EU policy mechanism tailored to carry out community tasks, and also within the 'third pillar' directed at internal and judicial matters. These connections and responsibilities amount to a decision-making structure of Byzantine scale, enormously complicating parliamentary control. As a result, neither parliamentarians nor the public have a comprehensive and transparent picture of ESDP decisions. Security and defence policy are not unique in that respect however.

Differences of opinion about the future of this area do exist in the various member states. While, for example, the Commission and the Benelux countries aim for a concentration of power in the hands of the Commission, thus strengthening the role of the Commission, other governments (particularly France and the United Kingdom) want to enhance the role of the EU Council and its presidency. Both concepts would strengthen the executive but not parliaments. The latter position could possibly lead to the establishment of a security council that would strengthen the inter-governmental structure. It is not to be expected that ESDP will be decided on the basis of majority rule in the near future. Only a gradual and step-by-step approach seems momentarily possible.

Three central parliamentary rights – access to information, participation in decisions on the deployment of troops and budget decisions – illustrate the scale of the democratic deficit in ESDP (Gourlay 2004).

First, access to information: The responsibility to inform and consult the European Parliament is being taken more and more seriously. During the last few years the EU Presidency, the High Representative for Common

Foreign and Security Policy and the EU Commissioner for Foreign Policy have regularly informed the Foreign Policy Committee of the European Parliament with regard to their policies. However, there is no uniform criterion or constitutional right for national parliaments to be informed about ESDP. This means that at the national level ESDP information is requested and given on an ad hoc basis only, depending on the interest of the parliamentarians and the willingness of the governments concerned.

Second, deployment of troops: Given the fact that deployment of armed forces is decided at the inter-governmental level and that competencies rest with national governments the European Parliament has no formal rights in this area. At the national level a formal parliamentary decision is necessary in Germany and Sweden; in other countries, for example in Denmark and the Netherlands, the same procedure is practised. In further countries parliament is only involved in the declaration of war, as in France, whilst in the United Kingdom this is the prerogative of the Prime Minister (Born and Urscheler 2004, 63). To complicate matters even more, deployments of crisis reaction forces, both in the EU and in NATO, normally require immediate decisions to react flexibly. From the perspective of the executive such decisions cannot wait for an intensive public debate or parliamentary scrutiny. In reality there is an acute democratic deficit as it relates to ESDP.

Third, budget authority: The European Parliament has important functions in decisions concerning the EU budget. It is involved, as it is, for example, in budgetary decision in crisis management as this is also part of the 'first pillar'. Included herein are the Rapid Reaction Mechanism and the authorization of the overall budget of the CFSP. Although the CFSP is part of the 'second pillar', its budget is included in the Community budget. In reality, however, the room for manoeuvre of the European Parliament to reject or freeze the total budget is limited. National parliaments in many countries have more far-reaching budget authority. They can play a role in the overall budget all the way down to decisive votes on individual procurement decisions. There are also national parliaments within the EU, for example in the United Kingdom, though with rather limited authority in defence and procurement policy as illustrated in Table 5.3.

In conclusion, this unbalanced structure of control concerning ESDP decision-making amounts to a double democratic deficit. At the European level there are no parliamentary controls over security and defence decisions (neither the Commission's nor the Council's). The

Table 5.3   Parliamentary participation in ESDP

	European Parliament	National parliaments
Information access	Yes	Ad hoc
Participation in troop deployment decisions	Formally none	Yes in some countries, no in others
Budget authority	Generally limited, yes in civil crisis management	Wide-ranging in many countries, limited in others

Source: Based on Gourlay 2004, 187–196.

European Parliament has no decision authority, although it does have the right to access information. At the national level parliaments can control the decisions of their governments, but not, however, ESDP decisions at the European level; in these cases the access to information is limited in practice given the complicated European bureaucracy. Therefore, civil–military relations are endangered and the civil and democratic control over the military is not guaranteed.

The new constitution

Will the democratic deficit be changed through the new EU constitution? The text of the draft constitution of 2004 includes the following provisions for ESDP (European Union 2004):

The European Security and Defence Policy (ESDP) is an integral part of the Common Foreign and Security Policy (CFSP). Within this policy the EU aims not only at strengthening its military power but also its civilian capacities. In reality however, the commitment for the establishment of crisis reaction forces is on a substantially larger scale than the civilian capacities.

Member states will have the possibility to 'establish permanent structured co-operation' (Art. I-41,6) to allow those countries with a higher binding commitment to military co-operation to speed up this integration. The intension of this provision is to prevent a slowdown of the co-operation process for countries such as France, Germany, Belgium and Luxemburg that desire to co-operate more intensively at the EU level. This stipulation cannot, however, resolve the existing differences in foreign and security policy that are the cause of divergent views among members about the institutional development of ESDP.

According to article I-41,3 member states may form ad hoc coalitions to make civil and military capabilities available to the EU. The countries can do this through their own means within the framework set by the EU Council. As long as there is no agreed common defence, member states have an 'obligation of aid and assistance' if a member state is a victim of armed aggression (Art. I–41,7).

To progressively improve military capabilities an 'agency in the field of defence capabilities development, research, acquisition and armaments (European Defence Agency)' will be established (Art. I–41,3). The agency is tasked to identify the operational requirements of the forces and to strengthen the industrial and technological base of the defence sector. This article in the constitution is tailor made according to the wishes of the defence producers' lobby, which fears the competition from the big US arms manufacturers. While important decisions of a common EU defence policy are still outstanding, the defence industry has already formed an effective lobbyist network. The defence industry contributed successfully to these passages of the constitution and secured the funding for military technology development from the EU, and no longer only indirectly through dual-use projects. As of 2004 the defence industry can be directly funded within the 6th framework for research and development (EU Commission 2003b).

In some parts of the constitution detailed micromanagement is being planned, such as, for example, the establishment of the European Defence Agency – an unprecedented paragraph for any constitution – while vital global programmes such as disarmament and arms control policy are not mentioned in the constitution at all.

The ESDP is stipulated in the constitution in vague formulations and indistinct compromise formulas that can hardly hide, and will certainly not contribute to, removing the divergences that already exist among the member states. The democratic deficit in security and defence policy is not eliminated by the new constitution. The European Parliament in the future will be as in the past 'regularly consulted on the main aspects and basic choices of the common foreign and security policy' and shall be 'informed of how it evolves' (Art. I–40,8).

The differences on security and defence policy in the EU and the competitive nature of the EU–NATO relationship will remain, and controversies and divisive debates are predictable. The different interpretations by the member states of the EU's future armed forces will continue to shape the debate. Whether these armed forces will be multinational or eventually become supranational – and thus truly EU armies – is a contested and open question. The various initiatives to upgrade military capacities, for example through the Capacity Action Plan, the calls for intensified defence efforts, and an increase in military expenditures are so far mainly paper commitments.

Nevertheless, the EU now has some operational capability across the full range of Petersberg tasks, but is still constrained by a number of shortfalls (EU Council 2003a, 8). The discussion and political attention focuses on improving military capabilities whilst the political dimension of CFSP and ESDP remains unresolved. In military operational terms these policies are a basket of various different options without clearly defined missions. The EU's defence, industrial and budgetary ambitions are illusionary. National parochial policies have not yet been eliminated, and inappropriate and missing equipment as well as missed opportunities for reform of the armed forces constitute serious stumbling blocks as the EU muddles through on the road to an autonomous force. The present and the planned democratic controls of ESDP in the new constitution have such a low profile that the democratic deficit will not be eliminated.

The need for civilian primacy in EU foreign policy: CFSP prior to ESDP

Legitimizing security policy can, according to Bono and Mawdsley (2002) be guaranteed through three connected processes: performance, institutional accountability and identity. During the Cold War period security policy was primarily legitimized through national symbols and identity, most clearly characterized by a visible and unmistaken enemy image. Security policy was based at that time, despite many and long lasting protests, on the support of a large part of the population. Such an identity to ESDP is so far non-existent, as first the argument for establishing European military capacities capable of humanitarian interventions is still contested, and second it is not clear if a majority of the population would support this policy if asked in a democratic process. Democratic accountability is, as suggested earlier, at present not given. Rather, today the security policy elites base their decision on the performance argument: that the EU should be militarily capable of humanitarian requirements since there is need in many crisis areas.

In democratic societies it is essential to establish a foreign and security policy that exists in reality prior to the institutionalization of the armed forces, which are otherwise merely the result of numerous ad hoc decisions. European security and defence policy would then follow an agreed foreign and security policy and not vice-versa. This is presently not the case. The foundation of CFSP is too vague and too controversial to function as a basis for ESDP. Nevertheless, the current initiatives that establish facts through creating armed forces can be compared to trying to fix a roof in a damaged house, but ignoring the dangers of subsistence or potential collapse of the structure.

The present debate and the concrete developments in ESDP are primarily directed at creating military capabilities. Europe should concentrate on what it can do best: development assistance, diplomacy and crisis prevention. Part of the catalogue of instruments could be military capacities, especially for UN stand-by. Such troops are available in the EU member states; but they are not organized and deployed in a coordinated fashion but rather decided upon largely on national lines. Too many resources are still invested in antiquated military structures, resulting in a scarcity of resources for other tasks. What is therefore needed is the setting of new priorities in security policy instead of continuing to muddle through on the road to an autonomous force.

The member states of the EU spent at present about 2.5 times more in development assistance than the United States. Here lies the competitive advantage of the EU. To compete with the United States for a 'better world' in this area and for more efficient policy concepts, the EU would do better service by pushing for civil power, aid and trade more self-consciously rather than competing in the area of military power.

Consequently, the priorities in formulating strategic aims in the European security strategy would have to be reversed. The first priority would be a world order on the basis of an effective multilateralism including the goal of international disarmament, which is presently missing from the constitution. The political declaration in the European strategy document, that 'our own experience in Europe demonstrates that security can be increased through confidence building and arms control regimes' (EU Council 2003b, 12) sounds hollow without concrete measures and without mentioning Europe's practical contributions.

At present, development experts, both in government and non-governmental organizations, hesitate to actively promote the civil arm within ESDP for three reasons: First, there continues to remain traditional resentment and fear of close contact between developmentalists and the military. Second, the development and humanitarian organizations fear that the military might encroach into their traditional areas of vocation. And finally, development policy is afraid to take on responsibility for security policy as a third mega-agenda, in addition to meeting the UN millennium goals of 2015 and fighting the negative effects of globalization, without being given additional financial resources.

Despite the fact that the EU strategy documents are much clearer than the US National Security Strategy of 2002 concerning the commitment to international law and internationally negotiated norms, multilateralism and assistance to the UN, and even though civilian means are given a prominent place – at least conceptually – an unambiguous statement is lacking that the military can only be used as a last resort in otherwise unsolvable conflicts. The vague security concept and insufficient analysis of the root causes of conflict must lead necessarily to contradictory options when choosing between civil or military instruments in the operative part of the strategy. This might be an understandable reflex of the most recent history and disruptions of international relations, which have led to the softening of taboos of military deployments and the blurring of the border between war and peace. But these crises are largely the product of political and economic processes with consciously operating actors, both governmental and non-governmental. Since the EU foreign policy has for the most part been characterized by the incoherence of their member states' viewpoints and their resulting inactivity, the EU members cannot overcome their differences by strengthening their military power alone. The weakness that still exists of CFSP is not the function of lacking military power and strategy, but of the institutional and constitutional flaws of the gradually integrating and expanding political and economic area of the EU. The situation of the present disagreement in important and central political questions, reflected in the formula compromises of the new constitution and security doctrine, offers room for pragmatic decisions on controversial issues in defence. The question remains if the concept of the EU as a civil and peaceful power will be strengthened or replaced hereafter by military-based concepts? Will the EU be a civil power or a power in camouflage?

6
Co-operation, Competition and Collateral Damage in Humanitarian Interventions

The large number of so-called humanitarian interventions in which military power has been applied in wars or violent conflicts during the last 15 years is unprecedented in the history of the United Nations (UN). The reconstruction and post-conflict programmes, which are carried out with explicit reference to humanitarian concerns by the UN, are also of a new quality. Beyond such UN deployments in wars and violent conflicts the military assists occasionally when natural disasters or catastrophes require quick and bold operations, as for example on a smaller scale following the floods in 2000 in Mozambique and on a larger scale after the Tsunami devastation in Asia at the end of 2004.[25]

This chapter deals not only with the different levels of co-operation between the external actors, but also with the competition amongst them and the resulting collateral damage. The main actors in the new type of interventions are humanitarian organizations and the armed forces, as well as increasingly private military and security companies. The assistance provided by humanitarian organizations and especially that following the deployment of troops usually takes place in an unstable environment since this work is directed at assisting in war and crisis situations. Complex and often complicated networks of relations are established that are characterized by one common goal, namely to assist and resolve conflicts, but the methods applied are quite different and often controversial – or even mutually exclusive. Thus, a network of divergent interests and competition for leadership in an operation evolves which is often sub-optimal or counterproductive.

The role of the armed forces in humanitarian crises is contentious. Humanitarians often criticize the strategic and security related goals that are explicitly or implicitly embedded in many interventions, and they fear that their relief work could become instrumentalized to legitimize military actions.[26] It should be equally noted that the 'humanitarian' activities of the armed forces are not always liked in the armed forces themselves; military reactions to these new tasks range from total rejection to enthusiasm. Military involvement in peace support operations and humanitarian actions has already had and is likely to continue to have consequences for the work of relief organizations. In the past, it was possible for military and humanitarian organizations to exist in parallel solitude. However, given the new and broadly accepted trend towards intervention in wars and conflicts, the isolation of military and civil action seems no longer possible. Humanitarian organizations today are discussing amongst themselves their own role and asking themselves if they should not try to maintain the distance that characterized relations during the 1970s and 1980s. In particular they raise the issue as to whether the relief worker has already become an instrument of foreign and security policy or – at worst – of war and power politics. Practical experience has shown that warring parties can misuse humanitarian assistance (Leriche 2004) and some humanitarians fear that they will become de facto assistants for war with a humanitarian label (Füllkrug-Weitzel 2003). The code of conduct of humanitarian organizations obliges them to act independently from the foreign policies of their governments, but it is not just up to such organizations taking a firm position themselves for their efforts to remain impartial and neutral. Warring parties as well as donor governments that are engaged in post-conflict programmes try to integrate relief into their strategy – 'as a publicly relevant humanitarian component to soften the painful war' (Füllkrug-Weitzel 2003, 64). The US military tried to apply this policy unashamedly after the Iraq War in 2003; the humanitarians reacted with sharp protest and some of them withdrew from Iraq (Misereor, EED and Brot für die Welt 2003, OXFAM 2004).

The military-relief relationship was less strained and less controversial in a number of other conflicts, particularly so in the UN peace operation in East Timor. The German weekly *'Die Zeit'* compares this relationship with the division of labour between a surgeon and assisting nurse. The surgeon cuts the malign cancer and the nurse sees to it that the cut does not bleed too much (quoted in Füllkrug-Weitzel 2003, 65). Others fear that humanitarian assistance might be misused as 'band aid in a manifold wounded world, and might contribute to make a policy acceptable which itself adds ever new wounds' (Brock 2003, 59).

Military mission creep or humanitarian necessity?

The expansion of the functions of the military to undertake international tasks can of course be documented historically. French and British armed forces operated internationally during and also after the period of colonialism, whilst US forces are long since designed as a force with global reach. The international deployment of armies is not new; what is new is the urgency with which the opinion leaders of the international community (particularly in the framework of the UN) have felt a need to intervene in cases of war and other complex emergencies (Roberts 1996).

Judgements about the need, efficiency and long-term consequences of the internationalization of military functions differ widely. Assessments of the new roles range from descriptions of opportunistic mission creep to humanitarian necessity and are very controversial (Pelton 2000) – as visibly demonstrated by the debates around the international military non-action in Rwanda in 1994 and the air war in the former Yugoslavia in 1999. It is argued that the new missions might lead to a detraction from the armed forces' core functions, namely to fight, or unclear civil–military relations. The number of UN missions has increased but UN peacekeeping has also been critically evaluated both from outside and within the UN, most recently in the so-called Brahimi report (UNGA 2001a), even though alternatives to such missions in critical international situations often seem non-existent.

The sociological literature on the new military engagements has for some years consistently reported the resistance of military personnel to missions that diverge from their primary goal of fighting and winning wars (Miller 1997). The US soldiers deployed in 1992 in Somalia agreed with Huntington's conclusion that a peacekeeping role for the armed forces was conceptually principally wrong (quoted in Kartsen 2001). Although the criticism within the armed forces might have been exaggerated, this sentiment had already been voiced in 1976 by the dictum that 'peacekeeping is not a soldier's job, but only a soldier can do it' (Moskos 1976, quoted in Miller 1997). In the US armed forces, for example, there were clear differences of opinions between Colin Powell, the former Secretary of State, when he was chairman of the Joint Chiefs of Staff and his successor John Shalikashvili (Goldstein 2000). While Powell was reserved or even strongly opposed to a US armed forces' role in peacekeeping, Shalikashvili opted for engagement and demonstrated a 'can-do' attitude.

The reluctance of the military, which is by no means universal, is attributable to three fundamental sources (Goldstein 2000):

First, there is the *victory problem*: Peacekeeping seldom yields the satisfaction of clear-cut victory; conflicts are often confusing. Furthermore, the deployment is often not well-liked since it does not concur with the 'hard-fighting' soldier image. Soldiers have mixed feelings about non-core deployments such as peacekeeping and emergency aid, as noted previously when in 1960 Janowitz wrote in his seminal book *The Professional Soldier*, that non-core functions are not popular since they are less prestigious and less honourable (Janowitz, quoted in Miller 1997). However, military journals also criticize the bias that a 'peace mission is for wimps' (Bellamy 2001). Indeed, it seems that peacekeeping is quite popular in some countries. A study on the attitude of the officer corps in Belgium, Italy, Slovenia and the Netherlands showed that peacekeeping and 'helping in the case of disasters' was favoured while national defence was not among the top priorities in any of these countries (Manigart 2001, 11).

Second, there is the *politics problem*: Political motivations 'to do something' against war and genocide might lead to inappropriate military actions and result in undesired political effects. The effects can be particularly negative if no exit strategy is planned and if the deployment drags on over a long period of time. The promoters of international military deployment and peacekeeping who consider these tasks as a worthwhile challenge, criticize the fact that the military does not get the required resources to do the job effectively. But there is also the opposite argument raised by humanitarians. Gebauer (2003, 16), the head of the relief organization Medico International, commented on the military action in the floods in Mozambique by concluding: 'The white helicopter pilot, who rescues a new-born baby from the top of a tree surrounded by floods, is the emblem for "humanitarianism" and the symbol for "interventionist" aid, flying in externally and often disappearing again.' The sustainability of such assistance is questioned because – as a CARE director has put it – the military has an almost 'bomber pilot' mentality for aid delivery: 'give me my orders and I will go in, do the job and leave. Follow-up and long-term impacts do not seem to be part of the equation' (quoted in Pelton 2000, 13). This flawed concept was drastically demonstrated when the US Air Force, after the fall of the Taliban Government in Afghanistan, dropped bombs and food packages from the air at the same time.

Third, there is the *readiness and resource problem*: Many armies are often not in a position to react to the humanitarian demand. Restructuring of the armed forces after the Cold War is still not completed and military leadership feels that forces have been stretched too thinly in the 1990s in terms of both equipment and personnel.

These different reactions prove that humanitarian interventions are contentious within the military. The military has in part chosen to expand its roles voluntarily, occasionally even by pushing its way in. On the other hand, the new assignments are to some degree the result of intensified requests from the international community. Both supply-side and demand-side factors have contributed to the international mandate or mission expansion of the military. There is not only the demand for action by the international community but also the military's search for new vocations and the need to demonstrate their validity after the Cold War. Rather than accepting drastic reductions, soldiers are in search of new areas of operation. This is a reaction typical of large organizations faced with structural changes, and the armed forces, faced with rationalizations and cut backs in the 1990s, are no exception. Furthermore, the armed forces have excess capacities (especially large air transport and other logistical capacities) as a result of the military draw back after the end of the Cold War, which now function as stand-by capacities. The intention is to put these capacities to good use, hence the 'natural' reaction by governments to use their armed forces for relief action. Most non-governmental organizations do not have such capacities readily available for immediate action and feel disadvantaged since the military has got more resources at their disposal to react speedily in times of crisis.

In addition, though from a different perspective, another resort to the additional uses of the armed forces can be viewed in what Musah and Fayemi (2002, 3) note as a return of the era of 'intervention' of the Western powers, which is accepted 'so long as that intervention can be suitably dressed up for public consumption'. Pugh (2004, 39) suggests that militarized peace operations 'sustain a particular order of world politics that privileges the rich and powerful states in their efforts to control or isolate unruly parts of the world'.

The motives for military interventions since the end of the Cold War have varied greatly, as the examples of Somalia beginning in 1992, Kosovo since 1999, East Timor since 1999, Mozambique in 2000 and Afghanistan since 2001 illustrate. The alleged aims included the protection of refugee camps and convoys of relief agencies, the stopping of the flow of refugees and of genocide, the toppling of dictatorial regimes and the assistance for the emancipation of women.

Conflicts of interest in civil–military co-operation

Growing military engagement

The experiences of the military during their interventions of the complicated co-operation with numerous autonomous and independent non-governmental organizations made the military aware of the need for a concept of co-operation. Civil–Military Co-operation (CIMIC), the concept that had already been developed in NATO for domestic civil–military relationships, has recently been adjusted so that it fits situations of co-operation in humanitarian interventions. It developed more incrementally than planned being both a reaction to and a result of the many hands-on experiences in a number of crises where the military had to relate to humanitarian organizations. CIMIC is a tactical doctrine from a military and security policy perspective and was intended to regulate the relationship to relief organizations and civil society in general. The military emphasizes that it is not a concept of military control over civil organizations but one of co-operation.

Most military interventions of the last few years led to more or less far-reaching transfers of central state functions to the armed forces, including the establishment of UN protectorates (Heinemann-Grüder and Pietz 2004). According to NATO doctrine the role of the armed forces is normally the responsibility for security and assistance in that realm relevant to civil public authorities. Only in exceptional cases might the armed forces be required to take over the functions of civil authorities (NATO, no year). In practice all large peace operations have shown that troops have taken over a wide range of state functions, far beyond traditional military tasks.

The civil–military relationship in crises is not always harmonious. Despite NATO's CIMIC doctrine there are big differences (both within and outside of NATO) as to how civil–military relations should be practiced. Although most governments stress that the military should only be tasked in a subsidiary role, for example in reconstruction or development work when the task cannot be performed by civil organizations, with the creation of the so-called Provincial Reconstruction Teams (PRT) in Afghanistan this relationship has entered into a new phase. Civil organizations and the military act in the case of the PRTs in Afghanistan in concert in a common organizational frame. In Germany, for example, the Ministry of Foreign Affairs, the Ministry of Economic Co-operation and Development and the Ministry of Defence pursue what is called an integrated approach. This means the three ministries share the responsibility for the PRT programme in Afghanistan. Heinemann-Grüder and Pietz (2004, 203) conclude that PRTs 'are the precedent for political organizational integration of civil and military activity in a state intervention strategy'. Controversial discussions preceded the introduction of this concept and several relief and development organizations refused to participate; the official development policy of the German government, however, accepted the plans of the military.

Reactions

Amidst all of these unresolved controversies and practical difficulties, the humanitarian relief and aid community stands divided on the issue of the expanded role the military is assuming. The humanitarians are trying to position themselves in this new environment.

First: At one extreme, UN peacekeeping missions operate under the notion of *integrated military and civilian peace-related operations*. The dilemma of independent and impartial relief work versus dependence on the military was most drastically demonstrated during the 2003 Iraq War and its aftermath. Not only were journalists affected by the 'embedding' strategy declared by the US and British governments, but relief organizations were also affected. All activities were planned so as to be under the command of the coalition forces. The Coalition Provisional Authority, the US-dominated civil authority in Iraq, tried to enforce a co-operation agreement on all non-governmental organizations and demanded that they reported to them quarterly. Most institutions refused to meet this demand and several stopped their work in Iraq altogether. They correctly feared that their status as impartial and neutral organizations would be damaged. But in such circumstances not all organizations are free to decide. In Iraq, US AID, the governmental aid organization of the US, threatened to withdraw funding from organizations that would not comply with the governments demand. Some of these organizations depend on state subsidies for their own survival.

Second: In the middle of the spectrum of opinion is the view of a *division of labour*, emphasizing that mandates of civil humanitarian action should be recognized and protected from the compromising involvement of the military, whilst nevertheless keeping the option of coordinated action open (Smillie 2000, Mayhew 2000). This position of a necessary division of labour with the armed forces and a clearly visible distinction between relief workers and armed forces was further underlined in mid-2004 in a non-binding 'reference paper' of the UN (UNIASC 2004).

Third: At the other end of the spectrum is the traditional standpoint which was held for a long time by the International Committee of the Red Cross (ICRC), and is in part still its position today, that *humanitarian operations should proceed independently* from the political and security activities of military forces (Tauxe 2000, Studer 2001). The provision of humanitarian assistance invariably takes place in a political or security vacuum, and the Red Cross recognizes the importance of the protection and the logistical capacities of the armed forces (Tauxe 2000). But relief should not be conflated with the efforts of an 'integrated' peace operation. The raison d'être of humanitarian action is not peace, and most certainly not the enforced peace of the UN Security Council, but to protect human dignity (Studer 2000) and to deliver aid – hence the need for a clear separation of activities.

Impact

In practice, however, there is no strict separation of 'spheres of competence' and actual overlaps abound. Relief workers have to work in volatile and high-risk environments. But here again, controversies in assessing the situation and conflicts of interest are not unusual. The German Minister of Defence, Peter Struck, tried to legitimize the PRTs in Afghanistan by stressing the required protection for relief workers. The protest of a number of relief organizations against this assessment, however, was hardly recognized by the public (Medico International 2003, 10). Humanitarian organizations emphasize that their insistence of their impartiality is not indifference with regard to political realities (Gebauer 2003, 19); they are fully aware that they can hardly influence the political conditions that they are working under.

Humanitarian organizations remain concerned about several consequences of the expanded military role in humanitarian actions (Smillie 2000):

First: The actions of military peacekeepers can threaten NGO impartiality and harm the quality of aid delivery in the field. Impartiality as it is understood by humanitarian organizations (e.g. members of the Steering Committee For Humanitarian Response) is based on the delivery of aid for people in need, regardless of the race, creed or nationality of the recipients and without adverse distinction of any kind according to The Code of Conduct for the International Red Cross and Red Crescent Movement and NGOs in Disaster Relief (quoted in OXFAM 2000). The UN has recently formulated a number of principles as a condition for co-operation between relief organizations and the armed forces.

The prime criteria are humanity, neutrality and impartiality. OXFAM (2003, 6) has concluded that – except for in extreme situations – civil humanitarian organizations are better qualified for effective relief work. The UN underlines the need for a clear distinction between civil relief workers and the armed forces (UNIASC 2004). Yet this visible distinction between civil work and military deployment is sometimes purposely blurred by the armed forces, for example when Special Forces in Afghanistan do not wear uniforms in their fight against terrorists and use the same type of vehicles as the relief organizations.

Second: Military engagement might lead to a militarization of aid (Forrari 2000, Auswärtiges Amt 2000). This concern is particularly relevant to decision-making about humanitarian assistance, which seems to reside increasingly in the hands of military, rather than civilian, leadership (Pelton 2000, Wright 2000). Even before the war in Iraq, then US Secretary of State Colin Powell declared with regard to Afghanistan that humanitarian organizations are 'an important part of our combat team' (quoted in Brock 2003, 61). NATO calls humanitarian relief programmes, which they themselves carry out in parallel to military operations, 'force protection' and hope that civil programmes will increase the acceptance of the public to the military deployment, both at home and in the deployment region. NATO nations raise quite openly the expectation of military co-operation with humanitarian organizations and thus underline the fear of the civil organizations that they might be manipulated to be part of power and war politics. The opposition in Iraq against the occupying forces and the Taliban in Afghanistan interpret the role of the relief organizations similarly; according to them they work in the interest of the United States, and critically, when the distinction between the military and humanitarians gets blurred, the relief workers will be attacked too. This background is the explanation for the attack on the Red Cross in 2003 in Baghdad, and also subsequent attacks on several relief organizations both in Iraq and in Afghanistan. It should be noted also, however, that in less extreme situations, such as for example in East Timor, the division of labour between the military and the humanitarian organizations was quite successful.

Third: Relief organizations complain that the military tends to establish its own long-term projects such as the building of wells, hospitals and schools, often unsustainably and without necessarily having sufficient experience in aid projects. Examples proving this claim are easy to find. VENRO (2004, 13), a network of relief organizations, has criticized the air drop of food packages in Afghanistan by the US air force with the statement that this action has 'grossly violated standards of humanitarian aid' since the relief neither reached the most needy nor was the selection of food included in the packages adequate for the Afghani's diet. Occasionally, a long-term military engagement is undertaken because of the existing excess capacities of the military (as for example in the 1990s in Somalia) and because there is often little practical work to be done to keep the peace. Such an approach might be well intended but not well implemented and over time in Somalia this was proved by the fact that the wells built then have now deteriorated.

Fourth: While the military usually has an impressive capacity for logistical support, the cost of military operations are often much higher than that of civilian aid, as evaluations have shown. The OECD (1997, 8–9) concluded in a report that the civil sector purchases relief goods at lower prices, that their medical service is better suited to the local conditions, that they make more effective use of local resources, and that they manage refugee camps comparatively better than the military. These results are confirmed in other studies (Pelton 2000, Smillie 2000). The United States spent in Afghanistan in 2001 US$40 million for the air supply of food; this amounted to a price of US$7.50 per kilogram – in comparison the World Food Programme of the UN delivers food for 20 cents per kilogram (OXFAM 2003, 7).

'Help – the helpers are coming'[27]

Relief organizations are themselves also part of the problem of collateral damage in relief operations. They do their work not only for altruistic reasons and engage in crisis situations not just to supply aid. Relief work has become an important economic activity too, with the growth rates during the last few years being substantial. Fairs are being held for this market segment where everything required is exhibited and sold – blankets and tents, water purification equipment and logistical services, food and medical kits, rescue boats and four-wheel drive vehicles, mine clearing equipment and body bags. Ethical and social criteria seem to be less relevant than statistical indicators for the relief provided.

Ultimately, relief organizations have to care about donations in their home country if they want to remain in business or to increase their share of the 'relief cake'. Among the humanitarian organizations one can hear the exaggerated formula: 'A year without a disaster is a disaster for the relief organizations'. Self-critical humanitarians ask: Are we, in cases of doubt, giving in to economic interests or to the pressure of governments, and what about our independence if we depend increasingly on government subsidies (Medico International 2003)? The armed forces are a potential competitor; this might be one of the reasons for their often-harsh criticism of military deployments. Despite numerous positive examples of excellent co-operation amongst different relief organizations they do compete amongst themselves too, and there is rivalry to gain the most prominent place in the media since this is likely to increase their donations. This reality, together with the commercialization of relief, results in a lack of co-operation. Help for self-help, the motto of many relief organizations, can also develop into self-legitimization.

It can also be noted that the lack of local knowledge in crisis areas that humanitarian organizations hold against military deployments is true for some relief organizations too. In their efforts to advertise their work in order to collect funds for aid and relief, they might rush into war-torn areas with no local knowledge and without properly investigating the problems and begin their work immediately without proper assessment of the impact (Leriche 2004, 106).

Additionally, the use of an often-large number of expatriates in relief operations might marginalize local structures and lead to the pushing aside of local non-governmental groups. The often desperate economic situation of locally available professionals forces them to accept jobs with a foreign organization below their qualification. They are often employed as drivers or translators. Furthermore, the larger the foreign presence (of civil and military personnel) the more likely is the probability of the evolution of a black market and prostitution. Large numbers of expatriates and the enormous amounts of financial resources flowing into a country initiate an economic path that can devastate existing local structures.

Indeed, relief and aid, even if it is neutrally and impartially intended, can exacerbate conflicts. Neutrality means that an organization does not take sides in a conflict. But all relief work can become political; for example, when para-military groups profit from food supplies in refugee camps one or several of the warring parties might be strengthened. In this way humanitarian work has political and sometimes even military repercussions (Anderson 1999, Lischer 2003). Refusing aid is immoral because people need to be protected, and yet the supply of relief can also have effects other than those intended. Sadako Ogata, then UN High Commissioner for Refugees, complained at the end of the 1990s about the Rwandan refugee crisis in Zaire: 'Probably never before has my office found its humanitarian concerns in the midst of such a lethal quagmire of political and security interests' (quoted in Lischer 2003, 108).

This moral dilemma is not only of relevance for the relief organizations but for the military units in their deployments abroad as well.

Competition on various levels

It is an irony that at a time when ever more police forces are required in humanitarian interventions it is the armed forces that are being deployed. The Brahimi report of the UN called for a change in doctrine to primarily deploy police and civil personnel to establish law and order. Yet, due to the lack of available police recruits, it is military personnel who are taking on more and more police jobs in post-conflict pro-grammes – from traffic regulation in Kabul to election monitoring in the Balkans. Condoleeza Rice, at that time National Security Advisor to the US president, advised against the use of the military for non-military functions that made no sense – she urged, for example, not to use para-troopers for taking children to school (quoted in NATO 2001). Wesley Clark (quoted in Field and Perito 2002/3, 86), the former NATO Supreme Allied Commander in Europe, in describing the wars and the post-war programmes involving police functions in the Balkans concluded that 'most military are simply not capable of performing such functions effectively and should not be the primary element responsible for them'. Apparently thus it is not always the soldiers who are pushing to take over humanitarian tasks, but rather they are often used as substitutes when intervening states do not have enough civilian personnel at their disposal. Furthermore, it is obviously not as easy to deploy police or civil-ians into conflict zones as it is to deploy soldiers; police and judiciary experts are not as easily available and also often not under the jurisdiction of the central state authorities.

A second contradiction can be noted in the allegedly necessary use of military power to prevent war. More than ever before, including during the time of the Cold War and the East–West antagonism, troops are involved in war fighting in the name of preventing conflict and build-ing nations. The use of military power, so the expectation goes, should stop wars or prevent them. But catastrophic situations are often exacer-bated, as was the case during NATO's air war in Kosovo that was intended to stop the stream of refugees. This is probably not the result of a lack of preparation or training on behalf of the military for that task, but rather inherent in the inconsistencies of crisis prevention and conceptual insufficiencies.

Due to these political reasons set out earlier, two classical principles of UN blue-helmet mandated deployments have been dented through a number of recent military interventions: the role of the peacekeepers as neutral mediators in a conflict, and the denial of troop contributions from permanent members of the UN Security Council and neighbouring countries to the conflict. Though troops from these countries are now deployed in peace operations the UN often requires many more resources (military, police and financial) than the member states are willing to contribute, and hence the discordance of the lack of capabilities in face of the new and ever-increasing additional requests for crisis management.

The competition and often overly complicated co-operation between the military and relief organizations contribute to the negative impacts and inefficient implementation of interventions. The very different cultures and ethos of military and civilian organizations do make co-operation difficult (Minear, van Baarda *et al.* 2000, Minear and Guillot 1996). This is reflected particularly (but not exclusively) in the non-coercive nature of the work of humanitarian organizations (Studer 2001). Whereas the threat or the application of force to achieve their aims is a characteristic of the armed forces, many humanitarian organizations reject the use of force or are at least committed to not using force themselves. Many NGOs, based on their long experience in humanitarian aid projects, expect the military to consult with them before they act, but are instead often faced with the military's reluctance to co-operate with others and their lack of transparency. Thus, practical experience has led to much frustration among the humanitarian organizations (Wright 2000, Auswärtiges Amt 2000, Pelton 2000) but also to second thoughts on the part of the military (Lanman 1998a, and b).

While there is no dissent about the fundamental principle that military resources should complement – not replace – civilian resources, roles have become dangerously blurred. Although Guidelines on the Use of Military and Civil Defence Assets in Disaster Relief (referred to in Pelton 2000) exist, in practice the relationship is often strained (Forrari 2000, Gourlay 2000) and has been intensified during the last few years in Iraq. The experience of the 1990s now suggests that the euphoric hope at the end of the Cold War that uncomplicated humanitarian action in war could be increased, was misplaced (MacFarlane 1997). The major impacts of the competitive military-relief relations have been often inefficiency of actual relief efforts and in critical cases even unintended new conflicts or collateral damage. Today, different organizations have reacted by defining codes of conduct for co-operation (UNIASC 2004, BMZ 2004, UNHCHR 2004, OXFAM 2004), though the original almost total refusal of co-operation by the humanitarian organizations has not completely disappeared. There have been a number of occasions during the last few years, however, where numerous organizations were prepared to engage in an agreed framework to co-operate with the military. It seems that the contrary positions are somewhat softening and compromises for the sake of effective relief are being sought (Heinemann-Grüder and Pietz 2004).

The business of peace missions

Companies to the front

Private military and security companies are increasingly interested in doing business with relief organizations by contributing to the security of their relief work. Correspondingly, the relief organizations are interested in some of the services of these firms. So far the UN has not engaged private military firms to fight in peace enforcement operations, although the issue has been discussed. However, only few companies are prepared to contribute combat troops. Companies are often tasked as suppliers of materials or providers of logistics. The permanent shortage of resources for UN mandated peace operations, the chronically difficult search of the secretary general to mobilize enough peacekeepers, and the growth of specialized private military firms has brought the question to the fore as to whether the capacity of the private sector could not be used in future peace operations.

A 1998 study of the International Institute for Strategic Studies (IISS) had addressed the possibility of using private military companies and concluded optimistically that this opportunity should not be forgone (Shearer 1998). In 2004, political analysts of the Brookings Institution (O'Hanlon and Singer 2004) published a detailed proposal for UN use of the services of private military companies in peace missions. The head of now defunct Sandline International, Tim Spicer, who had previously engaged with combat troops in several conflicts, had offered his 'good services' quite frequently (Spicer 1998). Such past isolated advances by companies seem to be now transferred into a concerted action. A small group of over a dozen companies has formed the International Peace Operations Association (IPOA), an association which, according to its mission statement, provides 'services related to conflict alleviation and avoidance, post-conflict reconstruction, and emergency humanitarian rescue worldwide'; to propagate a code of conduct for companies who offer such professional services; and to 'raise the profile and acceptance of association members' (http://www.ipoaonline.org/background.htm, accessed 6 January 2005). The companies want to provide peacekeepers for the benefit of international peace and human security. They believe that long-term, sustainable peace in the trouble spots of the world depends on the know-how of such specialized companies. The association does not just publish general intensions but has made a concrete offer to the UN. It offered to participate in the UN peace operation in the DRC (MONUC) and promises to provide, under the command of the UN, the necessary services that are still lacking. According to a January 2003 paper of IPOA, MONUC 'cannot successfully fulfill its peace mission, stabilization and humanitarian protection without these services' (International Peace Operations Association 2003, 1).

Furthermore, the paper claims, the UN would need for a successful mission in the DRC US $ 1 billion annually. The estimated costs of an IPOA consortium providing the critical peacekeeping services would amount to 'between 100 and 200 million dollars' depending on the scale of the mission (ibid., 6). The companies would provide services in three areas: *First*, Security and stabilization services with protection for civilians; monitoring the withdrawal and redeployment of forces; protection of UN personnel, facilities, installations and equipment; deterrence and interdiction of armed factions; disarming irregular forces; training of security and border protection forces; and so on. *Second*, Humanitarian services such as locating and monitoring internally displaced persons and vulnerable population groups; mission security for international humanitarian operations; demining and ordnance disposal; and logistical needs for non-governmental and humanitarian organizations. *Third*, Humanitarian support services such as an improved communications network; a 24-hour rapid rescue service; 24-hour emergency medical facilities; and emergency evacuations for key personnel.

Five companies have formed the support consortium for the MONUC mission: PAE, a logistics provider; ICI, an international air charter and air security company; MPRI, the military training provider that is mainly under contract by the US Army; AirScan International, an air, ground and maritime surveillance company; and TASK International, a company of Nepalese Gurkha veterans who served in the British forces. All five companies have been publicly implicated in allegations of involvement in war-related activities or human rights violations. Since there is no legal basis for prosecution, they have not been formally charged. The cynical question inevitably arises: Is this public criticism of the private military companies' behaviour possibly the reason for trying to create a respectable image by offering a code of conduct that promises transparency, the observance of ethical principles and of human rights, and praises disarmament and mine clearing as particularly useful tasks? Proudly the consortium announces that the 'IPOA consortium is prepared to offer a greater degree of transparency and accountability than any UN peacekeeping operation *EVER* provided' (emphasis in the original, IPOA 2003, 4).

Individual firms have offered their services too, such as, for example, the British company Northbridge, which offered in 2003 to deploy 2000 soldiers in Liberia (O'Hanlon and Singer 2004, 92) and promised to seize indicted former Liberian President Charles Taylor and hand him over to an international tribunal if the company was rewarded a honorarium of US$2 million (BBC News 13 December 2003, http://news.bbc.co.uk/1/hi/world/africa/3309203.stm, accessed 25 October 2004).

Reservations and rejections at the UN and from humanitarian organizations

How do the UN Department of Peacekeeping Operations, the responsible UN Departments and humanitarian organizations react to such offers? There is no systematic or comprehensive data available about the use of private security and military firms. The present situation is characterized by general reservations and rejections of companies with a military or combat image. This attitude towards private military companies is grounded on the image of the companies as 'modern mercenaries', and as such the privatization of peace missions seems presently unacceptable for the majority of the UN member states. The business practices of companies, which are by no means always transparent, also contribute to reservations and suspicions. There are also practical considerations. Most of the companies are too small to regard them as a realistic alternative to member states' contributions in UN peace operations, and even if the companies would in reality be in a position to deploy large contingents of troops this would still need to be proven in practice.

Even so, all large donor governments and the large and globally operating relief organizations, as well as the UN, have already made use, in one form or another, of the services of private security firms, for example for the protection against violence of their personnel (Vaux *et al.* 2002, 16). As a rule, the UN and relief and aid organizations inform each other about the required and to be implemented security precautions in conflict and crisis situations. The UN Office for the Coordination of Humanitarian Affairs (OCHA) had already at the end of the 1990s published guidelines for their field officers with regard to hiring private security companies. The main criterion for hiring them is the registration of the company with the government of the host country (Vaux *et al*. 2002, 15).

The UN is in a dilemma. They lack not only the necessary number of well qualified military and police personnel for their peace operations due to member countries' reservations in contributing resources, but are also not flexible enough as noted when the secretary general has to beg for contributions after each and every Security Council resolution for a peacekeeping operation. The stand-by force, requested in the Agenda for Peace in 1992, has no chance of implementation. The conclusion of Kofi Annan, mentioned in the preface of this book, that apparently the world is not ready for privatizing peace is still true today. In a television interview in 2002, in which Tim Spicer was also interviewed, the former UN Undersecretary General and 'inventor' of the blue-helmet concept, Sir Brian Urquhart, said the UN should actually have a small rapid reaction force based on member contributions at its disposal. This is, however, not the case. He drew the conclusion that 'there are security questions, there are special areas, there are all sorts of special tasks which possibly these companies are better-trained to perform than a UN force put together at the last minute for the particular purpose' (Australian Broadcasting Corporation 2000). In contrast, the UN Special Rapporteur on mercenaries wrote in 2001 that no matter how difficult a situation might be states have a responsibility for law and order, and security and protection should not be handed to private entities. The international community can neither allow the formation of private armies nor the privatization of war (UN ECOSOC 2001b, paragraph 66).

A search at the UN proved that there is currently no intention to deploy private military firms in peace operations; the relevant policy papers do not exist.[28] A search amongst UN specialized agencies and relief organizations had similar results.[29] The buying of the services of unarmed private security companies for protection of personnel and buildings as well as for the provision of logistical service is generally accepted and common, but armed services are generally strictly rejected. OXFAM, for example, has a 'no armed private security guards policy', although in exceptional circumstance this policy could be overwritten. The hiring of private military companies would need to pass OXFAM's ethical purchasing policy, which prevents the organization hiring or using services from companies that have an involvement in arms. Due to a serious incident in 2004 OXFAM introduced advance screening of those companies who might be contracted.[30]

German relief organizations have been offered the services of private military companies too. In one letter a military company offers 'unconventional combat, guerrilla warfare, evacuation, intelligence gathering, anti-terror deployment' and many other services. To tempt the addressee, a relief organization, the company also wrote that 'we are always happy to offer humanitarian relief too'.[31]

The UN High Commission for Refugees (UNHCR), an organization often confronted with violence in conflict regions, considers private military companies' services as not in conformity with its mandate and mission. Occasionally, UNHCR has sought the protection of refugee camps from the police of the host nation. Security companies are used by UNHCR to protect offices and stores, but these services are not hired for the protection of its personnel during official mission or private travel. Contracts for protection services are publicly tendered, and the contracts are awarded based strictly on economic considerations. For an assessment of security situations UNHCR has established its own Field Safety Section, which advices in-country UNHCR authorities. Private security companies, some of them large transnational concerns, are normally hired locally only if they are officially registered with the government. As an alternative the organization employs its own security guards but it also seeks security services from the host country. Governments are committed by the Vienna Convention to protect the privileges and immunity of UN personnel and to guarantee their security; they are, however, often not in a position or willing to do this. In such situations UNHCR might assist the host country with a so-called security package for the necessary training and supply of equipment to enable the government to meet its obligation. With regard to the protection of refugee camps, UNHCR is hesitant to make use of the security services of the host country since the refugees often had to flee precisely because of these security agencies.[32]

The International Committee of the Red Cross has the function of a relief organization and the responsibility to monitor the implementation and development of International Humanitarian Law (IHL). It is a policy of the ICRC not to use armed security guards. However, this is a sensitive subject. In accordance with a resolution of the International Red Cross and Red Crescent movement, the organization never uses armed escorts in areas against the wishes of those controlling that territory (Sandoz 1999). The Red Cross has expanded contacts to private military and security companies on an ad hoc basis with the aim of ensuring that the companies operating in conflict regions are familiar with and observe IHL. This, in effect, means that the Red Cross recognizes the existence of companies in this particular sector; which, in turn, makes it necessary to train the personnel of these companies from an ICRC perspective. The ICRC makes it explicitly clear that it 'does not plan to take a position on the legitimacy of private military and security companies but will insist that the trend toward privatising military functions should not open the door to a weakening of respect and implementation of IHL' (ICRC 2004).[33]

7
Countering Terrorism Through Military Means?

Priorities for military-based policies

Terrorism is not a new phenomenon. Yet our concern of it seems to evolve in proportion to its affect upon us. Today, first and foremost it is the US government that is requesting the countries of the world to actively and effectively fight terrorism. This was different in the 1970s when it was the European countries who were most affected by terrorist acts and they tried in vain to convince the United States of the dangers of terrorism (Jenkins 2003). The reactions of governments against this threat were until recently conditioned by the type of single terror attacks themselves; the various terrorist activities did not seem to be interconnected. Today, for the first time, a systematic – although not necessarily successful – security strategy to counter terrorism is being pursued. US President George Bush called the terror attacks of 11 September 2001 the first war of the twenty-first century, which would also require a military strategy of the twenty-first century (US Government 2002b). The present security situation is drastically changed since the fight is against an almost invisible enemy. The global dimension of terrorism, though at least partly rooted locally and regionally, is the central defining element of US, and a number of other countries', military strategy.

Global politics are more militarized today – and not only since the 2003 Iraq War. The indicators of increasing military expenditures and the willingness to first react to conflicts with the assessment of military options have been observed for a few years now. The terrorist attacks of 9/11 and the subsequent declaration of 'war on terrorism' by the United States have graphically exposed deep changes and divergences in international relations, which have to be understood as conflicts of interest of global dimensions. Zones of differing levels of security with

149

life-threatening inequalities already existed before 11 September 2001; but they are now more apparent and manifest because of the overwhelming technical, economic and military dominance of the United States.

Confrontational patterns are prevailing and have been more noticeable than behaviour of co-operative conflict resolution. The 2002 US National Security Strategy (US Government White House 2002a) favours threats with military power, and the Iraq War illustrates that this policy concept is not a mere verbal warning but practiced when considered necessary. Arms control policy, based on multilateral treaties and internationally accepted norms, has lost its priority and is no longer a focus on the political agenda. This trend has been enhanced by the newly emerged terrorist threat.

These new patterns of international relations correlate to domestic processes in a large number of conflict-prone societies in which the military or other security agencies no longer seem to be perceived by large parts of the population as guarantors of security but rather as a latent and often blatant risk to their survival. As a reaction to the 9/11 attacks the armed forces in many countries are used both as protection forces as well as for combating the terrorists. This is mainly the case in Central, South and South-East Asia, the Middle East and the Horn of Africa.

The terrorist attacks gave counter-terrorist concepts greater urgency. The notion of a 'war on terrorism' progressed quickly from a first phase, aiming at the annihilation of Al Qaeda and the overthrow of the Taliban regime in Afghanistan, into a second phase in which the US government presumes an alleged direct relationship between the terrorists, weapons of mass destruction and so-called 'rouge states'. To take this connection between terrorists, weapons of mass destruction and 'rouge states' for granted proved, even against the empirical evidence in the case of Iraq, to have important functions and consequences.

For one, this point of view is supposed to legitimize the global reach of the military. In addition, reference to the state sponsors of terrorists is used to justify regime change, as aspired to and implemented in the cases of Afghanistan and Iraq, despite important reservations in international law. If the US government were to classify the terrorists as 'mere' criminals, it would soon be confronted with having to present proof of criminal acts acceptable in courts. This is obviously difficult in the terrorist environment, as has been shown by several court cases already. However, when terrorists are defined as hostile combatants, intelligence service information seems sufficient for a majority of the voters to legitimize military-based counter-terrorism policies. The alleged trinity of terrorism, weapons of mass destruction and 'rouge states' thus has a domestic dimension too. Finally, the 'war on terrorism' is not only used to justify international interventions, including the war in Iraq, but also to expand the defence budget and procurement of new weapons in numerous countries. But interestingly, in the order books of defence producers one does not find weapons systems or other equipment especially designed and developed to counter terrorists, but rather the typical big ticket items, the large weapons platforms, which were conceptualized during the Cold War and already then on the shopping list of the armed forces. Yet due to arms control policies in the early 1990s and budget constraints in later years these items could not be procured earlier (Brzoska 2002).

However, this concept of 'old wine in new bottles' is being rejuvenated not only in the United States. The blue print of internationally operating terrorists, sponsored by rouge states and striving to possess weapons of mass destruction is the concept Russian President Putin uses to legitimize his war in Chechnya. The danger that terrorists will really be able to acquire weapons of mass destruction should not be belittled, and some of the state-sponsored nuclear programmes in the Middle East and Asia are frightening as well. But one particular aspect of possible counter-measures is usually not mentioned or considered, namely that the terrorists can obtain these weapons or the relevant technology only from those who already possess them and this group of countries includes not only a few of the so-called dubious ones.

There is no doubt, given the dimension of the new terrorist attacks, that this terrorism is more than organized crime. But the classification as 'war' is inappropriate in several respects. From an international law perspective such a classification means upgrading the terrorists in as much as they are allotted the status of combatants (Howard 2002). Consequently it would mean that this status serves to recognize them as representing a 'party' and negotiating counter-part. Almost no country has refused the US government's wish for co-operation after the 9/11 events and its military-based counter-terrorism policy. In public debates and in policy prescriptions to counter terrorism the possible role of the military is an important ingredient. But what can the military actually do? In the former antagonism between capitalism and communism the antagonist was clearly visible and recognized as the enemy, and communism eventually 'lost' the battle. In the 'war on terrorism' the enemy is hidden and very difficult to track down. Relying on military means without a recognizable enemy is bound to be open-ended and every unsuccessful military action will make future efforts even more difficult.

Discussion in the United States embraces the whole spectrum of viewpoints and motivations, from the hardliners who want to erase all evil whenever there is the possibility (Frum and Perle 2003), to the analysts in the military realm, who warn against too heavy a military hand and who prefer low-key military action (Gray 2002, 6).

Combating terrorism as a military task

Military strategic concepts

NATO's Strategic Concept of 1999 includes only two references to the term terrorism. Paragraph 24 mentions risks, including terrorist attacks, sabotage and organized crime, while paragraph 53i requests that the armed forces and the infrastructure of the alliance are protected against terrorists (NATO 1999). Terrorism has become a focus in strategic debates only since the attacks in New York and Washington. In contrast to the earlier periods the US government gradually began to recognize terrorism as a serious threat to security only during the 1990s; this is reflected in the relevant strategy documents. A chain of terrorist acts against US installations, naval ships and embassies forced a debate about the security risks, and by the time of the 1997 report of the US Ministry of Defense, a whole chapter was devoted to finding answers to counter terrorism. The 2001 report stresses the need for military capabilities to counter asymmetric threats. This report is particularly concerned about the threats of nuclear, biological and chemical weapons and suggests strengthening the ballistic missile defence system and the fight against terrorism. There had already been an earlier discussion about low intensity conflicts, but this debate did not deal primarily with combating terrorism. The former US Secretary of State, George Schultz (1984, quoted in Sloan 1986, 46) had wanted as far back as in 1984 to pursue an 'active strategy [that] should go beyond passive defense to consider means of active prevention, preemption, and retaliation'.

Low intensity conflicts comprise, in the usage of the US armed forces, combating guerrillas, uprisings and the drugs trade; but they also include combating terrorism. In 1990, the then US Minister of Defense, Richard B. Cheney, stated in his annual report to the Congress that he expected that low intensity conflicts would be the most probable form of violence endangering US interests. Furthermore, he called for an active and timely defence that would act as a credible deterrence against this type of violence (US Department of Defense 1990, quoted in Adolph 1992). The Clinton Administration followed this assessment and published

Presidential Decision Directive 39 in 1995 that underlined that terrorist attacks against US installations would not be a question of if, but of when (Weiss 2001).

The US strategy of preemptive military-based security comes closest – both conceptually and in reality – to a change of security paradigm. Terrorism is today seen as *the* key threat while the 'old' security paradigm was geared at defending against security threats by states. This conceptual change was already in the making before the Bush Administration came into office (Andreas and Price 2001). Despite intensive strategic debates about the dangers of terrorism the US forces are still not in a position to present an effective concept for the prevention of such attacks. Even today, the question as to what the armed forces can concretely do in order to combat terrorism, and how they should be restructured for this task and what weapons and equipment are best suited, remains largely unanswered. Military journals continually discuss experiences of counter-terrorism and the results of protection as well as retaliation programmes against supporting governments, whilst in addition the difficulties of asymmetric warfare and experiences in low intensity conflicts are revisited and controversially debated. Although this debate does not give clear answers to a possible role of the military, the 9/11 attacks added to the 'appetite' of combating terrorism with military muscle, and although this has often been publicly declared as policy these calls remain unspecific and vague. After the 9/11 attacks and the perceived urge to do something, qualified and constructive criticism of the militarily based counter-terrorism strategy is almost absent or is not taken seriously at all when such criticism is raised.

Military doctrine and security policy journals and documents broadly agreed until the 2001 terror attacks that military measures could not be the primary answer and certainly not the sole reaction to combating terrorism (US Department of Defense 1997). To try to fight terrorism through military means alone is described as 'mission impossible' (Gotowicki 1997). Politicians in other countries faced with similar threats came to the same conclusion. For example, the then Prime Minister of Israel, Yitzhak Rabin, often criticized his domestic opponents in the mid-1980s, the Likud Party, for relying entirely on the application of violence and military power to solve the Arab–Israeli conflict. He concluded during the first 'Intifada' that there was a need for a political concept as well and that the strategy should be two-legged, political and military (Inbar 1991).

Characteristics of terrorism

Terrorism attacks the values of the international community. It flourishes, as the UN report of the High-level Panel of 2004 has concluded, 'in environments of despair, humiliation, poverty, political oppression, extremism and human rights abuse' (UNHLPT 2004, 47). The fact that for some they are 'freedom fighters' while they are 'terrorists' for others, illustrates how difficult it is to arrive at an unequivocal and accepted definition of terror, terrorism and terrorists. The above-mentioned UN report of the High-level Panel has greatly contributed to clarifying the definition of terrorism by defining it as any action, in addition to actions already specified in the relevant treaties (especially the Geneva Conventions and UN Security Council resolution 1566 of 2004), 'that is intended to cause death or serious bodily harm to civilians or non-combatants, when the purpose of such act, by its nature or context, is to intimidate a population, or to compel a Government or an international organization to do or to abstain from doing any act' (UNHLPT 2004, 52). The report makes it clear that not only non-state actors but also states are covered, and it concludes that international norms against state violations do exist and are in fact far stronger than in the case of non-state actors; furthermore (with a view to the Israeli–Palestinian conflict) nothing in the occupation of a territory by a state justifies the targeting and killing of civilians (UNHLPT 2004, 51).

However, even after the presentation of this authoritative definition it will still be difficult to decide on the effective role of the military as a counter-terrorism instrument. Can the military prevent such attacks as in New York and Washington and those in several other cities in Europe and Asia that followed? Is the main military purpose to prevent the acquisition of weapons of mass destruction by terrorists? What about so-called cyber terrorism? And should nationally based or ideologically orientated, religious, one-issue or state-sponsored terror be combated by the armed forces (Wilkinson 2002)? Obviously a convincing and thorough military answer to respond against such a diffuse picture of various different types of threat is not possible.

During the 1970s and 1980s the terrorist groups in Europe and Japan aimed at catching as much public attention as possible, but without however expecting to have to kill people in as large a number as possible. The terrorism of today, sometimes called mega- or hyper-terrorism, is different in that respect. Mass casualties and unbearable suffering are intended to affect the attacked society to its core.

Al Qaeda is the first terrorist network with a global reach. Its activities have greatly added to the threat perception and the change in the

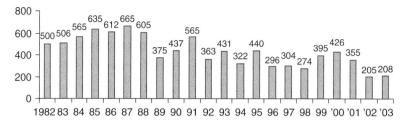

Figure 7.1   Number of acts of international terrorism, 1982–2003
Source: US Department of State 2004a, Appendix G.

security paradigm. The 9/11 attacks illustrated in all their brutality that Al Qaeda is not interested in the support nor concerned about the suffering of its 'enemy's' populations. It hopes to inflict the highest possible damage in the countries of its 'enemy' without regard for innocent victims by using unconventional means.

Despite this intensified public attention, the number of globally registered acts of terror has – with some fluctuations – declined over a long period of time, according to a statistic of the US Department of State. The report on patterns of global terrorism of June 2004 lists 208 acts of international terrorism in 2003, a slight increase from the previous year but a 42 per cent drop from the level in 2001 (US Department of State 2004a). During the 1980s this annual figure amounted to over 500, while during the 1990s it fell much lower, as Figure 7.1 indicates. The number of casualties, however, increased – as the terrorists intended.

From a military perspective terrorism is a surprise attack that requires much less logistical effort than a military intervention, for example, since the terrorists do not depend on sophisticated weapons. This gives them flexibility and opportunities to strike with no or limited advance warning. Their attacks receive great public attention, both in the attacked society as well as among the terrorists' potential clientele. In contrast to guerrilla fighters they do not rely on the support of the population but instead make use of the attacked society's infrastructure. They do not only ignore the possibility that resultant casualties of their actions might be innocent victims, but in fact also abolish the very differences between civilians and combatants enshrined in the international humanitarian law. Normally, terrorists prefer to hit soft rather than hard and protected targets without any forewarning. They carry out precisely planned attacks, in which they themselves are prepared to commit suicide, or withdraw without engaging in combat after the act of terrorism.

The difficulties of military reactions

The fight against terrorism therefore is a conflict without any frontline in the military sense. Comparing the equipment of the military and terrorists or their personnel size, the terrorist groups are inferior. This makes them look for asymmetric combat in which modern and sophisticated weapons are of minor importance. Terrorism is a strategy in which the militarily speaking weaker group can act to its own advantage by applying violence. Terrorists change the form and methods as well as the time and place of their attacks, and thus are impossible to predict. This strategy makes it extremely difficult to combat them through military means alone.

There is a consensus that acts of terror cannot be tolerated and that the attackers should be punished. This is normally the task of the judiciary. However, international terrorism operates usually from across borders and thus challenges the typical constitutional characteristic in democracies of limiting the role of external security institutions (Slocombe 2003, 293). In principle terrorism can be combated by prevention, by deterrence/dissuasion or prosecution. It is controversial which of these three areas should be emphasized and what role the military might play in each. Fighting the potential nuclear threats of terrorists no doubt needs to be done by prevention, namely by non-proliferation of the weapons and the relevant know-how. This is not primarily a military task but rather needs to be guaranteed by control regimes. It is questionable if at all terrorists can be deterred if they are willing to give up even their own lives in a terrorist attack for the cause of their conviction. As regards punishment it may be questioned if this, for example through military sanctions, will result in a new upsurge of terror attacks and a spiral of violence or if they will stop. The modern equipment of the armed forces, with typical large weapons platforms, may result in a military supremacy that is, however, only of limited or even no use in fighting terrorists. The armed forces with their equipment can only find militarily relevant targets if the terrorists concentrate their forces or when they organize themselves into a military-like structure. Therefore, the attacks against the training centres of Al Qaeda in Afghanistan by the US forces made military sense, since this complicated the recruiting and training process for Al Qaeda.

Experiences of armed forces in combating terrorism

Instead of speculating if the present military counter-strategy will eventually be successful or not, I analyze previous experiences of armed forces in this area. The use of the military as a tool against terrorists was not invented in 2001. The armed forces of numerous countries have had rich experiences, partly over extended periods of times, in fighting insurgencies, uprisings, partisans, guerrillas and terrorists: the United Kingdom in its former colonies (Palestine, Malaya, Burma and Kenya) and until recently in Northern Ireland, Russia currently in Chechnya and during the 1980s in Afghanistan, Spain in the Basque country, the Philippines in Mindanao, India in the North-Eastern provinces (Manipur, Assam, Tripura and Nagaland), Sri Lanka in the Jaffna region, Israel in the occupied territories and in Lebanon, Columbia in the fight against drugs, and so on. To avoid any misunderstanding, I want to underline that not all the groups fighting their governments or occupiers can be classified as terrorists. It is not of interest here how the different groups are classified, but the primary question is what experience the armed forces had in these conflicts against militarily weaker groups; this will enable an assessment of the potential role of the military in combating terrorism.

The conceptual spectrum of governments that engaged the military in these conflicts varied greatly. Some military actions reminded of police methods, some governments used carpet bombings or extinguishing of the leadership, others attempted to win the hearts and minds of people. Although some actions were militarily successful, such interventions seldom had political success in the sense that they ended violence or led to a peace treaty or resolution of conflict. The long periods of protracted fighting in some conflicts and the open violence in others – as for example in the Middle East – are evidence enough of the small chances for military success. The experiences of Russia in the past in Afghanistan or today in Chechnya and the consequences of deploying British troops in Northern Ireland demonstrate that military strategies did not resolve these conflicts. What lessons can be learned for today's role of the armed forces in combating terrorism? From the numerous possible historical examples I have looked at the experiences of the Israeli, the United States and the British forces in several conflicts.

The role of the Israeli armed forces in the Palestine conflict

Israel's armed forces have reacted with different concepts at different times against the resistance and the fight of the Palestinians in which acts of terror have played an important role. Originally the armed forces were tailored, on the basis of the experience gained in several wars, to apply quick and decisive military actions to win wars. While the Israeli military played hardly any role in countering the aircraft hijackings by Palestinian groups during the 1960s, gradually the military was reformed and reequipped to fight 'small wars', especially to prevent suicide attacks or at least to minimize the damage.

The first 'Intifada' during the 1980s, the intervention of Israeli forces in Lebanon in the mid-1990s and the current second 'Intifada' forced the readjustment of the armed forces. Today, the armed forces have the full spectrum of tactical means typical for 'small wars' at their disposal. This includes, besides interventions by ground forces, planned bombings of relevant objects as well as the elimination of key figures (Inbar 1991, Ganor 1997). The government of Premier Sharon tries to use massive military power to react to Palestinian attacks, which in turn leads to further reactions and a spiral of violence where nobody can tell who started it.

The 'Intifada' is an unusual mixture of non-violent civil disobedience and the application of force below the level of conventional war. Independent of the fact that the 'Intifada' is a phenomenon 'sui generis', and is neither a guerrilla war nor a terror campaign, conclusions can be drawn from this conflict of what military counter-terror measures might or might not achieve. The government of Prime Minister Rabin reacted against the first 'Intifada' in the beginning with economic measures. Those Palestinians, who behaved 'well', according to Israeli assessment, could expect the proverbial 'carrot' while 'unacceptable' behaviour was punished with the 'stick'. The Israeli defence forces were requested during this opening phase to keep away from the Palestinian leaders, although at the same time they were asked to try to isolate the hard core of the leadership who would take part in terror acts.

During the next phase, which was perceived in Israel as a heightened risk that could possibly threaten the existence of the state of Israel, the armed forces were called upon to stop the violence seen as being initiated by the Palestinians. The object of the intervention of the military was to deter and control the situation by using limited power. The government increased the military presence substantially; it relaxed the possible use of firearms, introduced more effective modern munitions, and the armed forces shifted Special Forces and elite units into the occupied territories. Besides these military measures the government implemented administrative tools, such as arrests, indictments, detentions and tried to apply economic pressures.

By the end of the 1980s the Rabin government had become gradually convinced that the application of military force was not an effective strategy to stop the violence. The government admitted that the armed forces were not successful in controlling the uprising. The change of government under the Likud Party and the change in the Ministry of Defence did not, however, result in an immediate change in the concept of the armed forces. Additional troops were deployed on the main roads to strengthen the police efforts, though the total strength of the Israeli military in the occupied territories was not increased (Inbar 1991). A mixture of a more visible military presence, the specialized training of soldiers for this form of intervention, the deployment of Special Forces and comparatively more professional soldiers, intensified intelligence gathering and the development of a tactical doctrine for differentiated actions resulted in an adjustment of the armed forces for this type of conflict. At the same time a more restricted use of firearms led to a lessening of tensions, a reduction in the number of casualties among the Palestinians and a noticeable pacification in the occupied territories, although not to an end of the conflict. Eventually it was possible, with strong assistance and pressure from abroad, to initiate the Oslo peace process and to end the first 'Intifada'.

The military operations of Israel against the Hezbollah in Lebanon in 1996 under the code name 'Grapes of Wrath' also graphically demonstrate the limits of military counter-terrorism – they were not successful. A small number of committed suicide assassins were eventually successful in driving out the French, the US and finally also the Israelis from Lebanon (Ganor 1998). The main objective of Israel's armed forces intervention was to stop the rocket attacks of the Hezbollah against Israeli settlements. After the policy of US mediation had failed Israel's air force got the green signal in spring 1996 to start its operation 'Grapes of Wrath' (Eshel 1996). To minimize the casualties amongst civilians, Israel defined a certain area in Southern Lebanon as a war zone and requested the population to leave this area.

The Hezbollah operated in small teams without a broad-based or sophisticated infrastructure. The majority of their fighters moved together with the local population to the North at the beginning of the Israeli operation, while small and well-organized rocket crews who constantly changed their positions remained in the declared war zone in South Lebanon (Eshel 1996). The Hezbollah applied a hit-and-run tactic. With the assistance of Iranian experts, some of whom had trained in the United States for the fight against the Soviet Union in Afghanistan, the Hezbollah fighters used technically simple, portable rockets, which were fired by a timer so that the rocket team had already left their positions by the time the rocket was fired. They avoided using Russian produced multiple-radar-guided missiles to evade detection by the Israeli armed forces. Therefore, it was nearly impossible for Israel's air force to discover the Hezbollah rocket positions. Even the flight of Israeli unmanned air-breathing vehicles did not put the air force in a position to gain real-time information about the locations of the Hezbollah teams. Of course, when the Israeli air force had finally detected their original positions they had usually already moved on to a different location. Although Israeli patrols and checkpoints were able to catch some of the heavy equipment of the Hezbollah, the number of rocket attacks increased. The Israeli population demanded and pressed increasingly for the elimination of the Hezbollah rocket attacks on the Kiryat Shmone settlement – a settlement close to the Lebanese border. Israel's modern and technically sophisticated fighters were not equipped for this kind of mission, thus clearly showing that technological advantage was insufficient for a military victory. When an Israeli artillery shell mistakenly and tragically hit the camp of Kafr Quana, which was under the protection of the UN, and resulted in numerous civilian casualties, Israel had to stop the operation due to intense international pressure.

Despite these experiences the Sharon government has based its strategy in the occupied territories during the last few years mainly on military interventions; the tensions have only increased and the military objective has been completely missed. Rejection of this policy is mounting, even from within the military, and a small number of high-ranking officers have distanced themselves from the official policy and decline to serve in the occupied territories.

US retaliations against terrorism

Terrorist attacks against the United States have in the past mainly been directed at US installations, such as the embassies in Kenya and Tanzania or against US military bases and naval ships abroad. Terrorist organizations have carried out numerous attacks during the last few decades. The US Department of Defense distinguishes between anti-terrorism and counter-terrorism, although the term anti-terrorism is presently hardly used. The former mainly means defensive measures to reduce the vulnerability of personnel or to intensify protection of installations, but also refers to the gathering of intelligence information. This is called the first line of defence. Counter-terrorism is defined by the Pentagon as prevention, deterrence and retaliation against acts of terrorism (US Department of Defense 1997). The 2001 annual report of the Department of Defense adds two further aspects: the management of the impact of acts of terrorism, to minimize the damage caused, and intelligence gathering as an independent counter-measure (US Department of Defense 2001a, 26). The particular emphasis on the need for more effective intelligence is a consequence of the omissions and absence or inefficiency of co-ordination in the period before the 9/11 attacks in 2001, despite several early indications the intelligence agencies failed to suggest counter-measures or take the initiative.

The definitions of anti- and counter-terrorism sound somewhat like an artificial separation and might be an indication of the difficulties in designing relevant military concepts for the prevention or combat of terrorism. Although US forces no longer pursue the simple and catastrophic strategy developed by General William C. Westmoreland to combat your militarily inferior enemy with overwhelming firepower – 'find em and fight em' – (quoted in Wallace 1996, 213), nevertheless, so far they have yet to find a convincing counter-terror doctrine. The Quadrennial Defense Review Report (of 30 September 2001, mainly prepared before 9/11 but with explicit reference to the acts of terror in New York and Washington) does not include a specific military strategy to fight terrorism exactly because this is objectively difficult if not impossible. This report mentions a general conceptual change in which the armed forces will no longer be directed against steadfast threats, but instead they will be 'capability' oriented to forego the asymmetric advantages of enemies (US Department of Defense 2001b).

In the meantime much has been written, somewhat controversially, about the possibilities of military counter-terrorism. The government implemented institutional changes, particularly the establishment of the Ministry for Homeland Security. In general – and much unlike Europe – the armed forces are used to perform tasks that have been traditionally located within the legal services. This change in policy did not begin with the priority placing of terrorism on the political agenda but was already the case, as the application of military power in fighting drugs or in high-crime rate urban centres suggests. Mixing the domestic judicial-executive with external security tasks is problematic however (Slocombe 2003). Governments in a number of countries, particularly in Europe, and civil society organizations complain 'that the "war on terrorism" has in some instances corroded the very values that terrorists target' (UNHLPT 2004, 148) and that fundamental human rights are being violated. The previously mentioned connection between terrorism, weapons of mass destruction and state sponsors of terrorism has become a central pattern of explanation to counter such 'liberal' claims. However, the experiences in Iraq are the most manifest evidence for the doubtful assumption of the alleged connections, as well as for the military difficulties in attempting to solve them. The justification for the war in Iraq in spring 2003 to fight terrorism sounds rather empty given the lack of supporting evidence and given the fact that the Saddam Hussein regime had rather little sympathy for terrorists. The reference to terrorism is more an embarrassing afterthought used when the original claim for a need to destroy weapons of mass destruction also failed to materialize.

It is not only since 9/11 that the US forces have realized that combating terrorism cannot be successful in the short term but that this is a long-term and protracted conflict (US Department of Defense 1997, Chapter 9). Some military operations against terrorists have to be characterized as complete failures, despite overwhelming military power and the availability of modern weapons systems and equipment. One such example is the 1980 failure of operation 'Eagle Claw', which was intended to free US hostages in Iran. The US forces not only never got anywhere near to the hostages but managed to damage with their own helicopters the transport plane that was intended to return the hostages home. Two acts of military retaliation – bombing several targets in Libya in 1986 and the parallel sorties against Sudan and Afghanistan in 1998 – are analyzed here to throw light on the further possibilities and limitations of military power.

Muammar Gaddafi, the President of Libya, was considered anti-Western and anti-American from immediately after his coup to overthrow the King in 1969. He was seen as the main stately supporting force of the Red Brigades in Italy, the Red Army Fraction in Germany, and Hezbollah and Islamic Jihad in the Middle East. President Reagan recognized in him the pivotal source of terrorists' threats. Shots from within the Libyan embassy at demonstrators in London in 1984, the damage to 19 ships from Libyan sea mines in the Red Sea in the same year, and the bomb attack against the Berlin discotheque La Belle on 5 April 1985 were enough reasons for the US government to look for military options against Gaddafi. President Reagan authorized operation 'Eldorado Canyon', a nightly air strike against targets in Libya nine days after the bomb attack in Berlin. Eighteen F-111 fighter-bombers fired on three targets in Tripoli, and over 70 Marine Corps fighter and support aircraft started a simultaneous attack from the aircraft carriers 'America' and 'Coral Sea' against two targets in Benghazi (Kosnik 2000).

Comparing the military targets to the actual damage inflicted by the bombing, these raids cannot be called a success. Only two of the F-111 fighter-bombers were able to drop their bombs or fire missiles, whilst one aircraft was downed and both pilots died. Further, the aircrafts that took off from the aircraft carriers also ran into difficulties. Only 10 per cent of the aircrafts hit their targets, yet even worse than the poor quota of hits against military targets was the collateral damage. US fighter jets dropped bombs on a gas station and a dispensary in Benghazi killing innocent civilians. In Tripoli the US weapons damaged the French embassy and several other buildings. The collateral damage and especially the unintended human cost raised loud international protest against the US policy. Weapons might be 'smarter' today and targeting might be more precise, but nevertheless the missile that hit the Chinese embassy during the Kosovo air war and the collateral damage caused in Afghanistan sound peculiarly ominous and are reminders that even the technically dominant US air force is far from being able to always inflict the intended damage by 'surgical' strikes. The present protracted and costly attacks against foreign and Iraqi forces in Iraq prove that a seemingly quick military success and the occupation of the country can in fact provoke terrorist counter-attacks.

The impact of retaliatory measures against acts of terrorism is disputed. Will terrorists be deterred or encouraged? According to some observers operations such as 'Eldorado Canyon' can have an impact, despite the military inefficiency of the air strike, as the terrorists operations could be disrupted (Jenkins 2003, 217). While the supporters of military retaliation point to the fact that Libya is today no longer a promoter of terrorism, the sceptics conclude that a spiral of violence was initiated or strengthened. They draw the conclusion that the bomb attack against Pan Am flight 103 and the crash of the airliner over Lockerbie in Scotland in 1988 was a direct reaction against the US air strikes in Tripoli and Benghazi (Kosnik 2000, 21). Equally open to debate is the question as to whether the recent agreement with Libya, in which the government renounced the development and possession of weapons of mass destruction, is a reaction of Gaddafi considering the Iraq War or if it is instead the result of the secret talks and political efforts of the United Kingdom and the United States that led to reversing the Libyan government's policy. Both these positions pro and contra military retaliation can point to plausible arguments.

In a second example, the US government believed that Osama bin Laden's network was responsible both for the bombing of a military installation in Saudi Arabia in 1995, an attack which took the lives of seven people, as well as for the bomb attack in 1996 against the Khobar tower in Dharan costing the life of 19 US air force soldiers (Kosnik 2000, 27). Despite many hints and warnings, the attacks against the US embassies in Nairobi, Kenya and Dar es Salaam, Tanzania on 7 August 1998 could not be prevented. Almost 5000 people were wounded and 224 people died. The Clinton Administration held bin Laden's group responsible and concluded that Sudan and Afghanistan were its most important supporters. On 20 August 1998, less than three weeks after the bombings, President Clinton authorized operation 'Infinite Reach'. US war ships fired around 70 Tomahawk cruise missiles at targets that were considered to be terrorist positions in Khartoum, Sudan and Khost,

Afghanistan. The damage caused by these missile strikes in the camps in Afghanistan was substantial. All the people killed and wounded – according to the Taliban government 21 fatalities and 30 wounded casualties – were considered in the United States to be terrorists. In Sudan, the cruise missiles hit a pharmaceutical factory in the centre of Khartoum that was allegedly financed by bin Laden and producing chemical weapons. One of the missiles hit a nearby candy factory. During the investigations that followed it was proved that the US government could not produce any evidence to support the claim of chemical weapons production; the decision had been a mistake, a product of the secrecy and lack of co-ordination about the intelligence gathered (Kosnik 2000, 30). This might remind one of the 'evidence' presented in the UN Security Council by then US Secretary of State, Colin Powell, about the Iraqi weapons of mass destruction programme and the regime's connection to Al Qaeda. The difficulty of collecting precise information about terrorists' plans seems to remain one of the inherent weaknesses of combating terrorism.

In spring 2000, a year and a half before 9/11, experts in the US marines believed that the August 1998 strikes in Sudan and Afghanistan 'do appear to have put bin Laden's terrorist organization on the defensive. Instead of focusing resources and attention on planning or executing new attacks, the group must have had to step back and regroup' (Kosnik 2000, 31). Unfortunately, this was too optimistic an assessment, but the fact that the declared objective of eliminating Osama bin Laden as the head and financier of Al Qaeda has so far failed, should however not be seen as proof of the impossibility of assigning a role at all to the armed forces in counter-terrorism. The fall of the Taliban government in Afghanistan has limited the terrorist group's room for manoeuvre and has taken away some parts of its sanctuary. Direct operations to fight terrorists are difficult and with regard to some of their activities impossible; but the control of the territorial environment of the terrorists can effectively limit their operational base.

The United Kingdom's experience in their former colonies and in Northern Ireland

The experience of British armed forces in combating mutinies, insurgencies, rebellions and uprisings in their former colonies led to a focus on the doctrine of 'small wars' in British military and security thinking and practice. In essence, military strategists and force commanders have drawn the conclusion that controlling uprisings or combating terrorism is *first* of all not a primary or sole military task because the legitimate reasons for such uprising need to be considered in stopping or preventing them. It is extremely important to win the hearts and minds of the people. This concept was successfully applied by the British during the 1950s in their then colony Malaya to counter a communist rebellion. *Second*, counter-measures should firmly rest in civil–police action with the military acting in a supporting role for police and judicial services. The UK government was reminded of this experience after many years of ill conceived and unsuccessful military engagements in Northern Ireland. *Third*, an important conclusion drawn in the United Kingdom is the need for reserved and restricted deployment if forces are tasked at all. Large military contingents and massive accumulations of weaponry are considered to be counterproductive. *Fourth*, collective retaliation measures or punishment have mostly the opposite of their intended outcome and result in a boomerang effect. Military deployments might help the terrorists in recruiting, young people especially. *Fifth*, it is important to have an option for an exit strategy if the military is deployed. Today's assessment of these experiences is usually not given without reference to the model of the great military strategist Liddel Hart (1954) who developed military strategies with regard to small wars (Mockaitis 1993, 12).

The analysis of the deployment of British military forces against terrorism in Northern Ireland demonstrates that the various governments in London did not always take these assessments into account. To stop the revolt of the Catholic working class and to keep peace in the province the government deployed armed forces for the first time in 1969. In parallel a reform plan was proposed, which was too late in the eyes of the Catholic part of the population and too early according to the Protestants. The army was largely pro-Protestant and tried to eliminate the Irish Republican Army (IRA). They burned houses of alleged IRA sympathizers and detained them. This facilitated opposition and the protest against the army mounted and gave support to the Provisional IRA, the militant wing of the protest.

While the military had been fairly defensive in the first phase, they dominated all security matters in the next. In Northern Ireland, a part of the United Kingdom, the government tried to quell the protest through military methods that had been successfully applied in the former colonies. The army operated in an unstable political environment, without however being allowed to use – as in the former colonies – all the so-called emergency measures, including curfew, collective punishment, forced resettlement, torture, death penalties and so on. The conflict escalated and the army lost the last bit of its already marginal support in Northern Ireland.

The third phase in Northern Ireland clearly shows the possibilities and limits of military operations in such situations. During this phase the role of the armed forces was considerably scaled back. From about 1975 the British government emphasized police operations again; public order and security were placed under the authority of the Royal Ulster Constabulary, though this was still largely recruited from the Protestant community. The government withdrew the overall responsibility for combating terrorism from the armed forces. The intention was to contain the violence or at least bring it down to an acceptable level.

In secret talks between the British government and the IRA since the end of the 1980s both sides admitted that the development of the conflict was in military terms a zero-sum-game. This appraisal in fact opened the door for a political avenue to resolve the conflict. The peace process of the 1990s eventually led to the political recognition of the former terrorists and their co-operation in the Good Friday Peace Agreement. This happened in parallel to constitutional agreements – with active assistance from abroad – and regulations for the demilitarization of the paramilitary organizations and a reform of the state security forces, including the police. Even if the process of normalization has not been fully completed at the beginning of 2005, the experience of the process demonstrates the central function of political rather than military solutions (Hauswedell and Brown 2002).

The limits of military power

There can be no doubt that the 9/11 acts of terror have expanded the spectrum of military missions in many countries. Many armed forces are now tasked with counter-terrorism and in several cases there is an apparent priority for military operations. Most military strategists are aware – possibly more so than the politicians whose promises of serious action are perhaps made more for public consumption – that the armed forces can hardly contribute to removing the root causes of terrorism and that the military should not be the pivotal agency of the anti-terrorist policy. Evidently there is a discrepancy between political rhetoric, pressures from within societies and actions requested by the public on the one hand, and the rationality and possibilities of the military on the other.

Typical military tasks are logistical support, protection of installations, surveillance of shipping routes, surgical air strikes and occasionally possible deployment of ground troops for the purpose of intelligence gathering or protection and evacuation of people. These are short-term operations that might be necessary to prevent acts of terror or avoid or ameliorate their impact. The long-term objective to eliminate the root causes of terrorism cannot be achieved this way.

The UN High-level Panel of Experts suggests a comprehensive concept and a broad-based approach, especially in the states from which terrorists originate. Such a strategy requires more than coercive measures and should include (1) 'dissuasion, working to reverse the causes or facilitators of terrorism' including the promotion of social and political rights and the rule of law, reduction of poverty and unemployment, and so on; (2) 'efforts to counter extremism and intolerance, including through education'; (3) better global co-operation to counter terrorism, including areas of law enforcement and intelligence-sharing; (4) 'building State capacity to prevent terrorist recruitment and operations'; and (5) 'control of dangerous materials and public health defence' (UNHLPT 2004, 48–49).

The likelihood of direct and open combat with terrorist groups or their networks through military means is possible only in rare cases. This is because, *first*, the international terrorism of today relies to a lesser degree than in the past on its own fixed infrastructure. An attacked country might – still under the shock of attack – want to react immediately. But the military will find it difficult to locate militarily relevant targets. Military operations of this type uncover very few lucrative targets and these operations cannot most likely be sustained beyond a first strike (Jenkins 2003, 217). International terrorism operates in a de-territorialized environment and requires only few training centres and sanctuaries (Münkler 2002). *Second*, the military cannot make use of its own advantages, namely prevailing military power and weapons dominance, because of the asymmetric combat. This disadvantage is difficult to compensate for, or indeed to turn around to become a possible asymmetric advantage for the military. The guerrilla type of combat during the Vietnam War is evidence of this assumption; here, the massive deployment of troops still found it generally difficult to operate against small and autonomous cells. In this respect, the experiences of US troops in Iraq are similar to those in Vietnam. Terrorists too operate in small units; they are militarily weaker than the armed forces and cannot defeat them, but neither can the armed forces completely eliminate the terrorists.

In essence, this means that to successfully fight terrorism what is required first and foremost is not a military but a political strategy in which the armed forces need to play a supportive role. The military can be tasked to restrict the operational territory of the terrorist, they can protect installations against attacks or they can apply deterrence or retaliation to prevent governments from supporting terrorists.

At the same time the international deployment of armed forces in counter-terrorism raises a number of unanswered questions, for example with regard to the international norms of such deployments. Are they based on article 51 of the UN Charter stipulating the right of self-defence, or are they completely different and rather are there not very credible reasons at play – such as the domestic difficulties of the Clinton Administration at the time of the strikes against Sudan and Afghanistan (Kosnik 2000, 21)? Similarly doubtful reasons can be mentioned with regard to Iraq and the 2004 election campaign in the United States.

What is the long-term impact of blurring the otherwise clear separation between the domestic use of police and the external deployment of the military, a separation and division of labour that has long been cautiously guarded for well-founded reasons in democracies (Andreas and Price 2001, 48–52, Slocombe 2003). Will the military reactions against terrorism lead to the militarization of whole societies? Will the purely military retaliatory operations strengthen the terrorists' network and thus achieve the opposite of what was intended? The answers to these questions vary greatly. But that the military should only have a limited and supportive role in a comprehensive political strategy is supported by the past and current experiences.

8
Rent-a-Soldier: Privatization in the US and UK Armed Forces

Privatizing military services fits neatly into the general market-oriented privatization concept favoured by conservatives in the United States, particularly the resultant fact of making the armed forces fit for combat without expanding their size. In the United Kingdom, the main driving force for privatization is budget constraints.

Privatization and outsourcing are, in recent decades, *the* favoured strategies for the transformation of the relationship between the public and the private sector. This is the case almost universally. The governments of Ronald Reagan in the United States and Margaret Thatcher in the United Kingdom pushed through these concepts systematically, including the defence sector – first the defence industry and then military research and development institutions. It is therefore no surprise that the two leading countries in these previous privatization efforts are now advancing other military services systematically for privatization too.

After a boom of company mergers, takeovers and joint ventures in the defence sector, resulting from cuts in the procurement budgets of many defence ministries after the end of the Cold War, the remaining defence producers no longer based their business plan on a broad-based and diversified product range but on specialization in defence products. Wall Street had encouraged companies to concentrate on what the stock market called 'pure play' and 'core competencies' (Markusen and Costigan 1999). This trend of the 1990s is now complemented by a business model in which companies aim at opening new markets in a whole range of public services including traditional military functions.

This kind of company policy of taking over functions from the public sector is not new. Kaldor had already published in 1981 the thesis that

169

companies try hard during recurring industrial depressions to expand their business interests at the expense of the public sector. She describes the survival concept of the British shipyard Vickers during the seventies of the nineteen hundreds century, a company that was burdened by large over-capacities, to put pressure on the government in order to close down public sector shipyards and instead contract private yards for fighting ship production (Kaldor 1981). This hypothesis of reductions in the military sector and parallel outsourcing to private companies could well explain several privatization periods in the history of the defence sector: during the 1950s in the United States and Europe, during the 1970s in the United States and the United Kingdom, and during the 1990s globally. The private sector increased its pressure on governments to reduce their state functions and to provide new business areas for companies at common moments of lulls in production and financing – after reductions in the military budget after the Second World War, after the Vietnam War and after the end of the Cold War. Usually this trend is fed by a combination of commercial interests with strong lobbyist activities based on a political–ideological concept.

A diversified supply of military services

Manifold service areas

Although no comprehensive database or even a complete overview of the companies in this business sector is available, the compilation of companies (in the appendix) with 118 firms can illustrate and give an impression of the companies' fields of activity. The information about these companies stems from newspaper reports, annual company reports and their own websites. Half of the companies are based in the United States and are for the majority of their business contracted by the US forces. The next largest group of companies operates in the United Kingdom (30 of 118), whilst the remaining firms can be identified as spread amongst several other countries, either individually or at most a handful based in one place. This area is a fairly new sector and many entrepreneurs are hoping to make a profit; amongst the many new companies there are also many unreliable or even dubious actors. Some of the companies had a short lifespan and went out of business quickly. It is most likely that some of those listed in Table 8.1 are no longer registered as companies. This list can therefore only give a general overview.

Table 8.1 Origin of private military companies

Number of companies	Country of origin
58	United States
30	United Kingdom
21	other countries
9	not known
118	Total

Source: Appendix.

Privatization in the military sector takes place, often quite comprehensively, in a number of countries. Companies profit from the many outsourced military service areas. How manifold these activities are is demonstrated by the following examples:

When, for example, American tanks rattle through the Joint Readiness Training Center of the US Army in Fort Polk, Louisiana, and suddenly civilians appear in the midst of the simulated battlefield then this is not an unplanned or unwanted disturbance of the training exercises. On the contrary, the army had contracted Cubic, a private company, to simulate as realistically as possible the advance of the US troops into Baghdad. While Military Professional Resources Incorporated (MPRI) trained the American GIs in house-to-house combat in Camp Doha in Kuwait, Cubic flew in Bosnian refugees into Fort Polk from all over the United States to simulate their war experiences as realistically as possible. Cubic hired over 600 people for an exercise of 6500 soldiers (Schwartz 2003).

Kellogg, Brown & Root (KBR), a subsidiary of Halliburton, for which US Vice President Dick Cheney had served as CEO, provided food, water, clean laundry, mail and heavy equipment for some 20000 US troops in the Balkans. KBR delivered some 42 million meals and cleaned 3.6 million bags of laundry. The Pentagon contracts amounted to US$3 billion. The company is one of the main contractors of the armed forces in Iraq and is tasked amongst others in rebuilding the infrastructure. In the Enduring Freedom mission KBR builds new military installations and bases in Afghanistan and trains the forces in Georgia (www.halliburton. com/services/sl0900.jsp).

The list of the managers of MPRI, founded in 1987, reads like a Who's Who of retired US armed forces officers. Director of the company is ex-General Carl Vuono, the commander of the US Army during Desert Storm in the 1991 Gulf War. A dozen retired generals and admirals are on MPRI's pay role, plus former high-ranking CIA officials and former ambassadors. The company claims (according to the *New York Times* 13 October 2002) that it 'can muster more generals than the Pentagon'. In contrast to a few other companies MPRI does not participate directly in combat. According to its information 'MPRI has conducted successful programs in every region of the world' (www.mpri.com, accessed 18 January 2005). For example, MPRI employees are working on behalf of the US government in the police and military forces of Colombia to combat drugs. They were also engaged in a 'military stabilization program' in the Balkans and maintain a combat simulation centre and a combat training camp. The company was publicly criticized for the training of the Croatian army at the time of ethnic cleansing in the Krajina region. Whether or not MPRI was directly involved cannot be proven. The training was carried out with the agreement of the US government when the UN had agreed on a mandatory embargo against the former Yugoslavia.

The examples are extensive. The British company Defence Systems Ltd (DSL), founded in 1981 by the former General Sir David Ramsbotham, had worked during the time of Milton Obote in Uganda and Mobuto Sese Seko in Zaire. The company used former Special Forces to protect these regimes, as well as the oil exploration of large multinational companies in Angola and United Nation's personnel in peacekeeping operations in the Balkans. Pacific Architects and Engineers (PAE) and International Charter Incorporated (ICI) carried out logistical tasks, paid by the US government, for the Economic Community of West-African States (ECOWAS) troops in Liberia (O'Hanlon and Singer 2004, 87). The air transport and surveillance company AirScan, based in Florida, has been involved in several scandals. The company has allegedly illegally supplied weapons into South Sudan to support the Sudanese People's Liberation Army (O'Brian 1998, 95). In Colombia, AirScan was hired by oil companies to protect pipelines against attacks from rebels. Within this contract AirScan experts coordinated an air attack of the Colombian air force against a rebel base; a village was bombed and 18 unarmed civilians were killed (Singer 2003, 221).

The policy of outsourcing, as stated, is most systematically pursued in the United States and the United Kingdom and governments in other countries have shown an interest too. In Germany, for example, privatization is primarily focused on service companies in such inconspicuous areas as the management of car fleets, military barracks, uniforms, the running of canteens and so on. Repairs and maintenance of weapons are outsourced to private companies, and the sale of surplus military installations is managed and sold by a government-owned company, Gesellschaft für Entwicklung, Beschaffung und Betrieb (GEBB). The main purpose of this privatization policy is to make additional funding sources available for the military budget. But a few companies want to move into the military service market too. The company Optronic, based in Königsbronn in Southern Germany, whose CEO received a four-year prison term for the illegal trade of weapons (Frankfurter Rundschau 27 May 2004), offered on its internet site job opportunities for 'civilians on the battlefield'. The applicants were asked to serve in US army training exercises in Germany and would be paid €80 per day, plus travel costs, accommodation and food. The short-term employees were to live within the military barracks and were not allowed to leave the compound during the exercise (www.optronic-online.de).

The jobs in the civil war in Sierra Leone, where principally British companies were contracted, were less playful. Even before the 2003 Iraq War private military and security companies already worked in combat zones, and this was the case during the 1990s in Sierra Leone – where company personnel were also killed. The Green Paper of the British government 'Private Military Companies: Options for Regulation' lists a number of companies and their involvement in Sierra Leone throughout the 1990s (see Table 8.2). While the participation of the company Sandline

Table 8.2 Sierra Leone: a profitable market for military and security companies

Dates	Companies	Recruited by	Objective	Outcome
1991	Specialist Services International	government*	port security	
1992	Marine Protection Services	government*	policing of fisheries; tax collection	
1994	Special Protection Services	mining companies	mining facilities security	failed
1994	Frontline Security Services	Sierra Rutile and SIEROMCO	mining facilities security	failed
1995	Executive Outcomes, South Africa	government*	to counter rebel movement	rebels were driven back
1995–96	Ibis Air International		air logistic support; combat air support	
1995	J&S Franklin (Gurkha Security Guards Ltd)	government*	military training; mining facilities security	terminated a few weeks later

Continued

Table 8.2 Continued

Dates	Companies	Recruited by	Objective	Outcome
1995	Control Risks Group; Group 4		mining facilities security	terminated
1995	Defence Systems Ltd		mining facilities security	terminated
1996	Executive, Outcomes South Africa		military training and support; rebel HQ 'seized'	
1996	Sandline International Executive Outcomes, GB	government*	military training	
1996	LifeGuard Management (Executive Outcomes)		mining facilities security	
1996–97	Teleservices International		mining facilities security	
1997	LifeGuard Management		mining facilities security, military training, intelligence gathering	
1997–98	Sandline International		logistics, intelligence and air support to ECOMOG troops, military training	
1997–98	Cape International Corporation	Kamajor fighters	mining facilities security, military training	
1997–98	ICI (Pacific Architects and Engineers)		Logistics and air support security; personnel protection	
1998	Executive Outcomes		management services to LifeGuard and Sandline	
1998	LifeGuard Management		mining facilities security, military training and support; intelligence gathering; counter-insurgency	
1998	Defence Systems Limited	UNDP	security for UN humanitarian relief convoys	

Note: * Government of Sierra Leone.

Source: Extract from UK Government (2002, Annex A, 28–38).

International in combat led to a public debate and a parliamentary enquiry in the United Kingdom, the London-based company DSL provided logistical support for UN peacekeepers in the same conflict.

The paychecks for the employees of private military companies fluctuate widely. As a rule they are higher than the pay in the armed forces. During the war in the Balkans MPRI hired personnel locally, paying US$5000 cash upon signing the contract and a monthly pay of US$1500 tax-free (Hutsch 2003). Military companies also pay much more for specialists than the US armed forces – up to US$100,000 per year and according to some sources US$1500 per day (*Washington Post*, 13 May 2004). This is so attractive to military personnel that some have asked for a leave of absence and signed contracts with companies, to join the armed forces again later. As a result the Pentagon is reconsidering the pay-scale of the US military. The highest-paid company employees are former members of special units such as the US Navy Seals, Delta Forces and Rangers, the British Special Air Service, Airborne Commandos and Special Boat Service, Russian soldiers of the Alpha Team and former KGB members as well as from the Spetsnaz of the former Red Army (Schreier and Caparini 2005, 20). Although there are many interested in being recruited by companies, due to the explosion in the volume of contracts companies are finding it difficult to locate enough qualified candidates.

Profile of private military companies in the various service areas

The different types of company activities can be illustrated more thoroughly by the profiles of military companies. I use for this illustration the typology of military companies developed in Chapter 2, Table 2.1:

Consulting and planning: SOC-SMG, USA   The company from Nevada calls itself the 'Ferrari' and the only 'five-star-company' in the security sector; SOC-SMG works in Iraq, Oman and Indonesia. The company was founded by former Special Forces and Rangers and consults on strategic questions, intelligence gathering and protection for international armed forces. Amongst its customers are large companies, the CIA and FBI, the US Department of Defense, the Drug Control and Enforcement Agency as well as the weapons labs in Sandia and Los Alamos in the US (http://www.soc-smg.com/ company.html).

Logistics and support: CACI, USA   The Arlington, Virginia, headquartered company works under the motto 'ever vigilant'. The company's turnover passed the US$1 billion threshold for the first time in their

2003/2004-business year, mainly from engineering work. Originally, CACI was specialized in information technology but now offers the 'full spectrum of engineering services from concept definition through life cycle support across the defense establishment'. The company offers logistics and supply chain management functions, it reverse-engineers older systems and designs software, tests and evaluates optimal performance, provides C4ISR operations analysis, research and development and supports field services, including intelligence and electronic warfare. The main customers are the US Marines, the Air Force and the intelligence services. With about 9400 employees CACI is one of the largest companies of the sector (http://www.caci. com/business/engr.shtml). CACI has developed more and more into a prime contractor of the US Department of Defense and signed a so-called blanked-purchase agreement to work for the Pentagon. The large, only vaguely worded contract is designed so that the agencies can react flexibly if so required. This contract has a limit of US$500 million and as an after-thought a contract for the interrogation in Iraqi prisons, worth US$19.9 million was added. CACI employed intelligence specialists who used dubious methods to interrogate the prisoners in Abu Ghraib (*Washington Post*, 17 May 2004).

Technical services and repairs: DynCorp, USA   The company was founded in 1946 by former military pilots and offered support for the US Air Force during the Korean War. Today, the company is specialized in logistical services, maintenance and surveillance technology and offers its services worldwide including in relief operations. Until the end of 2002, when DynCorp was purchased by the computer and defence company Computer Science Company (CSC), DynCorp was owned by its approximately 26,000 employees who worked in 550 different locations. During the mid-1990s the company diversified and has since then offered information technology services too. DynCorp complements the programme of CSC in as far as the latter's business with US federal agencies is concerned, especially that with the Pentagon. CSC employs 90,000 people who are, amongst others, responsible for the logistical systems of the US Army. A team of technical experts helped the crippled destroyer USS Cole to return to sea again after a terrorist attack in October 2000 in Yemen. In addition, they have helped to establish mobile military hospitals for the US forces during the wars in Afghanistan and Iraq. CSC ranks 22 in the list of the top 50 US military contractors (www.csc.com, accessed 23 October 2004). DynCorp is part of the anti-drug programme of the US government in Colombia and operates helicopters to fight guerrillas. In 2000 one of the helicopters was downed (Reuters 23 January 2002). In

April 2003 DynCorp was awarded a US$50 million contract to support law enforcement functions in Iraq and the US Department of State has tasked the company to provide 1000 civilian advisors to support the Iraqi government's law enforcement, judicial and correctional agencies (www.csc.com).

Training: Blackwater, USA   The company motto is 'in support of freedom and democracy everywhere'. This group of companies consists of Blackwater Training Center, Blackwater Target Systems, Blackwater Security Consulting, Blackwater Canine (K9) and Blackwater Air (AWS), which are specialized in several areas, particularly training in firearms and personnel protection. Most of the top management are former US Navy Seals. Blackwater works globally for law enforcement agencies, the US Department of Defense, the US Department of State, the Department of Transportation, multinational companies and, according to the company internet site, 'for friendly nations from all over the globe' (www.blackwaterusa.com, accessed 23 October 2004). Presently, the main business lies in the Middle East where the programme is managed by two recently established subsidiaries in Kuwait City and Baghdad. In the United States, Blackwater established a training centre specialized in firearms training. More than 50,000 persons have been trained in the over 6000 acres area in Moyock, North Carolina.

Blackwater Security Consulting employees were killed in Fallujah, Iraq, and their bodies hanged from a bridge on 31 March 2004 – an event that served to greatly publicize the use of private security firms in Iraq. The company is specialized in personnel protection and was, amongst others, responsible for the security of Paul Bremer, the former head of the US civil authority in Iraq. Due to a growing contractual volume Blackwater Security Consulting hires personnel for high-risk tasks from many parts of the world, especially from military commando units – this has included amongst them soldiers of the disgraced former Pinochet armed forces of Chile (The *Guardian* 2 April 2004). Such new employees' job descriptions may include: rescue of hostages, house-to-house fighting, intelligence gathering, sharp-shooting operations, search and rescue operations, combating drugs, sabotage operations, medical services and language services.

Peacekeeping and Humanitarian Assistance: Pacific Architects and Engineers (PAE), US   PAE, established in 1955, has worked especially in engineering and maintenance and employs 6000 people worldwide. Located in Los Angeles with offices in Singapore and New Zealand, the company functions, besides its original speciality in the design of bridges and oil platforms, as a provider of facilities management to the armed forces of Canada, New Zealand and the United States and has also worked for UN blue-helmets in Sierra Leone and East Timor. In 2001, PAE was awarded a contract by the UN in East Timor to operate and maintain the airports and aviation related facilities in support of the UN peacekeeping efforts (http://www. paechl.com.html).

Combat forces: Sandline International, UK   The company was founded in the beginning of the 1990s in London by Colonel Tim Spicer. The company's philosophy was 'to fill a vacuum in the post cold war era'. On two occasions company personnel participated directly in combat. In January 1997 Sandline signed a contract with the government of Papua New Guinea to fight against insurgent rebels. Sandline agreed to deploy Special Forces and to supply weapons. From 1997 until 1998 the company also deployed its personnel in Sierra Leone to support the Nigerian ECOMOC peacekeeping troops with logistics, intelligence gathering, air transport and surveillance. In addition, Sandline trained the Kamajor fighters of the toppled government (UK Government 2002, 35).

Public criticism and a parliamentary debate on 6 March 1999 found the Blair government in difficulty because of the Sandline activities in Sierre Leone (International Alert 1999). Sandline International had exported weapons into the war region despite an existing UN arms embargo, which was interpreted both in public and in parliament as to the government therefore being aware of this deal.[34] During the parliamentary debate Jack Straw, the Foreign Secretary, stressed the need for stricter controls of British 'mercenary activities' to prevent a repetition of the weapon supplies to Africa (*Financial Times* 11 February 2002). The Green Paper of the British government on private military companies, which was written due to the very reason of Sandline's Sierra Leone involvement, was presented in February 2002. It analyzes in great detail the legal and technical possibilities to regulate such companies (UK Government 2002). Sandline International has always tried to protect itself from being perceived as a mercenary group and emphasized its important 'peace' and 'life supporting' function (Spicer 1998).[35] On 16 April 2004 Sandline announced the closure of the company and argued that this was the result of 'the general lack of governmental support for Private Military Companies willing to help end armed conflicts in Africa' (www.sandline.com/comment/list/comment48.html, accessed 3 May 2004). Whether the activities of the company employees and the management in this area have really ended is doubtful. They probably lead a less visible, though similar existence. The CEO Tim Spicer and his small London-based company Aegis has been awarded a large three-year contract by the US Army and the government of Iraq as the company responsible for the security of the reconstruction programme (Schreier and Caparini 2005, 23) – a matter I return to later. A similar pattern emerged several years ago when Executive Outcomes closed down its offices in South Africa only to re-establish itself in the United Kingdom and the United States.

US: privatization at any price

The intense move for privatization of the defence sector began long before the Reagan administration's drive during the 1980s. Dwight D. Eisenhower presented not only the famous dictum during his farewell address of 1961 in which he warned against the military-industrial complex, but already knowing the intricate relations between the military, industry and bureaucracy his government had initiated during the 1950s a public–private competition, which was eventually codified into the so-called A-76 budget regulation (that is still in existence), in which both government agencies and private-sector firms are invited to bid for contracts. The present A-76, which was revised by Reagan's budget director David Stockman in 1983 and once more in 1996, pushed the emphasis away from the public–private competition towards a priority for private-sector preference. Stockman wrote that the government should 'rely on commercial sources to supply the products and services the government needs' (quoted in Baum 2003).

Today, privatization of the public sector in the United States is far advanced, with the military sector further privatized than many other public sectors. The most substantial move for privatization took place, in contrast to Kaldor's thesis about privatization during periods of depression, during a time of rapid growth of the public budget. In a time when the budget and the budget deficit climbed to hitherto unknown levels, the Reagan administration cut the services of the public sector and outsourced them to the private sector. All successor governments have pursued basically the same policy, although somewhat softened, and Vice President Gore pushed the privatization of government functions during the Clinton era under the slogan of 'reinventing government'.

At first, the main focus of privatization was on the supply of weapons and equipment for the armed forces. This was followed by military relevant research and development, which was transferred from the typical state-run weapon labs to private companies and university institutes. The borderline between the privatizing of weapons development and production on the one hand and the outsourcing of classical military services such as training of the forces or logistics on the other is not very distinct; these areas overlap, and it is not only newly formed private military companies that engage in this sector but also defence producers. The privatizing of military services is but the most recent pattern to develop. The reason for the outsourcing of logistics, training, combat support or maintenance and repair of weapons and equipment is only in part due to the difficulty of the armed forces in recruiting enough qualified personnel. Economic interests, industrial lobbyists and the political–ideological concept of the lean state are part of the equation too.

Secretary of Defense Donald Rumsfeld strengthened and expanded the initiatives of the Clinton administration and said: 'Only those functions that must be performed by the DoD [Department of Defense] should be kept in the DoD ... Any function that can be provided by the private sector is not a core government function' (quoted in Mother Jones 23 May 2002). He felt that there are 'something in the neighborhood of 300,000 men and women in uniform doing jobs that aren't for men and women in uniform' (quoted in *Business Week* 15 September 2003, 44). The Bush administration decided with the declaration of a general strategy of privatization in 2001, entitled The President's Management Agenda, to identify core and non-core functions of the Department of Defense to be able to outsource as many functions as possible to the private sector (USGAO 2003a and 2003b).

The Pentagon had already tasked a company, at that time still under the name of Brown & Root in 1992 when Dick Cheney was Secretary of Defense, to produce a classified report into how the logistics of the armed forces could be best supported in the conflict regions of the world. Shortly afterwards the company signed a five-year contract for the so-called Logcap-Program. Cheney took over in 1995 as CEO of Halliburton, the holding company of the then entitled Kellogg, Brown & Root (Baum 2003).

Industry reacted enthusiastically with lots of confidence and pride. David J. Lesar, a later Halliburton CEO, boasted in 2003, when the company was publicly criticized for insufficient services to the armed forces, 'we are very, very proud of what we do to support the military and, I think, save the U.S. taxpayer some money'. Robert Harl, his deputy, assisted by claiming: 'Our company has no higher priority than to support our military on the ground' (quoted in *Business Week* 15 September 2003, 45).

The US Department of Defense believes that the private sector is not only of benefit for the US armed forces. Deputy Assistant Secretary of Defense for African Affairs, James Woods 'believe[s] that privatized security efforts can help to relieve anarchy and chaos, keep local security disruptions from spreading, and provide sound defense against outside threat' (quoted in Mandel 2001, 135).

There can be no doubt that the trend to privatizing logistics, training and combat support has been strengthened due to the manifold deployments of the US forces in international conflicts. During the wars in the Balkans the government had the alternatives of increasing the troop strength, calling in the reserves and the National Guard or contracting private companies. Rumsfeld decided to contract companies and continued to reduce the number of uniformed and civilian personnel in the armed forces even at a time of an increasing defence budget (USGAO 2003b). A few years later, when the present conflict in Iraq escalated, the government felt that it did not have such alternatives any longer, and did both – that is, it called in the reserves and National Guard in great numbers and contracted private military companies.

The massively practiced outsourcing of numerous military tasks is highly controversial within the armed forces. The armed forces' top-level promotes this policy and signals limitless consent to the privatization policy. The US Army's journal *Parameters* is quite impressed by the services of the private military companies and writes, in the jargon of consulting companies, about the possibility of the armed forces to concentrate on 'core competencies', namely 'combat', when they are assisted by private companies. Peace operations, humanitarian missions, paramilitary operations, information warfare and asymmetric wars are mentioned as typical areas where private military companies could relieve the armed forces from an over-extended deployment (Smith 2002/03, 114–116). Army General Barry McCaffrey spoke in 2000 about the generally positive trend of privatization and said: 'I am unabashedly an admirer of outsourcing ... There's very few things in life you can't outsource' (quoted in Baum 2003). Shortly afterwards the General was hired into the management of one of the largest defence contractors, Raytheon Aerospace and Integrated Defense Technologies. Further, Thomas K. Adams (1999, 115), who actually criticizes the 'new mercenaries' in *Parameters*, emphasizes that 'even the US Army has concluded that in the future it will require contract personnel, even in the close fight area, to keep its most modern systems functioning'. A detailed 1997 report of the US General Accounting Office concludes regarding the improvement of logistics in the Logistics Civil Augmentation Program in the Bosnia deployment that, according to the army, the use of contract firms is a 'last resort but necessary in these missions because of troop ceilings, unavailability of host nation support, and the need to keep military units available to respond to a major regional conflict' (USGAO 1997a, 4).

But the privatization policy is also criticized. A paper of the US-Army War College questions the companies' reliability: 'Contractor loyalty to the almighty dollar, as opposed to support for the front-line soldier, remains [a] serious question' (quoted in *Business Week* 15 September 2003, 46). Colonel Bruce Grant of the army (1998, 106) fears that the armed forces could be seriously damaged: 'When former officers sell their skills on the international market for profit, the entire profession loses its moral high ground with the American people. The new paradigm of privatized international military assistance has far-reaching implications in the American democratic culture. It can profoundly change how we as a society interact with our military'.

United Kingdom: *Public–Private Partnership* Initiatives

The big push for privatization in the United Kingdom started with Prime Minister Margaret Thatcher taking office in 1979. Despite strong opposition the government implemented its so-called denationalization policy, the systematic privatization of the large public enterprises. The international reactions from the dominant economic theorists were quite enthusiastic and the concept was praised as a success story and a model for other countries. Despite the original claim made by the Labour Party and the unions to revise this policy once in office, this has not been the case since Tony Blair became prime minister in 1997. The Thatcher privatization drive affected a number of state-owned defence companies and the establishment of the world's third largest defence producer of today, BAE Systems, is a result of this policy and the subsequent series of joint ventures and take-overs.

As regards the present privatization of military services, the government distinguishes between the delegation of military missions within the policy concept of Public–Private Partnership Initiatives and the activities of private military companies that engage in wars and conflicts. Although the latter are not put on an equal footing with mercenaries they are discussed in this context. Foreign Minister Jack Straw writes in the preface of the government Green Paper of February 2002 about 'reputable and disreputable private sector operators', the former of which should be encouraged and supported by a licensing system or a regulatory mechanism while the latter should be eliminated (UK Government 2002, 5). According to the government, private military companies are not ipso facto bad while not all national armies are good. Private military companies can possibly be better controlled than uncontrolled operating rebel groups. But the government does not offer a clear and acceptable definition of the 'bad' and the 'good' guys. It finds the distinction between combat and non-combat operations often artificial. For example, the 'people who fly soldiers and equipment to the battlefield are as much a part of the military operation as those who do the shooting' (UK Government 2002, 8–9). The British government makes it quite clear that there 'is nothing wrong with governments employing private sector agents abroad in support of their interest; but where such links are transparent they are less likely to give rise to misinterpretation' (UK Government 2002, 18).

The regulation of contracting private military companies has, according to the Green Paper, a number of advantages since these companies' activities can have an immediate effect on British foreign policy, on the potential confrontation between British forces and British firms and because the life of UK citizens could be at stake. The government assesses the pros and cons of a regulatory control and refuses in no uncertain terms the prohibition of private military companies since it would not be possible to define what exactly is prohibited and which services would be allowed to be performed. In addition, the implementation of a possible prohibition would be extremely difficult to put into practice and such a policy might have negative effects on British defence exports (UK Government 2002, 20–26). The Green Paper enumerates and assesses several options for the control of private military companies – from a prohibition to licensing, from registration to self-regulation of companies. Yet at present, there is no existing legal control of private military companies, as I detail in Chapter 9. Private military companies were pleased when the government formulated its vague and cautious policy vis-à-vis military companies and were happy to signal their interest in a company-formulated code of conduct (Sandline International 1998). The government emphasizes that 'this Green Paper does not attempt to propose a policy' and the Foreign Minister concludes 'that a wide debate on the options is needed' (UK Government 2002, 5).

This Green Paper served its purpose of reacting to the public criticism of the UK government's own foreign policy and involvement in the case of the delivery of weapons into Sierra Leone by Sandline International despite the mandatory UN arms embargo. Today, since Sandline has ceased its operation, ostensibly because of a lack of government interest, the debate about private military companies in the United Kingdom is over. There has been no 'wide debate' as envisioned. This has probably also happened because there is much less interest in the role of British as opposed to US companies in Iraq.

The present active government privatizing initiative stands in stark contrast to the lack of interest in private military companies. In 1998 the UK government initiated with its Strategic Defence Review a so-called Public Private Partnership (PPP) Initiative, with a Private Finance Initiative (PFI) as the key instrument to use public resources in the defence sector more effectively. The Ministry of Defence has ambitious goals and mentions 'transforming defence support functions into quasi commercial organisations' (Davis 2000, 2). On the agenda are procurement and maintenance of modern weapons systems, which are planned to be privately financed – from tank transportation to air refuelling for the Royal Air Force, from construction of housing facilities for officers' families to the management of military bases. A whole range of services are to be privatized – including the comprehensive privatization of military-run laboratories and workshops and so on.

Privatization in the United Kingdom is a by-product of constraints of the government budget, a result of market pressures and a general belief in the effectiveness of the private sector. PFI is the key but not the only instrument for co-operation with the private sector. With the PFI the Ministry of Defence wants to make use of the management expertise, the innovative capabilities and the capital investment of the private sector. Ideally, large weapons systems, equipment and fixed assets should, if possible, no longer be purchased by the Ministry of Defence. Instead, the armed forces should purchase the services from companies but not buy the assets themselves. The Ministry will continue to be in charge of the delivery of the services, but the companies will invest in and manage the assets (UK Government 2004c) and thereby the Ministry hopes to get more value for money. It is hoped that the extremely high initial investment costs will be turned over to the private sector and the Defence Ministry will only pay for the leasing of the weapons or the equipment (similar to the leasing of a car) or simply pay for the services provided by the companies. Amongst the most ambitious projects is the future air refuelling for the Royal Air Force and the procurement of fighting ships for the Royal Navy.

The PFI is only part of the initiative; other aspects include 'Partnering Agreements' for long-term programme contracts with companies, 'Outsourcing' to purchase certain services from the private sector, 'Prime Contracting' for large procurement contracts if PFI-Projects cannot be implemented, and 'Wider Markets' to market surplus capacities of the armed forces for non-military purposes for the financial benefit of the Defence Ministry (UK Government 2004a, Downing 2004).

Military hardware such as weapons and non-military assets such as buildings should only be procured if the armed forces depend on them for strategic or other reasons. Services should be purchased from the private sector. PFI is located between these two components with an emphasis on strong management and investment of industry. If the demand of the armed forces is still relatively uncertain Partnering Agreements with the private sector are intended to bridge the time until the demand and the supply are exactly defined. The public–private co-operation should be further deepened by other programmes such as the concept of Sponsored Reserves, in which the partners of the Ministry of Defence not only agree to supply services but also employ reservists to provide such services (UK Government 2004b).

Since the initiative commenced in 1998 until the financial year 2003/04, 57 agreements with a total volume of almost five billion pounds have been signed and an additional 50 projects with a volume of almost two billion pounds have been authorized for bidding (UK Government 2004d and 2004e). Given the annual average total procure-ment budget of the Ministry of Defence of nine billion Pounds during the last half decade, the volume of the PPP projects is not overwhelming; but these contracts represent a growing share of the budget. It seems like the British government is set on tapping new financial sources for the military sector.

Economic rationality of privatization – uncertain data for decision-making

A central argument for privatization and outsourcing is the positive economic effects for the public budget. What, then, are the concrete economic effects of the policy of privatization in the military sector? Despite a whole range of detailed studies about the savings potential of privatization and public–private competition, it is not possible to give a definitive answer as to how much has or can really be saved. Numerous reports of the US General Accounting Office (USGAO) point out the potential for savings, but precise analysis and reports about the results of implemented programmes are still lacking.

A 1997 USGAO study assessed the result of the work of contract firms who provided logistical support for six peace missions (Somalia 1992 Operation Hope, Rwanda 1994 Operation Support Hope, Haiti 1994 Operation Uphold Democracy, Saudi Arabia/Kuwait 1994 Operation Vigilant Warrior, Italy 1995 Operation Deny Flight and Bosnia 1995 Operation Joint Endeavor). The report concludes in general terms that the use of private firms has indeed saved cost. However, in a detailed case study on Bosnia the report concludes that the need to speed up and expand the programme resulted in additional cost (USGAO 1997a). In another USGAO assessment about privatization and public–private competition of the same year, it is written that the Department of Defense expects that the reduction of 203,000 civilian jobs would save US$9.2 billion between 1997 and 2005. Yet due to uncertain data 'neither we nor DoD could precisely quantify the extent of savings from these nine [studied] cases' (USGAO 1997b, 4). Furthermore, imprecise data, wrong assumptions about the level of cost in the Department of Defense and ignoring of the cost of implementation of the programme 'made it impractical to identify precise amounts of savings' (USGAO 1997b, 5). The data, it was said two years later, was insufficient to make a realistic comparison (USGAO 1999a, 2 and 2000, 4). 'Estimates of savings in the 20- to 30-percent range or higher have been cited in some assessments of previous competitive sourcing studies but often have been based on initial savings estimates from previous competitions, rather than on actual savings over time. DoD has not systematically tracked or updated the savings estimates from competitions' (USGAO 1999b, 4). Nevertheless, privatization continues to be promoted with the argument of its economic rationality.

Markusen (2003, 480–481, 483) draws a critical conclusion: 'Extant studies compare bids by private and public agencies but, with few exceptions, do not track actual performance. In other words, they assess the *promise* of savings rather than their achievement ... In summary, this review finds that evaluations of the gains to Pentagon privatization are narrowly drawn, largely prospective rather than retrospective in nature, and confined chiefly to cost and not quality assessment. They lack the sophistication of social-science methodology applied in other areas of public–sector privatization.' Usually, the savings potentials are overestimated when companies are contracted; these estimates must then be revised in later studies or, alternatively, not all costs are included in the original cost estimates. It is surprising on what a meagre empirical basis such far-reaching decisions are being made – decisions which not only have economic effects in the defence sector but also fundamental social and political consequences.

Sloppily implemented privatization in the US military sector

This privatization, which has been inadequately and unsatisfactorily implemented from an economic perspective, has not been principally improved since the USGAO reports were published. Using the three criteria for successful privatization defined in Chapter 2 as a yardstick (the existence of real competitors, clearly formulated parameters of the expected service and monitoring and verification of the supplied services) the results of privatization in the US military sector are by no means as positive as the government likes to claim.

First, the number of competitors: Markusen (2003, 478), who analyzed primarily the results of privatization in the defence industry, draws a few general conclusions that apply to the private military firms as well. In arms procurement, with its reduced number of companies, there is no real competition; at best there is an oligopoly and in some areas a monopoly of bidders. The reduced number of companies undermines the economic success of privatization. This negative trend is strengthened by the exclusion of foreign competitors in the defence sector. The Pentagon signed 3061 contracts worth over US$300 billion between 1994 and 2002, but 2700 of these contracts were signed with only two companies – Kellogg Brown & Root (KBR, Halliburton) and the technology consulting company Booz Allen Hamilton (Kahn 2002). During the same period the number of contracts for non-public bids increased substantially. As a result higher costs were incurred, such as the cost for petrol supplied by Halliburton in Iraq that was 100 per cent over-priced (Schreier and Caparini 2005, 52).

Presently, numerous private military companies still offer military services. But the trend of takeovers and mergers, observed previously with the arms producers, has begun amongst the private military companies too. The result will be reduced competition and increased cost. Some bottlenecks are already visible. The boom of private military companies in Iraq has resulted in a long queue of security clearance applications for the employees of private firms. In spring 2004 there was a pool of 188,000 requests waiting for clearance. Five years ago, the total annual volume of applications was less than 50,000. The companies themselves are having difficulties in recruiting enough qualified personnel quickly and thus need to rely on people that are under-qualified. The pressure is so intense that representatives of the Information Technology Association warn: 'We're essentially creating a new class of people here, where a clearance takes precedent over skill or ability' (quoted in *Washington Post* 14 May 2004).

In addition, an essential principle for the success of privatization is often violated, namely to rely on competitive bids. Increasingly the Pentagon has offered so-called blanket-purchase agreements without public bidding. These are well-paid long-term contracts with vaguely formulated service responsibilities in which the companies agree to supply a wide variety of services quickly and on short notice, such as the previously mentioned blanket-purchase agreement signed by CACI (*Washington Post* 17 May 2004). According to a report of the Army Inspector General, 35 per cent of the 31 interrogators provided by CACI did not have any 'formal training in military interrogation policies and techniques' (quoted in Verlöy and Politi 2004). Kellogg, Brown & Root (Halliburton) received similar blanket-purchase contracts from the armed forces to rebuild the infrastructure of Iraq and for the US armed forces; these are guaranteed for many years to come and thus stifle the need for a competitive edge. The armed forces are especially keen on the fast services. KBR agreed, for example, to start establishing a military base in any part of the world at 72 hours' notice. Invoicing is done on a cost-plus accounting basis. As a rule the companies can add 1 or 2 per cent profit onto their incurred cost, with an option of up to 5 to 8 per cent for better than agreed performance (The Center for Public Integrity 2004, *Business Week* 15 September 2003).

Protagonists of these blanket-purchase agreements argue that this type of contract offers flexibility for the Department of Defense and the armed forces – flexibility which is essential to react quickly and decisively in crisis situations. But the argument of the alleged cost savings gets lost. The USGAO concluded in 1999 that savings are possible if there is competition, no matter if this is competition within the private sector or between the public and the private sector (USGAO 1999a, 4). The privatization gurus respond to such an argument by stating 'the cost-saving argument for outsourcing is not nearly as compelling as the potential improvement from quality of service or flexibility' (Steven L. Schooner, George Washington University, quoted in *Business Week* 15 September 2003, 45).

Second, clearly defined criteria for the supply of services: Long-term and open-ended blanket-purchase agreements do not include clearly defined services. On the contrary, to avoid public bidding and to be able to quickly request services and make use of the know-how of companies, the Pentagon prefers open and vaguely formulated contracts. Such contracts usually evolve into a bilateral monopoly, with a monopolist each on the demand and the supply side. This results in the often-criticized symbiotic relationship between the contracting parties with technical dependencies and the potential for corruption and political influence which question both the economic rationality as well as the security relevant assessment of the basis of these contracts. In addition, critics add, this policy weakens the long-term potential of the armed forces since they lose their know-how. The companies acquire the know-how, use it internally and protect it as an internal resource against requests from outside. Outsourcing can save money, but it can also weaken the combat potential of the armed forces since expertise is lost to the public sector (Avant 2002).

These blanket-purchase agreements encourage 'producing' high cost. Within the Army it was said that in the contract with KBR costs were almost marginal: 'Cost was considered but because of the nebulous nature of cost in the contract, it wasn't the most significant' (Dave Defrieze, an Army lawyer, quoted in Mother Jones, 23 February 2002). It is therefore no surprise that government documents show that ten companies with billions of US dollars worth of contracts in Iraqi reconstruction 'have paid more than $300 million in penalties since 2000 to resolve allegations of bid rigging, fraud, delivery of faulty military parts and environmental damage' (The Associated Press 29 April 2004). Essentially thus, private military firms are profit-oriented providers of military services that do not necessarily supply the qualified service that is required for security reasons. It was claimed that KBR, for example, had delivered insufficient services during the conflict in the Balkans and that in four out of seven contracts with the US Army they had billed too high a cost (Singer 2001/02, 205). According to Singer, the ratio of personnel of private military companies to the US Army was between 1 to 50 or 1 to 100 during the first Gulf War at the beginning of the 1990s; a decade later for every ten soldiers one company employee was hired to serve in Iraq (quoted in Schwartz 2003). Contracts in the order of a magnitude of US$30 billion (8 per cent of the total military budget) and a procurement budget of nearly US$100 billion were authorized by the Pentagon in 2003 (ibid. 2003). The dependence of the US armed forces on private military contractors for more and more military functions increased continuously with the March 2003 Iraq War and the subsequent reconstruction period – for Special Forces training and support, for the protection of military and civilian installations, for the maintenance of weapons, for logistics and so on. The US armed forces have long relied on the private sector but today's type of fusion between the military and company employee is something new – to the extent that it is becoming difficult to distinguish them. This form of mutual dependency is not only with regard to privatization in the United States. The deployment of private military firms in developing countries in combat or for the protection of weak or besieged governments has often resulted in a general mutual dependence between the two contracting parties. Governments depend for their survival on the support given by the companies and the companies must continue to support the governments to receive payment for their services.

Third, monitoring and verification: In addition to the necessity of competition and clarity about the contracted services, the third essential criteria mentioned above for the success of privatization was the ability of the government or its agency to monitor and verify the service delivery. The capacities in the US Department of Defense to oversee the private military companies are totally inadequate. This was already criticized in the USGAO report on the Bosnia deployment (USGAO 1997a, 5). Due to the boom of private military firms in Iraq this insufficiency has become even more obvious. In a letter to the secretary of defense several democratic senators expressed their concern about the role of the private military companies and particularly that private companies are supposed to control private companies; they urged for a review by the USGAO, calling this situation 'a dangerous precedent to allow private armies to operate outside the control of a governmental authority' (quoted in The Associated Press 29 April 2004). The previously mentioned contract of Aegis is a classical example of a case that should absolutely be avoided. Aegis, a small company, established two years back by the dubious ex-Colonel and ex-CEO of Sandline, Tim Spicer, received a large contract to coordinate protection measures in Iraq. The company had no prior experience in this area but no matter, the US Army seems not to care about the owner's previous business conduct (Schreier and Caparini 2005, 23).

The Pentagon does not pay enough attention to verification and monitoring of service supplies. For example, companies such as KBR are blamed for having invoiced for more personnel than they actually used. Yet after companies sign a contract there is hardly any responsibility for transparency (Avant 2000, Schreier and Caparini 2005, 54 and 81). American companies work with a license of their government. These licenses do not foresee any monitoring function that would allow the verification of the actual services provided. National embassies abroad are officially in charge of monitoring, but the embassy personnel are neither trained nor available for this job (Avant 2002). Singer (2003, 239) analyzed the case of AirScan, whose company employees had coordinated the downing of a civil aircraft. Asked if they would pursue this case a member of the Department of State stated: 'Our job is to protect Americans, not investigate Americans'. Bruce D. Grant (1998,

100), a Colonel of the US Army, wrote in an essay for which he shared third place in the 1998 Chairman of the Joint Chiefs of Staff Strategy Essay Competition 'a private firm can train another nation's army without congressional notification, much less congressional approval. Thus, significant foreign policy actions related to foreign security assistance do not receive the benefit of the checks and balances system inherent in our system of government'.

It is not by chance that the number of contracts with private military firms is increasing, that savings of outsourcing are expected but that the empirical proof is lacking, and that the dependence of the Department of Defense and the armed forces on private companies is growing. When the Bush administration started its privatization offensive a private military company was contracted by the Pentagon to write the very guidelines for the business of private military companies with the government. The business journal *Fortune*, certainly not a critic of privatization, asked disdainfully 'Guess who helped write the manual on dealing with private contractors? A contractor – MPRI' (Schwartz 2003, 6, Zamparelli 1999). Verification and monitoring of contracts becomes intricate and thorny because of the symbiotic relationship between politics and companies. A host of examples of conflicts of interest are published in the press that are a consequence of the changing functions of former company managers now serving in responsible ministries, and former officials of the defence ministry and high-ranking officers of the armed forces now serving in companies (Schreier and Caparini 2005, 70 and 94).

Critical questions regarding privatization in the United Kingdom

The results and effects of the privatization effort are disputed in the United Kingdom too. The dimension of outsourcing in the United Kingdom is much less pronounced than in the United States, probably because of the previous public debate about the role of private military companies in Britain. The main focus of the privatization drive in the United Kingdom is to use the private sector, including its capital, to reduce the public investments of the Ministry of Defence. Still, a number of open questions regarding the long-term effects of ideologically driven privatization in the military sector remain. Critical comments can be heard from within the Ministry of Defence itself. Neil V. Davis (2000, 5–8), Senior Economic Advisor in the defence ministry and himself a protagonist of privatization, does not hesitate to name a few drawbacks, obstacles and objections. He talks about 'sacrificing public service ethos' and 'excessive commercialisation'; he emphasizes that 'private finance costs more'; he identifies 'inflexibility' due to the difficulties of defining precisely in a contract of 'what will be required and when' and adds that 'it can be costly to renegotiate'; he is concerned about the 'loss of control' and the 'loss of accountability' in the Ministry of Defence; he also mentions the problem of 'surge capacities' and worries about the 'interdependence' since 'it may be that to ensure the best price one has to grant an effective monopoly to the supplier to encourage him to invest in highly specific assets'; and he warns against the 'potential for fraud and abuse' as well as the possible 'negative local economic impacts' of outsourcing.

What was relevant for privatization in general, back in 1989, still holds today for privatization in the military sector. Donahue (1989, quoted in Markusen 2003, 494–495) concluded: 'Links [between government and supplier] that begin as arm's-length transactions tend to evolve into closer relationships. Public officials who work daily with private suppliers, and who rely on these suppliers to accomplish their missions, come to care greatly about keeping contractors healthy and helpful ... If an organizational budget can be increased through political manoeuvring ... there will be little enthusiasm for driving hard bargains with suppliers. In any contractual relationship between government and private business, a key question becomes who is representing the broader public interests. Unless there are sturdy provisions to prevent it – and even if all parties are immune to corruption – the natural outcome is an alliance between private-sector suppliers and government officials at the taxpayers' expense.'

The state monopoly of violence traded at the stock market?

The successful business strategy of the private military companies has registered great interest amongst larger stock companies. The business journal *Fortune* published an analysis of the newly emerging industrial branch of military companies since this development is obviously of interest for investors (Schwartz 2003). The company CEO's talk with great confidence about the fact that the armed forces might still be able to fight a war but it would be difficult without the private military companies, according to Paul Lombardi, CEO of DynCorp (quoted in Schwartz 2003). DynCorp increased its turnover in 2002 by 18 per cent, reaching a total of US$2.3 billion, with one quarter in the sector of military services. Computer Science Corporation (CSC), a large contractor of the Pentagon itself, bought DynCorp at the beginning of 2003 and paid US$950 million. At the time of the takeover the CSC company management announced proudly that in the Department of Defense ranking DynCorp ranked 13th overall with US$1.36 billion in contract awards; and CSC placed 21st with US$808 million. 'When combined, the fiscal year 2002 total would have been $2.17 billion, placing CSC as seventh largest DoD contractor overall behind Lockheed Martin, Boeing, Northrop Grumman, Raytheon, General Dynamics and United Technologies Corporation' (www.csc.com/features/2003/7.shtml, accessed 23 October 2004). DynCorp had tripled its turnover from 1994 until the take-over. The company was so attractive for CSC as it has a strong presence in the area referred to in the government as 'sustainment', or providing operational and logistical support for base operations and aircraft maintenance for the US forces as well as with the British Ministry of Defence. CSC's 'back-office support', the management concludes, combined with DynCorp's 'front-line support' helps CSC offer a full spectrum of services. 'We now provide support for the warfighter from the day he or she joins the service until they're out in the battlefield actually at work. It's a whole life cycle support of the soldier' (www.csc.com/features/2003/7.shtml, accessed 23 October 2004). But the company also considered selling some of the risky business fields of DynCorp, such as its flight service in the Colombian anti-drug fight, because every loss of an aircraft or helicopter could also result in the drop of their share prices in the stock market.

CACI International Inc., mentioned earlier, was able to increase its 2003 profit by 33 per cent to US$11.5 million. Two thirds of all contracts came from the US Department of Defense. CACI took over Premier Technology Group, a company specialized in intelligence gathering and analysis, and also works for the Pentagon (*Washington Post* 25 April 2003). The stock market reacted promptly when the scandal about the interrogation practices in Iraqi prisons broke in May 2004. CACI's share price had risen from July 2003 until May 2004 from US$35 to over US$50, but then dropped by one-third until June 2004 when they were back to US$35. In October 2004 the stocks had reached a new high of US$56, and stocks were traded in January 2005 at about US$60 per share (http://www.shareholder.com/caci/quote.cfm, accessed 22 January 2005).

In 1997 the London-based company Defense Service Limited (DSL) was purchased by the US company Armor Holdings for a price of US$26 million. In the years 1999 and 2000 DSL was among the 100 fastest growing companies in the *Fortune* list. DSL claims to be the largest provider of contract personnel and worked at the time of the take-over in 44 different countries with the headquarters in London and offices in Washington, Jacksonville, Hong Kong, Singapore, Bogotá, Lima, Maputo, Kinshasa, Luanda, Port Moresby, Moscow, Kazakhstan, the Isle of Jersey and Sarajevo. Armor Holding was among the 200 Best Small Companies of the *Forbes* list in 2002. Bombs, war and civil unrest seem to be good for Armor's business. The business motto of Jonathan Spiller, CEO of Armor Holding is: 'When the world becomes less safe and secure, the demand for our products increases' (quoted by Nicole Ostrow in an article on the internet homepage of Armor Holdings) (www.armorhold-ings.com/whatsnew/ind_leader.htm, accessed 23 October 2004). But the business was not always as smooth. After a bankruptcy in 1992, the company recovered, but had to request Merill Lynch in 2002 to sell its Armorgroup SVC, a service subsidiary of Armor Holdings, as they had incurred losses in that sector (*BusinessWeek* online 15 July 2002).

L-3 Communications purchased MPRI in 2000 for US $ 35 million. MPRI was so successful that large defence producers became interested. The company now functions as an independent unit under the name L-3 MPRI. The New York–based L-3 enterprise is specialized in surveillance and intelligence technology and works mainly for the US Department of Defense, Homeland Security, the CIA and foreign contractors. L-3 emerged as an independent company after the merger of Lockheed and Martin Marietta to become the world's largest arms producer. Lockheed Martin L-3 Communications was in 2002 amongst the 100 fastest grow-ing companies and made above average profits of about 33 per cent dur-ing a period of three years at the beginning of the decade (Schwartz 2003). Lockheed Martin itself had – with the blessing of Wall Street – planned to takeover Titan Corporation of San Diego, another private military company. When employees of Titan, who were contracted as translators in Iraqi prisons, were charged with torturing in Abu Ghraib, the defence multinational Lockheed Martin dropped the plan (*Washington Post* 7 May 2004). The takeover fell through and the share price of Titan dropped from almost US$20 in June 2004 within a few days to US$12, and has fluctuated around US$13 to 15 since then.

Other examples point in the same direction. The fifth largest global arms producing company Northrop-Grumman took over Vinnell Corporation, a company which has been training the National Guard of Saudi Arabia within the US military assistance programme since 1975 (www.vinnell.com).

With a global branding strategy the private military companies hope to create a reputable image, and want to offer their services worldwide and not exclusively or primarily for the US forces alone.

Part III
Conclusions

9

The Need for the Control of Private Military Companies and Internationalized Armed Forces

The major impact of privatizing and internationalizing military functions is a fundamental change of the role of the military in its relation to the nation state and the long-term effects for the state monopoly of force. Globalization has changed the basic concept of the nation state. De-nationalization and a reduced role of the state can be observed on many levels of economic, social and cultural activity. Even the concept of nationally organized and orientated armies is questioned. In most cases national governments alone can no longer take decisions regarding war and the use of force. There is a real danger that the state instruments of force may fall into the hands of non-state actors such as criminal gangs, insurgents, militias and so on, or they will be handed over to privately operating companies. The trends to privatize and internationalize security exacerbate the already pressing problem of insufficient parliamentary oversight of the armed forces. A fundamental state function, the state monopoly of force, is being undermined or given up completely. Privatization does not mean the renunciation of state functions per se; delegation of state functions to reliable non-state actors can be rational. But in many developing countries the establishment of an efficient state monopoly of force and its proper use is not the rule but the exception. To complicate matters, in industrialized countries that outsource military missions, it is not clear to whom the private military and security companies are accountable. At the international level it is often unclear under whose control the internationalized armed forces operate and their democratic oversight is only marginally developed.

Three politico-legal areas are of great importance for the future development of security and peace and the regulation of force: the regulation and the strict legal control of private military companies, the reform of parliamentary control of the armed forces to overcome the democratic deficit in international interventions, and the improvement and development of the monopoly of violence beyond the nation state. These three tasks are analyzed below.

The control of private military companies: a legal grey zone

Regulations and control mechanisms for the production and distribution of food, for example yoghurt, and pharmaceutical products, or environmental regulations, are much stricter and clearer in many countries than the state control of the use of force by private military companies. Efficient rules are urgently required to uphold the public monopoly of violence.

Reputable companies are not opposed to some form of regulation. Since the activity of these companies is not just trendy or a short-term phenomenon and since a number of dubious companies operate in this emerging industrial branch – even large companies are trying to use opportunities to make a quick profit with dishonest or unfair practices – their oversight and regulation is urgently required. I have argued in Chapter 2 that international and national legal provisions are totally insufficient and that the companies operate presently in legal murkiness. Many legal questions that are of importance in the current conflicts remain still unanswered. This is, for example, demonstrated by the different treatment of soldiers as compared to company employees who both allegedly tortured prisoners in the Abu Ghraib prison in Baghdad. While the soldiers fall under international law, especially the Geneva Convention, and are faced with military jurisdiction, it was still disputed more than half-a-year after the scandal broke how the company employees were to be legally treated – on the basis of Iraqi, US or international law (Isenberg 2004, 51–67).

Several state authorities and international organizations are also interested in regulating private military companies, as for example the International Committee of the Red Cross (ICRC). The British Government wants – as expressed in its Green Paper (UK Government 2002, 20) – to bring non-state violence under control especially since 'actions in the security field have implications which go beyond those of normal commercial transactions'. So far the British government has not decided if and which of the different options discussed it wants to apply.

I distinguish three principally different approaches to deal with the increasing but unregulated practices of private military companies: prohibition, reliance on self-regulation of companies and national and international legally binding regulations.

First: A comprehensive *prohibition* of private military companies would be the most direct control, but there are a number of different reasons to make this an impracticable solution. Not the least of which is that it would be difficult to implement this prohibition on the basis of national laws extraterritorially. Also, as explained in Chapter 2, it is hard to define precisely who or what kind of activity would be covered by such a prohibition. Some companies offer useful services, for example in the logistics of relief operations. A general prohibition would also require ruling out such services. A general and far-reaching prohibition would affect weapon export regulations too, and it seems that there is no interest on the part of governments to tie their hands, both with regard to arms exports as well as services of private military companies.

Second: To ignore the problem and to hope for the *self-regulation* of the companies, as has been suggested by company representatives (Sandline 1998, IPOA 2004), seems totally unacceptable and inadequate given that companies cannot be forced to abide by certain behaviour or into acceptance of a code of conduct of an industry association. In any case, the 'black sheep' within the industry would not observe the self-regulation mechanism. In some areas (e.g. 'blood diamonds') such industry codes have improved the situation (Böge and Paes 2004) and some of the unfair practices have been stopped. The minimum norm for such a codex for private military companies would be observance of human rights, international humanitarian laws, the sovereignty of states and transparency about the business, and a readiness to be checked by state authority. Self-regulatory initiatives by companies and industry associations are positive, but they are not sufficient since neither the problematic cases in the grey zone between legal and illegal activities nor clearly illegal excesses can be prevented or prosecuted. The advantage of the self-regulation mechanism is its easy implementation, but it remains a soft regulation.

Third: A whole range of different, partly complementary options for *national and international regulation* are available.

1. *The expansion or reformulation of the Geneva Conventions*:   Since the contractors are not only engaged in logistical services but also operate

close to the battlefield or are directly engaged in combat it is essential to examine if the Geneva Convention needs to be reformed. Employees of private military companies are not civilians or 'non-combatants' as they are often armed and physically present at the request of governments in the conflict area. But they are neither 'lawful combatants' according to the Geneva Conventions since they do not wear regular military uniforms and are not under military command. Furthermore, they cannot be subsumed under the definition of mercenary. In legal terms they have presently the status of 'unlawful combatants' – similarly to the alleged terrorists held by the US government in Guantanamo Bay (Schreier and Caparini 2005, 57).

It is expected, according to international conventions on war that soldiers can distinguish between combatants and non-combatants. Armed contract personnel with quasi-military uniforms and military-type firearms are rather difficult to distinguish from regular military forces. Thus, as to whether they are, for example in Iraq, subject to Iraqi laws or the laws of their home countries is an open question. The definition of 'direct' participation in hostilities, as it is mentioned in the Geneva Convention, is also unclear. But this definition is a central criterion for the classification as combatant. Yet the Convention does not give an explanation or a precise meaning as to which of the companies' practices might be considered direct participation in hostilities or combat. Clarifications are necessary. However, the treatment of mercenarism in the Additional Protocol of the Convention and its implementation has proven that the international compromise that was reached after lengthy negotiations is not really a practical handle to prosecute mercenaries. It is likely that a revision of the Convention to include contract personnel would amount to similarly vague definitions that would leave governments enough room for manoeuvre to make use of non-state violence actors, including private military companies, if they so desire.

2. *Establishment of a licensing system*:   Licenses could be granted by national governments to companies that would authorize the holder to offer and undertake military services. Such a regulation would give them some sort of official legitimacy with implications for the government in case the licensee acts illegally. For stricter control, instead of such a general license for companies certain clearly defined services could be licensed; for other services no license would be granted. Further still, a licensing system could be feasible that is based on a case-by-case decision. Companies would have to acquire a separate license for each and every contract or transaction. These different licenses have distinct

parallels to the ones used for arms transfers and the experiences made in that area should be assessed and applied to private military company regulation too.

3. *National registration and notification*: Under such a system companies will have to register their activities and the home government as well as the government in the territory where the firms will work must be informed. The advantage of registration and notification is its easy, uncomplicated and unbureaucratic mechanism; a key disadvantage is the fact that governments would have to become more active in order to prohibit a certain activity. This, however, would require a legal basis. This regulatory mechanism is inadequate for systematic government control. The negotiation within the United Nations (UN) to register or establish a licensing system for arms brokers has shown how little interest a good number of governments have in regulating such activities under an accepted international norm.

4. *International registration, transparency and verification*: Companies and governments – both those that demand services from military firms and those that pay for them – could be required to report the details of contracts, including specifically the particulars about the volume and type of service, to a central international register. This universal format falls into the same category as the earlier-mentioned national registration and notification option. Such an instrument has distinct parallels to the UN Register of Conventional Arms. The advantage over the present situation would be enormously improved transparency. The UN or the International Committee of the Red Cross (ICRC) could function as the depository of the company register. However, the main disadvantages of the UN Register of Conventional Arms would also apply to a company register: Reporting will have to be done *ex post*, which is after the fact, and verification could only be done by comparing the data of the incoming reports from the companies and the governments (Laurance *et al.* 2005). Also, this form of registration would not cover the most problematic cases since dubious contracts would probably not be reported at all.

Without the introduction and establishment of regulatory mechanisms the companies can be held accountable only by their owners and shareholders or the governments who pay them. Yet all of the earlier-mentioned control instruments have gaps and loopholes, and some of the options require an elaborate government agency to implement effective controls. To clear up the present legal murkiness it is necessary – at a minimum – to introduce similar rules as those applicable for arms exports. As stated this would be a minimum: The numerous weapon scandals demonstrate just how porous the arms export regulations themselves are.

Governments are the key authorities to control private military companies. They have the responsibility for an effective state monopoly of force and are responsible if this authority is given up or undermined by privatizing war; they cannot, neither quietly nor publicly based on a political-ideological concept of assumed private sector efficiency, sneak out of this responsibility.

The democratic deficit

The role of parliaments in authorizing military interventions, such as peace operations, and their implementation varies greatly in different countries. Parliaments in only a few countries have the constitutional right to make decisions concerning the deployment of national troops in war and crises. Moreover, there is hardly any parliamentary role anywhere regarding contracting private military companies contracted to perform military services. National parliaments are in some cases part of the decision-making process when international interventions are planned, but in most cases the parliamentary role is marginal and not sufficient to facilitate the creation of democratic standards and norms at the international level. Damrosch (2003) concludes that parliaments have in recent years played a more intensified role in deployment decisions. This is indeed the case and a growing trend in a few West European countries and in several new EU and NATO member countries from central Europe. But the breadth of this trend should not be overestimated, because even in the countries with more explicit parliamentary decision-making tensions exist between parliamentary control and the internationally relevant decisions of the executive and their accountability vis-à-vis parliament and the public. Born and Urscheler (2004, 63) distinguish between parliaments without powers in authorizing the sending of troops abroad, parliaments with an authorization function, and parliaments with wider functions, including oversight functions during the implementation phase and the ending of an operation. Only in 5 of 16 countries analyzed (the Czech Republic, Denmark, Germany, the Netherlands and Sweden) do parliaments have authorization and control rights. In the United States, congressional approval as regards deployment is not required but Congress can decide the duration of the operation. There are only a few cases in which parliaments have pulled the plug on executive decisions. An example is the withdrawal of US troops from the UN mission in Somalia where Congress set 31 March 1994 as a deadline for the Clinton administration to bring the US troops back. Beyond the direct parliamentary role there are several indirect possibilities for parliaments to influence the executive's decision; these are summarized in Table 9.1. Beyond the legislative function the parliament can use its budgetary powers as a key function and effective instrument to strengthen the role of parliament to be able to influence or prevent the executive decisions. Nevertheless, while this is not uncommon with regard to the deployment of troops, contracts with military firms and the deployment of contract personnel are hardly on the agenda of parliaments.

Table 9.1   Parliamentary roles in deployment of armed forces and private military companies

Function	Instrument	Objective	Parliamentary practice
Legislative	law, codification of legal powers	• authorizing deployment and duration of mission • authorizing contracting private military companies	• increasingly practised • marginal or non-existent
Resource	budget	• approval of budget for the mission or withdrawal of financial means to end military operations • approval of budget to contract private military companies	• key function and effective instrument • key function, hardly practised
Elective	elections	• no-confidence vote	• only in exceptional cases
Oversight	consultations and committees	• scrutiny of government decisions, transparency and accountability of the executive; consultation rights	• effective means to enforce parliamentary
Representative	public debate	• facilitation of the consensus on or voicing popular disagreement to deploy forces	• key co-operation mechanism of the public beyond elections

Source: Expansion of a concept by Hänggi (2004, 12).

So far parliaments have not realized that they need to play a role in controlling the executive in this area too. Further, parliaments use their no-confidence power only in exceptional cases to enforce or prevent a government decision on the deployment of troops in international missions. A stronger check on the executive however, and contrary to the latter practice, is that consultation with the executive and parliamentary committees and enquiries are an often-used instrument usually applied on a case-by-case basis to facilitate the role of parliamentary powers. In certain cases parliaments have used parliamentary enquiries to uncover scandals or alleged serious faults or crimes of soldiers. The Belgian and the French parliaments assessed government decisions in the aftermath of the Genocide in Rwanda, whilst the Dutch parliament looked into the role of its armed forces in Srebrenica and the government decisions to deploy them. In the case of the Dutch, eventually the government stepped down because of the harsh and convincing criticism of the parliamentary report. In the United States, Congressional committees have looked into the Abu Ghraib prison torture scandal in which both soldiers and contract personnel of private companies were involved. Parliaments can also influence decisions by using their representative functions. Questions of war and peace often lead to emotional debates in parliament and in the public. The result-oriented legitimacy discussed in Chapter 1 plays a decisive role. Ideally parliament represents the people. The relations between the public and parliament can thus have a strong influence on the executive. But often it is extremely difficult for parliamentarians to get a precise picture of public opinion on the issue of military interventions. Opinions as they are reflected in representative polling are strongly influenced by how the questions are asked and by media reports. Current events can quickly evolve into strongly voiced opinions and then disappear again in a short time. Nevertheless, public discourse can influence decisions and can lead to a readjustment or strengthening of decisions on war and peace.

Constitutions were not designed originally with a view to cover UN peacekeeping or peace enforcement operations (Born 2004, 211). Given the large number and permanence of such international missions and relief programmes, constitutional amendments might be necessary in some countries. But the inadequate parliamentary and democratic control is not only the result of constitutional gaps. Often, parliamentarians are not willing or do not find the time to claim their parliamentary rights and make use of their control instruments in the area of security, war and peace. It is important not only to strengthen the various parliamentary functions but also the willingness of parliamentarians and their capabilities to engage in such issues (Hänggi 2004, 12–15). Parliaments must attempt to find the middle road between the present widespread absence of controls on the one hand and an overemphasis of parliamentary intervention on the other. Timing is important when deployments of troops are authorized since delays can exacerbate crises and can cost lives. But a tight schedule can be no reason for the executive to circumvent parliament.

The established, although often inadequate, control mechanisms at the national level are complicated when international missions are decided upon and the national control instruments are often unsatisfactory for this purpose. International law, as codified in the UN Charter, legitimizes the deployment of forces. This, however, does not mean that the authorization follows democratic rules. Even worse, the activity of the military companies is, as argued earlier, widely unregulated. In the public political discourse and in research publications there is no agreement on how to overcome this democratic deficit in international organizations. Dahl's (1999) question 'Can international organizations be democratic?' is not only rhetorical but an expression of his pessimistic assessment as to whether democratic rules are possible at all in the international arena.

Three possible models for democratization have been proposed (Greene 2004, 27): (1) The liberal-democratic internationalist agenda aims at the reform of international institutions and the establishment of liberal and pluralistic structures (Commission on Global Governance 1995). (2) The radical communitarianist democratic agenda is broadly to build on new social movements and the establishment of alternative structures that offer transnational and participatory governance; such communities are functional and not geographically orientated. (3) The cosmopolitan democratic agenda aims at establishing global governance that is based on democratic, elective principles and a cosmopolitan programme to overcome national sovereignty. The cosmopolitan concept is attractive since it envisions a step-by-step development and wants to make use of proven democratic mechanisms. It is a process in which new representative bodies develop on several levels.

Creating a multi-level public monopoly of violence

Thus far, parliamentary controls of the armed forces and of private military companies have not developed in parallel to the trend of internationalizing the military and the business practices of the companies. To overcome the 'double democratic deficit' in security at the international level, the nation state should not be seen a priori as the only legitimate authority to use the monopoly of violence; this is because the context for the functioning of the nation state has fundamentally changed.

Given the experience of the post–Cold War years in conflict prevention, peacekeeping, post-conflict reconstruction and nation-building, there was never a magic bullet or a panacea to ensure the security of people, the prevention or resolution of conflicts or the restoration of the state monopoly of force. The monopoly of violence of the nation state cannot easily be re-established. Each case of conflict has its own history and process, and there are no opportunities for quick fixes. The instant cure-all approaches usually have long-term negative effects and have often exacerbated conflicts and further shattered weak state institutions. The present military operations in Iraq are a case in point.

The Human Security Report (2005) hypothesizes that the declining rate of casualties who are directly killed in combat is a result of intensified UN peace missions. The UN High-level Panel on Threats, Challenges and Change (2004, 33) argues similarly and presents a correlation between the decreasing number of ongoing civil wars and the increasing number of ongoing UN peacekeeping and peace-building operations. Thus, interventions do have a positive impact. Yet, the international community usually treats peace-threatening crises as short-term problems which have to be solved as soon as possible. International relief and peace operations seem to follow a high-noon syndrome: They are expected to offer a final solution of the conflicts. But conflicts are usually the result of deeply rooted causes; they are protracted often going back several centuries. Short-term relief or humanitarian programmes can only be of limited value.

Today, when insecurity persists and violence effects large parts of populations, ready-made policy solutions are being implemented: conflict management and mediation, humanitarian intervention with civil and military means, emergency relief and aid, peacekeeping, peace enforcement and peace building, post-conflict reconstruction and nation-building, and democratization and development (Pape 1997, Debiel and Nuscheler 1996, OECE/DAC 2001). Most of these efforts are based on genuine humanitarian concerns. But a critical evaluation of the strengths and weaknesses of these approaches in concrete conflicts does not provide too encouraging a result.

The model

The reconstruction of the monopoly of violence is not just about re-establishing the state monopoly of violence. A more holistic approach is necessary to establish rules and regulations for the use of force that more effectively address both the legacy of conflict-endemic societies, the immediate security of the people and the external linkages. Given the violent fights and the breakdown of the rule of law in many societies it is virtually impossible for any of the warring parties to re-establish the monopoly of violence. Instead of addressing almost exclusively the level of the nation state, as external actors presently do, a legitimized multilevel public monopoly of violence is required.

As a result of increasing interdependence and globalization the nation state has lost or transferred part of its sovereignty to other entities: to the top (to supra national or multilateral organizations) and down to lower levels (such as local and district associations). This trend is most visible within the European Union (EU): Not only Brussels has taken over sovereignty rights from the member states but also some cross-border local groupings below the nation state level too. A system of a public monopoly of force should be based on at least the following four levels of authority:

- the local level, which offers proven forms of regulating violence with the inclusion of 'zones of peace' and 'islands of civility';
- the national level, with credible and accountable institutions of organized violence and good governance;
- the regional or sub-regional level, with regional organizations engaged in providing security and facilitating peace beyond the various national boundaries; and
- the global level, through the United Nations, including accepted international principles and agreed norms and with a legitimate authority to intervene for the protection of people.

Given the globalized world, with porous or non-existent nation state borders, with failing or collapsed states and with asymmetric zones of insecurity, the future lies not necessarily in the re-establishment of a nation state monopoly, but rather in a multi-level public monopoly of violence. A multi-level public monopoly of force comes closer to the present reality of the international system since it addresses the different levels of political decision-making.

Besides the daunting practical difficulties of implementing a multi-level public monopoly of legitimized violence regulation, such a system is faced with two conceptual problems: How shall the four different levels be legitimized, given the acute deficit in democratic processes at all four levels? And how can co-operation and a division of labour between these fragmented authorities at the different levels function? Top-down, bottom-up or through consent?

A multi-level monopoly is precisely speaking an oligopoly since the powers of a monopoly need to be shared between authorities at the different levels. Oligopolies are faced by definition with the prospect of competition and conflict. To create the suggested four-level public monopoly of violence as an efficient and functional instrument, a set of agreed rules is a precondition. Otherwise the system will be bogged down in fights over competencies and about who has the various authorities. And only if the system functions is there a chance to move from the present situation of the breakdown of the monopoly of force in many parts of the world to establishing a legitimate public monopoly of violence.

What could a set of agreed rules look like? The system must be based on security (not defence) and orientated to observe human rights; it should have clear political decision-making bodies on a multilateral basis and should encompass the rule of law for the use of violence (Study Group on Europe's Security Capabilities 2004).

Two basic principles should provide the basis. First, the monopoly of violence should be exercised according to the subsidiary principle, that is, in a bottom-up approach the lowest level should be the starting point and only when the local level is not capable or cannot be tasked with exercising the monopoly of force should the next higher level be entrusted with this mission. This concept is, for example, exercised in many federal states where a federal authority (or even local community) executes police functions. The central state (the nation state) will only become involved if the task goes beyond the local level or if the instruments of legitimized organized violence prove to be incompetent or inadequate. If the nation state level is ill-equipped or incapable of exercising the monopoly of violence the regional organization is tasked, for example to prevent the trade in humans, drugs or weapons. This would leave the UN as the highest authority to ensure peace and security only as a last resort.

The second principle is based on a hierarchy of authority. Norm setting takes place top-down. International norms prevail over regional, regional over national and national over local levels. The UN has higher authority than the regional organizations, the region is placed higher than the national level and the national level has prevalence over the local level. Given the realities of conflict-prone and war-torn societies, not all four levels will actually be functional, but the multi-level approach is designed precisely for such situations where one of the four levels is lacking or incompetent, namely, to compensate for the partial or prevent the complete breakdown of the monopoly of violence.

This suggestion is of course easier proposed than implemented. Numerous practical reasons and conceptual considerations can be listed to illustrate how difficult it would be to establish such a system. Not only is the local level in many societies haunted by corruption, dominated by criminal networks and suffering from weak public institutions; the nation state level is presently incapable in many countries; the regional organizations are often too inept to perform their missions, not just because of a lack of capabilities but more so because of deep-rooted political differences amongst their members; and at the global level, although the UN is the highest authority on peace and security, its activities are often heavily biased and contested. International norms are often selectively applied because the double standards of the members are all too obvious. Conflict regions are not only assisted with crisis prevention programmes but all too often they are at the same time at the mercy of the dominant powers.

Despite all these difficulties, such a proposal for a multi-level public monopoly of force points at an avenue out of the present crisis. The experience of the last four centuries in Europe demonstrates that security must be guaranteed by a monopoly of violence, and that privatizing or commercializing security will lead to the development of different zones of security and insecurity with effective protection only for the privileged who can afford to pay for their security.

Means for implementation

Militarily, if the aim is to control violence, force may have to be applied. But the criteria for the use or non-use of force need to be clearly spelled out in order to find an appropriate and effective compromise between the applications of massive firepower and doing nothing (Kaldor 1997). The International Commission on Intervention and State Sovereignty (2001) as well as the UN High-level Panel on Threats, Challenges and Change (2004) – extensively quoted in Chapter 3 – have given guidance as to under what circumstances force could possibly be applied. Their criteria demonstrate that the armed forces cannot and should not be used in every conflict, but they emphasize at the same time the need for protection, if necessary by military means, of people in need.

In *political* terms it must be clear that military intervention is not an alternative to diplomacy, negotiations, and conflict mediation or moderation. This was clearly spelled out, although often since then not practised, in the 1992 Agenda for Peace by Boutros Boutros-Ghali (1992). Despite the claim of governments, it is questionable if the military has only been used as a last resort, when political and diplomatic measures have failed. The political and economic changes in the process of globalization and their effects on conflicts have led to the new accent on quick military intervention. The cry for immediate military action is loud and Western governments often feel they have to do something to please their domestic audiences. The result for the population that this policy pretends to protect has not always been positive.

Arms control, especially small arms proliferation, disarmament and demobilization of combatants are prerequisites for the re-establishment of legitimate state force. Neglecting the 'revolving' door of combatants and mercenaries that wander from one conflict region to another and the weapons that are shipped from one war to the next is a guarantee for renewed fighting. There are both successful and unsuccessful examples of demobilization and reintegration of combatants in conflict-prone and post-conflict societies (Kingma 2000) as well as weapons collection programmes (BICC/SAND 2002). These experiences must be used in post-war reconstruction.

Economic reconstruction is a means to make societies (not necessarily the nation state) functioning again. If these efforts under the label of nation-building consist in practice only of economic liberalization in the international community's protectorates by reinforcing the old clientele structures and siphoning off scarce resources, continuation of fighting or re-emergence of conflict and the breaking of the fragile peace can be expected (Pugh 2004). A short- and medium-term measure is to demilitarize economic life, restrict the use of economic resources for violent purposes and to reallocate such resources for peace and development processes. This, of course, requires challenging the war and conflict profiteers.

Although the suggested multi-level public monopoly of violence is difficult to implement, a number of measures can be taken and policies introduced to aim for such a system.

Local level: The new wars arising from erosion or disintegration of the state is but one side of the coin. The other side is that the very emergence of the nation state has contributed in many cases to violence or has disrupted traditional local pre-state mechanisms for conflict management. Wars and large-scale violence have arisen as a result of state formation, as for example in today's Sudan where centuries-old conflict management mechanisms had previously been used (Deng 2000). The fact that Western researchers and media do not recognize such mechanisms working at the local level does not mean that they do not exist. Such traditional conflict regulations have their strengths and weaknesses. They are, amongst others, better suited to the local situation, offering inclusion and participation, but often disregard the essentials of democratic societies and might not be in conformity with Western standards of human rights (Trotha 1996, Böge 2004).

War-torn states may be dominated by warlords, organized crime, militias and unruly gangs of ex-combatants, mercenaries and corrupt officials, and so on – features to be found in countries like Afghanistan, Colombia, Sierra Leone, Liberia and many others. But such societies are also populated by citizens who form 'zones of peace' and 'islands of civility', as Kaldor (1999) has described them for the former Yugoslavia. The essential objective is not to exclusively address the nation state level. The long-term, bottom-up approach of co-operating with the non-violent factions in a society is of course more laborious and time consuming, but these processes might be a prerequisite for harnessing people's ambition for better times ahead. Civil society, although usually not well organized in war-torn societies, can be seen as the decisive societal pillar for reconstruction.

National level: Despite the predicted demise of the state and the dire experiences with weak, collapsed or failed states, it is still national governments which remain critical in international relations, whether it is a decision to fight war, intervene in conflicts, arm or disarm. Notwithstanding the intensification of globalization, the quest for global governance, international norm building and the growth of civil society, international policy remains decidedly state-centric.

Demilitarizing societies and the reform of the security sector have been described earlier as a necessary condition for peace and development. Such programmes need to be implemented chiefly at the national level. Development economists and politicians still have a great reluctance to engage in security sector reform, especially with the military. To the critics it still smacks somewhat of the old-style military assistance. To expect peace and to stabilize a society without touching the security-sector is wishful thinking. Since the military, police and judiciary are the ultimate agents of the organized institutions of state force it is essential to make them efficient and accountable (Ball *et al.* 2003, Brzoska 2003, OECD/DAC 2004, Wulf 2004a).

Regional level: The experience of UN peacekeeping during the 1990s, with partly catastrophic results, has led to the emphasizing of regional responsibilities for peace and security. Given their present structure, institutions such as the African Union (AU), the Organization of American States (OAS), the European Union (EU), the Association of South-East Asian Nations (ASEAN), the Organisation for Security and Co-operation in Europe (OSCE) and others are not in a position to apply the monopoly of violence effectively.

They suffer, in some regional organizations more than in others, from four weaknesses which need to be overcome to establish a functional multi-level monopoly of force: (1) The concept of the function of regional organizations with respect to the sovereignty of nation states remains in most cases contested. Delegating traditional nation state authority to a regional body is jealously guarded and opposed by most governments. (2) Similarly the division of labour among regional organizations (especially when there are geographically overlapping organizations such as the EU, OSCE and NATO or the AU and ECOWAS or SADC) is unclear and often competitive. (3) Another weakness is the existence of fundamental political differences in many organizations. Often a compromise, addressing emergencies, wars and other regional concerns is based on the lowest common denominator and mere lip service. (4) The final weakness is the absence of adequate institutions to implement decisions, for example to execute sanctions, and the lack of military muscle to project force if required in a crisis situation. The African Union (AU) is a case in point. Requesting coalitions of the willing to do the job is a natural reaction in such a situation. Such coalitions, however, can only be formed on an ad hoc basis and make long lasting and democratically legitimized structures impossible.

Global level: Peacekeeping as a global governance concept is not neutral. As long as it is subjugated by the dominating economic and military powers it serves primarily as a tool for problem-fixing or band-aid of the existing world system, even though such peace operations might be morally justified. The functioning of the international system, and with it the multi-level monopoly of violence, depends on the enhancement of international norms; a world order in which nation state sovereignty is limited in accordance to the existence of a higher-level executive authority and regionally and globally accepted legal norms (Weiss 2000, Messner and Nuscheler 1997). Despite these deficits in developing such norms there is no realistic alternative to the UN, even though there are specific limitations in creating the globally required and democratically legitimized monopoly of violence.

Conclusion

We can expect effective and sustainable peace processes only if the structural causes of conflict are removed, if political primacy over the military is established, if there is respect for traditional forms of conflict regulation, if the non-violent groups in conflict-endemic societies are strengthened, and if good governance and human security are observed at the local, national, regional and global levels. It is politically extremely problematic to give up or undermine the control over the armed forces and private military companies at the national level before new international control instruments are created. The established and endangered monopoly of violence must be reformed in order not to leave the internationalization and privatization of war and peace to market forces or uncontrolled non-state actors. The significant difference between outsourcing postal or railway services and outsourcing military or police functions is of a qualitative nature, and this is the public monopoly of violence. This ought not to be given up light-heartedly.

Establishing sound civil–military relations in democracies is a process to find a balance between complete civil control and the necessary autonomy of the armed forces so that they can perform professionally. The neo-liberal concept to introduce the forces of the market into the armed forces damages this complicated institutional balance. This leads to weakening the role and importance of public institutions. The security sector was already in the past a sector with insufficient parliamentary oversight; parliamentarians will have even fewer rights and possibilities when the military is primarily geared towards international tasks and when the outsourced military missions are beyond the control of parliamentarians.

Global governance, an accountable, globally oriented policy, is far from being implemented in the security sector. This has not changed after the call for a global fight against terrorism after the attacks of 9/11. Military resources are now available on a contract basis in the global market. Experts for almost any military job wait to be called. Economic power can now be quicker put into military power than before. Armies, created according to the nation state model of Max Weber, are intended for a general political objective: to ensure the security of the citizens. This function is now partly delegated to profit-oriented units. The nation state will not disappear completely, but private military companies work both for and against public interests. Can the present trend of leaving the instruments of war and violence and the control over them at the disposal of non-state actors be stopped? Will the armed forces sometime in the future fight against the citizens of their home country who serve in military companies on the other side of the front, as seemed to happen in the war between Ethiopia and Eritrea as mentioned in the preface of this book? Especially in democratic countries citizens must ensure that parliamentary control over the security sector will not be undercut and damaged by the privatizing of military functions.

Annex

Table A.1 Private military companies

Name	Country of origin	Website	Products and services	Major customers / areas of service	Comments
AD Consultancy	UK	www.adporta.com	Risk and threat assessment, surveillance and counter surveillance, escort drills, control and restraint training, firearms certification, close protection, body guards, residential and premises security, aviation security, close quarter combat	US Government, Home Office, Contracts in Iraq, Oil & Gas Companies, Ministry of Defence, Embassies	Subsidiary of AD Porta Group
Aegis Defence Services Ltd.	UK	www.aegisdef-webservices.com	Threat and risk analysis, close protection, studies on asymmetric threats, specialist military, police and intelligence training, overt and covert	US Government, Iraq	Contract to coordinate all security firms in Iraq ($293m.)
AirScan	USA	www.airscan.com	Military support and training, air combat support, military support to rebels (Uganda), air surveillance	Angola / Angolan government, Uganda (1997–1998) / Rebels, Latin America, Iraq	
AKE Limited	UK	www.akegroup.com	Hostile regions training, location security audits, body armour, medical audits, assistance and evacuation, intelligence and cultural briefings, risk and intelligence information	Iraq	
Al Hamza	Pakistan	www.alhamzagroup.com	Shipbreaking	Iraq	

Company	Country	Website	Services	Clients	Notes
AMA Associates Limited	UK	www.ama-assoc.co.uk	Security consultancy, aviation security, maritime security, specialist services, security training	UK government	
American International Security	USA	www.aisc-corp.com	Executive protection and vulnerability assessment	Iraq	
Applied Marine Technology Inc.	USA	www.amti.net	Threat analyses, exercises and drills, maritime tactical response, international and homeland security, information systems and communications	US Dep. of Defense, Dep. of State, Dep. of Homeland Security	240 employees
Archangel	USA	www.antiterrorconsultants.org	Foreign and domestic threat analyses, tactical training, VIP protection service, anti-terror preparation and response training	US businesses, government agencies, law enforcement departments	
Armor Group	UK	www.armorgroup.com	Global security risk management, security training and services, mine clearance	UN, NGO's, oil and gas industry, Dep. of State, Dep. of Defense, Iraq	Part of Armor Holding, 5500 employees, US$150 m. turnover
BDM International	USA		Military advice and training	Dep. of Defense	
Bechtel	USA	www.bechtel.com	Infrastructure reconstruction	Iraq, Dep. of State	With Halliburton largest contractor in Iraq, total turnover US$17 b.

Continued

Table A.1 Continued

Name	Country of origin	Website	Products and services	Major customers / areas of service	Comments
Beni Tal	Israel	www.beni-tal.co.il	Special security arrangements with sensitive equipment, security and investigative counselling, military and civil training, weapons training, body guards		
BH Defense	USA	www.bhdefense.com	Secure warehousing, logistics, support, convoy escort	CPA Iraq	
Blackheart International	USA	www.1stoptacticalgear.com	Equipment procurement services and training	Iraq, Afghanistan	
Blackwater	USA	www.blackwaterusa.com	Military training, weapons training, security consulting, air charter and special cargo transport, convoy protection	Dep. of Defense, Dep. of State, Dep. of Transportation, Iraq	
Blue Sky	UK	www.blueskysc.org	Intelligence gathering and analyses, VIP protection, surveillance and counter-surveillance, maritime security and detection, special forces	South East Asia, Southern Africa, West Africa, Kuwait, Afghanistan, Lebanon, Humanitarian Organizations	
Booz Allen Hamilton	USA	www.valuebasedmanagement.net	Management and technology consulting	Dep. of Defense, Govt. of Iraq	
BritAm Defense	UK	www.britamdefence.com	Security and risk management, aviation security, military training, maritime services	Iraq, UK company executives	

Company	Country	Website	Services	Clients	Notes
CACI Systems	USA	www.caci.com	IT solutions for defense and intelligence, interrogation, translation	US government, USA, Iraq	9400 employees, total turnover US$843 m.
Cape International			Military training, mining facilities security		
CastleForce Consultancy	UK		Security services in Iraq	Iraq	
Centurion Risk Assessment Services	UK	www.centurion-riskservices.co.uk	Training for dangerous work in extreme conditions	Media, NGOs, Humanitarians, Iraq	
Cochise Consultancy	USA	www.cochiseconsult.com	Security and VIP protection, ammunition clearing	US government, companies, Iraq	
Control Risk Group	UK	www.crg.com	Intelligence gathering, security and crime prevention services, mining facilities security, armed guards	Sierra Leone (1995), Iraq	500 ex-British military personnel
Combat Support Associates	USA	www.csakuwait.com	Comprehensive combat support services	US Army, Kuwait	Joint Venture of: AECOM Government Services, Research Analyses and Maintenance and SMI
Critical Intervention Service	USA	www.cisworldservices.org	Protection and investigative services	Iraq	
Custer Battles	USA	www.custerbattles.com	Business intelligence, global risk consulting, due diligence, litigation support, logistics	Iraq	

Continued

Table A.1 Continued

Name	Country of origin	Website	Products and services	Major customers / areas of service	Comments
CTU Consulting and Management	USA	www.ctuconsulting.com	Security consulting services, training services, operational services, close protection	Iraq	
Decision Strategies	UK	www.decision-strategies.com			Merged with Vance International
Defense Systems Ltd, (DSL)	UK		Military advice and training, security and crime prevention services, humanitarian assistance (UNDP Sierra Leone), guarding embassies	Uganda, Bahrain, Abu Dhabi, Angola, Ecuador, DCR, US Government, UN	Purchased in 1995 by Armor Holding, 4000 employees
Diligence Middle East	USA	www.diligencemiddleeast.com	Select security services, commercial intelligence gathering, due diligence, investigations	Iraq, Yemen, Saudi-Arabia,	Subsidiary of Diligence LCC
Defense Technology Systems (DTS) Security	USA	www.dtssecurity.com	Electronic security systems, physical security products	Iraq	
DynCorp	USA	www.csc.com	Intelligence gathering, logistical support	Afghanistan, Middle East / US Government	Subsidiary of CSC, main contractor for law enforcement support with 1000 civilians in Iraq

Company	Country	Website	Services	Clients	Notes
Eagle Group International	USA	www.eaglegroupint.com	Information technology security, military medical systems, fleet management	Iraq, UAE	Subcontractor of Vinnell in Iraq
EFFACT	Germany	www.effact.i110.de	Military training	Company executives	Subsidiary of EUBSA
EG & G Technical	USA	www.egginc.com	Asset management, IT, safety compliance	US Army, US Navy, NASA, Dep. of Justice	Subsidiary of URS, USA, turnover US$900 m.
EOD Technology	USA	www.eodt.com	Risk assessment, demining, disposal of unexploded ordnance	CPA, Dep. of Defense, Iraq, Kuwait, Dubai	
Erinys	UK	www.erinysinternational.com	Guarding oil pipelines, security services and consultancy, guard force management, site security, transportation and logistics security	US Government, CPA, Iraq	14,000 Iraqi Security guards
EUBSA	USA	www.eubsa.com	Security training	Company executives	
Evergreen Helicopters	USA	www.evergreenaviation.com	Security services, search and rescue	UN / Angola, Kuwait, Somalia, Yugoslavia	
Executive Outcomes (EO)	South Africa		Combat and operational support	Uganda, Botswana, Sierra Leone, Angola, Zambia, Ethiopia, Namibia, Lesotho	Company dissolved
Genric	UK	www.genric.co.uk	Risk assessment, close protection, training, surveillance, counter-terrorism, residence protection	UN, US government, Iraq	

Continued

Table A.1 Continued

Name	Country of origin	Website	Products and services	Major customers / areas of service	Comments
GeoLink			Military support (Zaire)		
Global Marine Security Systems	USA	www.gmssco.com	Port facility security assessment, ship security assessment		Part of the Hart Group
Global Risk International	UK	www.globalrisk.uk.com	Crisis management, close protection, residential protection, intelligence services, surveillance, electronic countermeasures, specialist training		
Global Risk Strategies	UK	www.globalrsl.com	Security, logistics and facilitation services	Companies, UN, US government, Iraq	1500 employees, 500 ex-members of British Army Gurkha regiment
Global Security Source	USA	www.globalsecuritysource.com	Security and protection services	US government, Iraq	300 positions offered in Iraq
Gormly International	USA	www.gormlyintl.com	Security consulting, anti-piracy countermeasures, counter-terrorism		
Gray Security	South Africa	www.graysecurity.com	Security and crime prevention services		Part of Group 4 Securicor
Group 4 Falck	UK	www.group4falck.com	Security and crime prevention services, mining facilities security, air marshals	Sierra Leone (1995), Iraq	Merger with Securicor and Wackenhut

Company	Country	Website	Services	Location/Clients	Notes
Gurkha Security Guards	UK		Combat and operational support, security and crime prevention services, military training, mine protection	Sierra Leone, Republic of Sierra Leone Defence Forces (RSLDF)	Connected to Global Marine Security Systems
Hart Group	UK/Bermuda	www.hartgrouplimited.com	Risk management		
Henderson Risk	UK	www.hrlgroup.org	Risk assessment, deployment of security professionals in high risk areas	Iraq	
Hill & Associates	Hong Kong	www.hill-assoc.com	Executive protection, information services	Iraq	
Ibis Air International (Capricorn)	South Africa		Air logistical support, combat air support, mine clearance, facilities security, establishing special rapid reaction police unit	Angola (1995–1996) Sierra Leone (1995–1996)	
ICI International Charter Incorporated	USA	www.icioregon.com	Aviation and security	Liberia, Sierra Leone, Haiti, US Dep. of Defense	
ICP Group Limited	UK	www.icpgroup.ltd.uk	Protection services, security equipment, logistics management	Iraq	
Intercon Consulting Services	Canada	www.interconsecurity.com	Military training, mining facilities security, protective services, protective hardware	Zaire / DRC	

Continued

Table A.1 Continued

Name	Country of origin	Website	Products and services	Major customers / areas of service	Comments
International Defence and Security			Military support, seizure and security, military training and support to rebels	Angola (1997–1998), Zaire (1997) Kabila	
International Rescue Squad	Germany	www.i-r-s@web.de	Unconventional warfare, anti-terror protection, anti-drug service, military training		Web no longer available
IRIS			Military support to UNITA? and DRC	Angola (1998) DRC (1998)	
ISI Iraq	Iraq	www.isiiraq.com	Object protection, security guards	Iraq	
Janusian Security Risk Management	UK	www.janusian.com	Corporate security analysis	Iraq	Part of The Risk Advisory Group
Kellogg Brown & Root	USA	www.halliburton.com	Logistics, infrastructure	US Dept. of Defense, Balkans, Iraq	
Kroll Security International	USA	www.krollworldwide.com	Intelligence gathering, close protection	USAID, Iraq	
L-3 Communications	USA	www.l-3com.com	Military communications, information security systems, intelligence, surveillance and reconnaissance systems		
Levdan	Israel		Military advice and training, arms procurement, presidential guard and armed forces training	Congo-Brazzaville	

Company	Country	Website	Services	Clients/Location	Employees/Notes
LifeGuard Management			Security and crime prevention, military training and support, intelligence gathering, counter-insurgency operations	Sierra Leone (1996 / 1998)	South African, Namibian, Angolan, Zimbabwean employees
ManTech International	USA		Telecommunications	US armed forces in Iraq	
Marine Protection Services			Policing of fisheries, tax collection for Sierra Leonean government	Sierra Leone / Government	
Meteoric Tactical Solutions	South Africa		Specialized training programmes, VIP protection, asset protection, risk management	Iraq	
Meyer & Associates	USA	www.meyerglobalforce.com	Military training, close protection, technical surveillance, special operations	USA, Central and South America, Philippines, Middle East, Iraq	
Military Professional Resources Incorporated, (MPRI)	USA	www.mpri.com	Military advice and training	US Government, Angola, Liberia, Croatia, Colombia, Macedonia, Nigeria, Iraq	Subsidiary of L-3, 700 permanent and 12,000 short-term employees
MVM	USA	www.mvminc.com	Training, security, management consulting	US government and companies	4300 employees
MZM	USA	www.mzminc.com	Interpreter and linguists support	US government, Iraq	
Near East Security	USA		Guarding embassies, museums, and so on in Baghdad, witness protection	US government, Iraq	250 employees

Continued

Table A.1 Continued

Name	Country of origin	Website	Products and services	Major customers / areas of service	Comments
New Korea Total Service	South Korea	www.nkts.co.kr	Military and police training, guarding services	Iraq	
Northbridge Services Group Ltd	USA	www.northbridgeservices.com	Weapons and weapons platform selection, operational and intelligence support, strategic communications	US government, Iraq	
Olive Security	UK	www.olivesecurity.com	Military training, close protection, residential security	CPA, Bechtel, Iraq	
Omega Support Ltd	Hong Kong		Military support to UNITA, military support against rebels in Zaire, mining facilities security	Angola, Zaire	Formerly Strategic Concepts Pty Ltd
Omega Training Group	USA	www.omegatraining.com	Training soldiers in Iraq	CPA, US Government, Iraq	Subcontractor of Vinnell in Iraq
Optimal Solution Services	Australia		Vigilance and security alert response	Iraq	
Optronics	Germany	www.us-statisten.de	Military training	US armed forces Germany	
Orion Management	USA	www.orionomi.com	Profession investigative services	Iraq	

Company	Country	Website	Services	Locations/Clients	Notes
Overseas Security and Strategic Information	USA		Protection of VIPs, convoy escort, training of security personnel	Iraq	
Pacific Architects and Engineers (PAE)		www.paechl.com	Logistical support, logistical support for peace keeping	Sierra Leone East Timor (UN)	
Panacec Corporate Dynamics			Military support		
Parsons	USA	www.parsons.com	Security consulting, rebuilding military bases	Iraq	
Pilgrims Group	UK	www.pilgrimsgroup.co.uk	Security services, risk management	Iraq	
Pistris	USA	www.pistris.com	Military training, equipment procurement, maritime force protection, security assessment, protective services	Iraq	
RamOPS Risk	USA	www.ramops.com	Security consulting, threat assessments, contingency planning	Iraq	Website not available
Ronco Consulting Corp.	USA	www.ronconsulting.com	Limited military training for Rwandan forces, mine clearance activities	Mozambique, Rwanda, Rwandan Patriotic Front, US government, Iraq	
Rubicon International Services	UK	www.rubicon-international.com	Personnel protection, asset protection	Iraq	
Science Applications International (SAIC)	USA	www.saic.com	Counter-terrorism, explosive ordnance disposal	US government, Dep. of Homeland Security, Iraq	Subcontractor of Vinnell in Iraq, 40,000 employees

Continued

Table A.1 Continued

Name	Country of origin	Website	Products and services	Major customers / areas of service	Comments
SafeNet (formerly Stabilco)	South Africa		Military support to UNITA, military support and training against Kabila, body guards	DRC	Owner: Mauritz le Roux, formerly EO
Safetynet Associates	USA	www.johngtarsikesjr.com	Military training, technical support		
Saladin Security	UK	www.saladin-security.com	Intelligence gathering, body guards, crisis management	Iraq	
Sandline International	UK	www.sandline.com	Combat and operational support, arms supply, military training	Sierra Leone Government, Zaire, Papua New Guinea	Company closure April 2004
Saracen International	South Africa		Mining facilities security	Angola, FINA	
Saracen Uganda	Uganda		Mining facilities security	Uganda (1996)	
SCG International Risk	USA	www.scgonline.net	Security, intelligence, technical and training solutions	Iraq	
SOA (Special Ops Associates)	USA	www.specialopsassociates.com	Special operations services	USA, Afghanistan	
SOC-SMG	USA	www.soc-smg.com	International force protection, convoy security operations, security consulting and risk assessment, surveillance	CIA, FBI, DEA, Dep. of Defense, Iraq	
Southern Cross Security	Sierra Leone	www.southerncross-security.com	Security management, guards, technical service, close protection, marine control and surveillance	Sierra Leone Ministry of Marine Resources, Ministry of Finance, UN World Food program, UNAMSIL mission, ICRC	

Company	Country	Website	Services	Locations	Notes
Steele Foundation	USA	www.steelefoundation.com	VIP Protection, armored vehicles, convoy security, force protection, worksite security, security planning	Iraq	
TASK International	UK	www.task-int.com	Security training, maritime security, military training, police training	Cyprus, Malaysia, Trinidad, Jamaica, Nigeria (presidential guards), UAE (special forces)	
Titan Corporation	USA	www.titan.com	Homeland Security, transformational programmes, airborne intelligence, technical services, providers of translators	Dep. of Defense, US Army, US Navy, UAE, Iraq	
The Sandi Group	USA	www.thesandigroup.com	Security guards, bodyguards, private police armed and uniformed	Iraq	Trained by DynCorp
TOR International	UK	www.torinternational.com	Risk reduction, security management, maritime security, military and police training, specialist equipment	Africa, Iraq, Asia	
Triple Canopy	USA	www.triplecanopy.com	Executive protection, site security, convoy security, security management, logistical support, medical support	Iraq	
Trojan Securities	USA	www.trojansecurities.com	Specialist training, counter-surveillance, executive protection, maritime security	Iraq, Ecuador	
UK Defence Services	UK	www.ukdefence.co.uk	VIP protection, site security, explosive ordnance disposal, maritime security		
Unity Resources	Australia	www.unityresourcesgroup.com	Protection, hostile area response	Iraq	

Continued

Table A.1 Continued

Name	Country of origin	Website	Products and services	Major customers / Areas of service	Comments
USA Environmental	USA	www.usa-environmental.com	Ordnance and explosive supplies, destruction of unexploded ordnance	Iraq	
Vance International	USA	www.vancesecurity.com	Executive protection, uniformed guards, security consulting, asset protection, education and training	Mexico, South America, Multinational Organizations, Iraq	Merged with Decision Strategies, Unit of SPX Corporation
Vinnell	USA	www.vinnell.com	Military advice and training	Saudi Arabia, Malaysia, Iraq, Dep. of Defence	Subsidiary of Northrop Grumman
Wade-Boyd and Associates	USA	www.wade-boyd.com	Armed close protection, undercover operators, K-9 dogs for explosive detection	US government, Iraq, Kuwait	

Sources: This table is based primarily on the newspaper archive of the author and the websites of companies. The services of Sebastian Wachendorf, BICC, for an internet search for this appendix is gratefully acknowledged. All websites were accessed 20 October 2004.

Notes

Preface

1. Quoted in *Financial Times* 25 July 2003, 10.

Introduction: New Wars and the Bumpy Ride to Peace Building

2. The terms bottom-up and top-down are used by Mandel (2001, 137).
3. I use the terms 'monopoly of violence' and 'monopoly of force' interchangeably.
4. I will not discuss the various different terms that are being used, although some reflect different approaches and concepts to explain these violent conflicts.
5. This agenda does not exclude the neoconservatives' quick resort to government action in order to apply financial sanctions when a situation such as 9/11 requires tight controls.

1 Internationalizing Armed Forces and their Deployment

6. I would like to point out that many military functions and planning capabilities within the NATO alliance are integrated. Nevertheless, the soldiers serving in such functions still remain under their various national authorities and will eventually return to their own national forces.
7. Sorensen (2000) uses the term 'selective defense'.
8. The EU is somewhat of an exception. The European Parliament does have certain limited rights (especially as regards requiring information and some budgetary rights) in foreign and security policy, as I detail in Chapter 5.

2 Privatizing Power: The 'Lean' State and the Armed Forces

9. I address this type of privatization here only as a reference point since much has been written about this aspect already.
10. Privatization of police is not addressed in this book either.
11. A partly different classification is given by Singer (2001/2002 and 2003).
12. For a list of private military companies see Annex.
13. Possible regulatory mechanisms are discussed in Chapter 9.
14. The Convention is reprinted in UNHCR (2002, Annex II, 33–38).
15. UN General Assembly Resolution 44/34 of 4 December 1989. It is a further development of the Additional Protocol of the Geneva convention.

16. The following countries have ratified the treaty: Azerbaijan, Barbados, Belarus, Cameroon, Croatia, Cyprus, Georgia, Italy, Libya, Maldives, Mauritania, Qatar, Saudi Arabia, Senegal, Seychelles, Surinam, Togo, Turkmenistan, Uruguay and Uzbekistan. Nine other countries have signed but not ratified the treaty (UN ECOSOC, 2002, 26).
17. The Green Paper of the UK Government (2002, 19) raises this issue too.

3 With the Highest Authority: UN-Peacekeeping Missions

18. A somewhat different classification is offered by Findlay (2002, 3–7); also Gareis (2002, 19–25).

4 South Africa: From Pariah to Regional Cop

19. The original engagement of South Africa, especially Nelson Mandela's activities to facilitate the peace process, was based on a mandate of the OAU. After the reorganization of the OAU and the transfer of authority to the AU, South Africa's peace mission in Burundi was mandated by the AU and eventually by the UN.

5 European Union: Civil Power in Camouflage

20. In this section I draw on a publication by Hauswedell and Wulf (2004).
21. In this part of the chapter I draw on Wulf (2004b).
22. 1999 prices and exchange rates (BICC 2004).
23. For the reporting of military expenditure data to the UN see United Nations, Department of Disarmament Affairs. (www.un.org/disarmament).
24. At the time ESDP was still called ESDI = European Security and Defence Identity.

6 Co-operation, Competition and Collateral Damage in Humanitarian Interventions

25. The latter use of the military in natural disasters is not being dealt with in this book. For the lack of democratic control in international military deployments and the implications for international law see Chapter 3.
26. I use the terms humanitarian organizations and relief organizations synonymously in this book.
27. Headline in the weekly *Die Zeit*, no. 19/1999, quoted in Eberwein and Peter Runge (2002, 10).
28. Correspondence of the author with the UN Department of Peacekeeping Operations in June 2004.
29. Telephone, written and personal interviews of the author in mid-2004 at the UN and several relief organizations.
30. Correspondence with the author of 19 August 2004.

31. A copy of the letter is with the author. The relief organization has asked not to be identified.
32. This information is based on correspondence with the author of 19 July 2004 and an interview on 10 August 2004.
33. Information based on a meeting with ICRC representatives in the margins of a conference on 5 October 2004.

8 Rent-a-Soldier: Privatization in the US and UK Armed Forces

34. Extracts of the parliamentary debate and comments from Sandline under www.sandline.com/site/, accessed 2 April 2004.
35. See especially the two statements on 'Private military companies – independent or regulated?' and 'Should the activities of private military companies be transparent?' (www.sandline.com/site, accessed 2 April 2004).

Bibliography

Adams, Thomas. 1999. The New Mercenaries and the Privatization of Conflict. *Parameters*, vol. XXIX, no. 2 (Summer), 103–116.

Adebajo, Adekeye and Christopher Landsberg. 2003. South Africa and Nigeria as Regional Hegemons. In Baregu, Mwesiga and Christopher Landsberg (Eds). 2003. *From Cape to Congo. Southern Africa's Evolving Security Challenges*, Boulder, Co and London: Lynne Rienner, 171–203.

Adolph, Robert B. 1992. Strategic Rationale for SOF (Special Operations Forces). *Military Review*, vol. 72, no. 4 (April), 36–46.

Anderson, Mary B. 1999. Do no Harm. *How Aid Can Support Peace – or War*. Boulder, Co and London: Lynne Rienner.

Andreas, Peter and Richard Price. 2001. From War Fighting to Crime Fighting: Transforming the American National Security State. *International Studies Review*, vol. 3, no. 3 (Fall), 31–52.

Annan, Kofi, 1999. Two Concepts of Sovereignty. *The Economist*, 18 September.

Aron, Raymond. 1986. Frieden und Krieg. Frankfurt/Main: Fischer Verlag.

Assembly of Western European Union/The Interim European Security and Defence Assembly. 2001. *National Parliamentary Scrutiny of Intervention Abroad by Armed Forces Engaged in International Missions: The Current Position in Law* (Document A/1762), 4 December.

Australian Broadcasting Corporation. 2000. Dogs of War, 18 May, manuscript. (www.sandline.com, accessed 15 August 2004).

Auswärtiges Amt. 2000. Protokoll der Klausurtagung des Koordinierungsausschusses. 'Humanitäre Hilfe' Protokoll 20 June (unpublished).

Avant, Deborah D. 2000. Privatizing Military Training. *Foreign Policy*, vol. 5, no. 17 (June). (www.foreignpolicy-infocus.org/briefsvol5/v5n17mil_body. html).

Ball, Nicole and J. 'Kayode Fayemi, Funmi Olonisakin, Rocklyn Williams, with Martin Rupia. 2003. Governance in the Security Sector. In Walle, Nicolas van de and Nicole Ball (Eds). 2003. *Beyond Structural Adjustment*. Basingstoke: Palgrave, 263–304.

Ballentine, Karen and Jake Sherman (Eds). 2003. *The Political Economy of Armed Conflict*. Boulder, Co. and London: Lynne Rienner.

Baum, Dan. 2003. Nation Builder for Hire. *New York Times Magazine*, 22 June 2003.

Bellamy, Christopher. 2001. Combining Combat Readiness and Compassion. *NATO Review*, web edition, vol. 49, no. 2 (Summer), 9–11.

Berdal, Mats and David M. Malone (Eds). 2000. *Greed and Grievances: Economic Agendas in Civil Wars*. Boulder, Co and London: Lynne Rienner.

Berman, Eric G. 2002. African Regional Organisations' Peace Operations. Developments and Challenges. *African Security Review*, vol. 11, no. 4, 33–44.

Berman, Eric and Katie Sams. 2000. *Peacekeeping in Africa: Capabilities and Culpabilities*. Geneva: UNIDIR.

Bertram, Christoph, Joachim Schild, Francois Heisbourg and Yves Boyer. 2002. *Starting Over*. Berlin: SWP-Studien: Stiftung Wissenschaft und Politik, November.

Bland, Douglas L. 1999. A Unified Theory of Civil–Military Relations. *Armed Forces & Society*, vol. 26, no. 1 (Fall), 7–26.

Böge, Volker. 2004. *Muschelgeld und Blutdiamanten. Traditionale Konfliktbearbeitung in zeitgenössischen Gewaltkonflikten.* Hamburg: Schriften des Deutschen Übersee-Instituts.

Böge, Volker and Wolf-Christian Paes. 2004. Rolle der Privatwirtschaft in bewaffneten Konflikten, Background paper for Gesellschaft für Technische Zusammenarbeit (GTZ) (unpublished).

Bonn International Center for Conversion. 1996–2004. *Conversion Survey (annual).* Baden-Baden: Nomos Verlag.

Bonn International Center for Conversion/SAND (Program on Security and Development). 2002. Tackling Small Arms and Light Weapons, A Practical Guide for Collection and Destruction. Bonn, February. (www.bicc.de/publications/books/guide_smallarms/guide_smallarms.pdf, accessed 25 October).

Bono, Giovanna and Jocelyn Mawdsley. 2002. Bridging the Accountability Gap in European Security and Defence Policy. Paper presented at the UACES 32nd Annual Conference and 7th Research Conference, Belfast, September.

Born, Hans. 2004. The Use of Force under International Auspices: Strengthening Parliamentary Accountability. In Born, Hans and Heiner Hänggi (Eds). 2004. *The 'Double Democratic Deficit'.* Ashgate: Aldershot, 203–215.

Born, Hans and Heiner Hänggi (Eds). 2004. *The 'Double Democratic Deficit'.* Ashgate: Aldershot.

Born, Hans and Marlene Urscheler. 2004. Parliamentary Accountability of Multinational Peace Support Operations: A Comparative Perspective. In Born, Hans and Heiner Hänggi (Eds). 2004. The 'Double Democratic Deficit', Ashgate: Aldershot, 53–72.

Boshoff, Henri. 2003. *Burundi: The African Union's First Mission.* (http://iss.co.za/AF/current/Burundimay03.htm, accessed 19 February 2004).

Boutros-Ghali, Boutros. 1992. *An Agenda for Peace: Preventive Diplomacy, Peacemaking and Peace-keeping.* New York: United Nations.

Brock, Lothar. 2003. Humanitäre Hilfe – eine Geisel der Außen- und Sicherheitspolitik? In Medico International (Ed.) 2003. *Macht und Ohnmacht der Hilfe*, Frankfurt/Main: Medico Report 25, 58–63.

Brock, Lothar. 2004. Alt und neu, Krieg und Gewalt. In Kurtenbach, Sabine and Peter Lock (Eds). 2004. *Kriege als (Über) Lebenswelten.* Bonn: Dietz Verlag, 11–19.

Brzoska, Michael. 2002. Von der 'Friedensdividende' zur 'Terrordividende'? In Schoch, Bruno, Corinna Hauswedell, Christoph Weller, Ulrich Ratsch and Reinhard Mutz (Eds). *Friedensgutachten 2002*, Münster/Hamburg/London: Lit Verlag, 167–176.

Brzoska, Michael. 2003. *Development Donors and the Concept of Security Sector Reform.* Geneva: DCAF, Occasional papers 4, November. (http://www.dcaf.ch/publications/Occasional_Papers/4.pdf, accessed 7 November 2004).

Bundesministerium für wirtschaftliche Zusammenarbeit und Entwicklung. 2004. *Zum Verhältnis von entwicklungspolitischen und militärischen Antworten auf neue sicherheitspolitische Herausforderungen.* Bonn: BMZ-Diskurs, no. 1.

Buzan, Barry. 2002. Who May We Bomb? In Booth, Ken and Tim Dunne (Eds). 2002. *Worlds in Collision: Terror and the Future of Global Order.* New York: Palgrave Macmillan, 85–94.

Buzan, Barry, Ole Weaver and Jaap de Wilde. 1998. *Security: A New Framework for Analysis*. Boulder, Co and London: Lynne Rienner.

Cawthra, Gavin. 2003. Security Transformation in Post-Apartheid South Africa. In Cawthra, Gavin and Robin Luckham (Eds). 2003. *Governing Insecurity*. London: Zed Books, 31–56.

Cawthra, Gavin. 2004. A Conceptual Framework for Regional Security. In Field, Shannon (Ed.). 2004. *Peace in Africa*. Johannesburg: Institute for Global Dialogue, 27–40.

Cawthra, Gavin and Robin Luckham (Eds). 2003. *Governing Insecurity*. London: Zed Books.

Cilliers, Jakkie and Peggy Mason (Eds). 1999. *Peace, Profit and Plunder? The Privatisation of Security in War-torn African Societies*. Pretoria: Institute for Security Studies.

Cleaver, Gerry and Roy May. 1998. African perspectives: regional peacekeeping. In Furley, Oliver and Roy May (Eds). 1998. *Peacekeeping in Africa*. Ashgate: Aldershot, 29–48.

Cohen, Eliot A. 2001. The Unequal Dialogue: The Theory and Reality of Civil–Military Relations and the Use of Force. In Feaver, Peter D. and Richard H. Kohn (Eds). 2001. *Soldiers and Civilians*, Cambridge, MA: MIT Press, 429–458.

Collier, Paul. 2000a. Doing Well out of War: An Economic Perspective. In Berdal, Mats and David M. Malone (Eds). 2000. *Greed and Grievances: Economic Agendas in Civil Wars*. Boulder, Co and London: Lynne Rienner, 91–111.

Collier, Paul. 2000b. Economic causes of civil conflict and their implications for policy. Washington, DC: World Bank, 15 June.

Collier, Paul and Anke Hoeffler. 2001. Greed and Grievance in Civil War. (http://www.worldbank.org/research/conflict/papers/greedgrievance_23oct.pdf, accessed 8 November 2004).

Collier, Paul and Anke Hoeffler. 2002. On the Incidence of Civil War in Africa. *Journal of Conflict Resolution*, vol. 46, no. 1, 13–28.

Collier, Paul, V. L. Elliot, Havard Hegre, Anke Hoeffler, Marta Reynal-Querol and Nicholas Sambanis. 2003. *Breaking the Conflict Trap*. World Bank, Policy Research Report. Washington, DC: Oxford University Press.

Commission on Global Governance. 1995. *Our Global Neighbourhood: The Report of the Commission on Global Governance*. Oxford: Oxford University Press.

Dahl, Robert A. 1999. Can International Organization be Democratic? A Skeptic's View. In Shapiro, Ian and Casiano Hacker-Cordón (Eds). 1999. *Democracy's Edges*. Cambridge: Cambridge University Press, 19–36.

Damrosch, Lori Fisler. 2003. The Interface of National Constitutional Systems with International Law and Institutions on Using Military Forces: Changing Trends in Executive and Legislative Powers. In Ku, Charlotte and Harold K. Jacobson (Eds). 2003. *Democratic Accountability and the Use of Force in International Law*. Cambridge: Cambridge University Press, 39–60.

Davis, Neil V. 2000. Outsourcing, Privatisation and Other Forms of Private Sector Involvement: Conditions and Requisites. Unpublished conference paper at the Euro-Atlantic Partnership Council Conference on Defence Reform, Defence Industry and the State, George Marshall Centre and NATO in Wildbad Kreuth, August.

Debiel, Tobias. 2002. Haben Krisenregionen eine Chance auf tragfähigen Frieden? In Debiel Tobias (Ed.). 2002. *Der zerbrechliche Frieden*. Bonn: Dietz Verlag, 20–63.

Debiel, Tobias. 2003. *UN-Friedensoperationen in Afrika*. Bonn: Dietz Verlag.

Debiel, Tobias and Franz Nuscheler (Eds). 1996. *Der neue Interventionismus*.

Humanitäre Einmischung zwischen Anspruch und Wirklichkeit. Bonn: Dietz Verlag.

Deng, Francis M. 2000. Reaching Out: A Dinka Principle of Conflict Management. In Zartman, I. William (Ed.). 2000. *Traditional Cures for Modern Conflicts, African Conflict 'Medicine'*. Boulder, Co and London: Lynne Rienner, 95–126.

Deutscher Bundestag. 2004. *Jahresabrüstungsbericht 2003*. Deutscher Bundestag. Drucksache 15/3167, 14 May.

Downing, Jon. 2004. Public Private Partnerships in UK Defence. DBSA-31. Directorate for Broadening Smart Acqusition. Präsentation, London. May (presentation at the disposal of the author).

Duffield, Mark. 2000. Globalization, Transborder Trade, and War Economies. In: Berdal, Mats and David M. Malone (Eds). 2000. *Greed and Grievances: Economic Agendas in Civil Wars*. Boulder, Co and London: Lynne Rienner, 69–89.

Duffield, Mark. 2001. *Global Governance and New Wars. The Merging of Development and Security*. London: Zed Books.

Dwan, Renata. 2004. *Civilian Tasks and Capabilities in EU-operations*. Paper presented at Study Group on Europe's Security Capabilities, London School of Economics and Friedrich-Ebert-Stiftung, Berlin 17–18 May. (http://www.lse.ac. uk/Depts/global/StudyGroup/CivilianTaskspaper.htm, accessed 8 November 2004).

Eberwein, Wolf-Dieter and Peter Runge. 2002. Neue Herausforderungen für die humanitäre Hilfe: Probleme und Perspektiven. In Eberwein, Wolf-Dieter and Peter Runge (Eds). 2002. *Humanitäre Hilfe statt Politik?* Münster/Hamburg/ London: Lit Verlag, 9–50.

Eisele, Manfred 2000. *Die Vereinten Nationen und das internationale Krisenmanagement*. Frankfurt/Main: Knecht Verlag.

El Baradei, Mohamed. 2003. U.S. Should Set Nuclear Disarmament Example, Reuters 26 August. Quoted in *Disarmament Diplomacy*, no. 73, October/November 2003.

Elwert, Georg. 1999. Markets of Violence. In Elwert, Georg, Stephan Feuchtwang and Dieter Neubert (Eds). *Dynamics of Violence: Processes of Escalation and De-Escalation in Violent Group Conflicts*. In *Sociologus Beiheft 1*, Berlin, Duncker & Humblot, 85–102.

Eppler, Erhard. 2002. *Vom Gewaltmonopol zum Gewaltmarkt?* Frankfurt/Main: Suhrkamp Verlag.

Eshel, David. 1996. 'Früchte des Zorns'. Aspekte einer Operation im Südlibanon. *Allgemeine Schweizerische Militärzeitschrift*, no. 162, 10 October, 12–15.

European Union Capability Improvement Conference. 2001. Statement by the EU Defence Ministers. Reprinted in Rutten, Maartje (Ed.). 2002. *From Nice to Laeken. EU Institute for Security Studies*. Paris: Chaillot papers, no. 51. April, 95–101.

European Union Commission. 2002. EU Presidency Report on the EU Programme for the Prevention of Violent Conflicts. In Haine, Jean-Yves (Ed.). 2003. *From Laeken to Copenhagen*. EU Institute for Security Studies. Paris: Chaillot papers, no. 57. February, 96–103.

European Union Commission. 2003a. *Action Plan for the Implementation of the Basic Principles for an EU Strategy against Proliferation of Weapons of Mass Destruction*. DG E VIII, Dokument 10354/1/03 REV 1 (en).

European Union Commission. 2003b. *Research for a Secure Europe – Report of the Group of Personalities in the Field of Security Research*. Luxemburg: Office for Official Publications of the European Communities.

European Union Council. 2001. Presidency Conclusions. In Haine, Jean-Yves (Ed.). 2003. *From Laeken to Copenhagen*. EU Institute for Security Studies. Paris: Chaillot papers, no. 57. February, 110–121.

European Union Council. 2002. Presidency Conclusions. In Haine, Jean-Yves (Ed.). 2003. *From Laeken to Copenhagen*. EU Institute for Security Studies. Paris: Chaillot papers, no. 57. February, 135–140.

European Union Council. 2003a. *General Affairs and External Relations*. 2509th Council meeting, Document 9379/03 (Presse 138). Brüssel, 19–20 May.

European Union Council. 2003b. *A Secure Europe in a Better World*. (http://ue. eu.int/uedocs/cms_data/docs/2004/4/29/European%20Security%20Strategy.pdf, accessed 30 December 2004).

European Union General Affairs Council. 2002. CFSP: *Implications of the Terrorist Threat on the Non-proliferation, Disarmament and Arms Control Policy of the EU – Council Conclusions*. (http://europa.eu.int/comm/external_relations/cfsp/intro/ gac.htm#sd150402a, accessed 25 October 2004).

European Union. 2004. *Treaty Establishing a Constitution for Europe*. (http:// europa.eu.int/eur-lex/lex/JOHtml.do?uri=OJ:C:2004:310: SOM:EN: HTML, accessed 30 December 2004).

Evans, Gareth. 2002. The Responsibility to Protect. *NATO Review*, no. 4 (Winter). (www.nato.int/docu/review/2002/issue4/english/analysis_pr.html, accessed 23 October 2003).

Feaver, Peter D., Richard H. Kohn and Lindsay P. Cohn. 2001. The Gap Between Military and Civilian in the United States Perspective. In Feaver, Peter D. and Richard H. Kohn, (Eds). 2001. *Soldiers and Civilians*. Cambridge, MA: MIT Press, 1–11.

Field, Kimberly C. and Robert M. Perito. 2002/3. Creating a Force for Peace Operations: Ensuring Stability with Justice. *Parameters*, vol. XXXII, no. 4 (Winter), 77–87.

Findlay, Trevor. 2002. The Use of Force in UN Peace Operations, Oxford: SIPRI. Oxford University Press.

Forrari, Marco. 2000. *Civil–Military Relations in Humanitarian Emergencies – The View of a Directly Operational Donor Country*. 2000. (http://www.isn.ethz.ch/4isf/3/ Elements/w_II-5/w_II-5_ab_Ferrari.htm, accessed 8 November 2004).

Freedom House. 2004. *Freedom in the World*. New York. (http:// www.freedomhouse.org/pdf_docs/research/freeworld/2004/map2004.pdf, accessed 18 October 2004).

Frum, David and Richard Perle. 2003. *An End to Evil: How to Win the War on Terror*. New York: Random House.

Füllkrug-Weitzel, Cornelia. 2003. Hilfe zwischen humanitärer Dienstleistung und sozialer Intervention. In Medico International (Ed.). 2003. *Macht und Ohnmacht der Hilfe*. Frankfurt/Main: Medico Report 25, 64–67.

Furley, Oliver. 1998. Rwanda and Burundi: Peacekeeping Amidst Massacres. In Furley, Oliver and Roy May (Eds), *Peacekeeping in Africa*. Ashgate: Aldershot, 239–261.

Ganor, Boaz. 1997. *Israeli Counter-Terrorist Policy*. Herzlia: International Institute for Counter-Terrorism. (www.ict.org.il, accessed 13 November 2002).

Ganor, Boaz. 1998. *A New Strategy Against the New Terror*. Herzlia: International Institute for Counter-Terrorism. (www.ict.org.il, accessed 13 November 2002).

Gantzel, Klaus Jürgen. 2002. Neue Kriege? Neue Krieger? In Schoch, Bruno, Corinna Hauswedell, Christoph Weller, Ulrich Ratsch and Reinhard Mutz (Eds). 2002. *Friedensgutachten 2002*. Münster/Hamburg/London: Lit Verlag, 80–89.

Garcia-Perez, Isolde K. 1999. Contractors on the Battlefield in the 21st Century. *Army Logistician*, vol. 31, no. 6, 40–43.

Gareis, Sven Bernhard. 2002. Der Wandel der Friedenssicherung durch die Vereinten Nationen. *Aus Politik und Zeitgeschichte*, B 27/28, 8 July, 19–25.

Gaultier, Leonard, Garine Hovsepian, Ayesha Ramachandran, Ian Wadley and Badr Zerhdoud 2001. *The Mercenary Issue at the UN Commission on Human Rights*. London: International Alert.

Gebauer, Thomas. 2003. Als müsse Rettung erst noch erdacht werden. In Medico International (Ed.). 2003. *Macht und Ohnmacht der Hilfe*. Frankfurt/Main: Medico Report 25, 13–19.

Goldstein, Lyle. J. 2000. General John Shalikashvili and the Civil–Military Relations of Peacekeeping. *Armed Forces & Society*, vol. 26, no. 3 (Spring), 387–411.

Gordon, Philip. H. 2004. American Choices in the 'War on Terror'. *Survival*, vol. 46, no. 1 (Spring), 143–155.

Gotowicki, Stephen H. 1997. Confronting Terrorism: New War Form or Mission Impossible? *Military Review*, May/June, 61–66.

Gourlay, Catriona. 2000. *Managing Civil–Military Co-operation in Humanitarian Intervention*. Geneva: UNIDIR, Disarmament forum, no. 3, 33–44.

Gourlay, Catriona. 2004. Parliamentary Accountability and ESDP: The National and the European Level. In Born, Hans and Heiner Hänggi (Eds). 2004. *The 'Double Democratic Deficit'*. Ashgate: Aldershot, 183–200.

Graduate Institute of International Studies. 2002. *Small Arms Survey 2002*. Oxford: Oxford University Press.

Grant, Bruce D. 1998. *U.S. Military Expertise for Sale: Private Military Consultants as a Tool of Foreign Policy*. National Defense University. Washington, DC. (http://www.ndu.edu/inss/books/books%20-%201998/Essays1998/ESSAY98. pdf, accessed 8 November 2004).

Gray, Colin S. 2002. Thinking Asymmetrically in Times of Terror. *Parameters*, vol. XXXII, no. 1 (Spring), 5–14.

Greene, Owen. 2004. Democratic Governance and the Internationalisation of Security Policy: The Relevance of Parliaments. In Born, Hans and Heiner Hänggi (Eds). 2004. *The 'Double Democratic Deficit'*. Aldershot: Ashgate, 19–32.

Hagman, Hans-Christian. 2002. *European Crisis Management and Defence: The Search for Capabilities*. London: The International Institute for Strategic Studies: Adelphi paper no. 353.

Haine, Jean-Yves. 2004. ESVP und NATO. In Gnesotto, Nicole (Ed.). 2004. *Die Sicherheits- und Verteidigungspolitik der EU*. Paris: EU Institute for Security Studies, 155–170.

Hampson, Fen Olser. 2003. Canada: Committed Contributor of Ideas and Forces, but Growing Doubts and Problems. In Ku, Charlotte and Harold K. Jacobson (Eds). 2003. *Democratic Accountability and the Use of Force in International Law*. Cambridge: Cambridge University Press, 127–153.

Hänggi, Heiner. 2004. The Use of Force Under International Auspices: Parliamentary Accountability and 'Democratic Deficits'. In Born, Hans and Heiner Hänggi (Eds). 2004. *The 'Double Democratic Deficit'*. Ashgate: Aldershot, 3–16.

Hart, B. H. Liddell. 1954. Strategy. *The Indirect Approach*. 3rd edn. London: Cassell.

Hartung, William D. 2004. *Outsourcing the Blame*. (www.tompain.com/print/ outsourcing_blame.php, accessed 8 November 2004).

Hassner, Pierre. 2002. *The United States: The Empire of Force or the Force of Empire?* Paris: EU Institute for Security Studies. Chaillot papers 54.

Hauswedell, Corinna and Herbert Wulf. 2004. Die EU als Friedensmacht? In Weller, Christoph, Ulrich Ratsch, Reinhard Mutz, Bruno Schoch, and Corinna Hauswedell (Eds). *Friedensgutachten 2004*. Münster/Hamburg/ London: Lit Verlag, 122–230.

Hauswedell, Corinna and Kris Brown. 2002. *Burying the Hatchet*. BICC Brief 22, Bonn: Bonn International Center for Conversion. (http://www.bicc.de/publications/ briefs/brief22/content.html, accessed 15 March 2004).

Heinemann-Grüder, Andreas. 2003. *Im Namen der Nato*. Berlin: Agenda Verlag.

Heinemann-Grüder, Andreas and Tobias Pietz. 2004. Zivil-militärische Intervention – Militär als Entwicklungshelfer? In Weller, Christoph, Ulrich Ratsch, Reinhard Mutz, Bruno Schoch, and Corinna Hauswedell (Eds). 2004. Münster/Hamburg/London: Lit. Verlag, 200–208.

Heitman, Helmöd-Romer. 2002. Crisis Response Capability. A Role for South Africa. *African Security Review*, vol. 11, no. 1, 61–71.

Hendrickson, Dylan and Adrezj Karkoszka. 2002. The Challenges of Security Sector Reform. *SIPRI Yearbook 2002, Armaments, Disarmament and International Security*. Oxford: Oxford University Press, 175–201.

Hippler, Jochen. 2003. *Nation-Building: Ein Schlüsselkonzept für friedliche Konfliktbearbeitung?* Bonn: Dietz Verlag.

Hirsh, Michael. 2000. Calling All Regio-Cops. Peacekeeping's Hybrid Future. *Foreign Affairs*, vol. 79, no. 6 (November), 2–8.

Hooker, Richard D. 2003/4. Soldiers of the State: Reconsidering American Civil-Relations. *Parameters*, vol. XXXIII, no. 4 (Winter), 4–18.

Howard, Michael. 1976. *War in European History*. Oxford: Oxford University Press.

Howard, Michael. 2002. What's in a Name? *Foreign Affairs*, vol. 81, no. 1, January/February, 8–13.

Human Security Report. 2005. Vancouver: Liu Institute for Global Issues (Summer 2005). Oxford University Press.

Hummel, Hartwig. 2003. Die Europäische Union und der 'demokratische Frieden': Zur parlamentarischen Kontrolle der Euroopäischen Sicherheits- und Verteidigungspolitik. In Peter Schlotter (Ed.). 2003. *Macht – Europa – Frieden?* Baden-Baden: Nomos Verlag, 159–178.

Hunter, Robert E. 2002. The European Security and Defense Policy: NATO's Companion – or Competitor? Rand Corporation. Santa Monica. MR-1463-NDRI/RE. (www.rand.org/publications/MR/MR1463/, accessed 2 December 2004).

Huntington, Samuel P. 1957. *The Soldier and the State: The Theory and Politics of Civil–Military Relations*. Cambridge, MA: Harvard University Press.

Hutsch, Franz-Josef. 2003. Beitrag im Hörfunk NDR 4. *Streitkräfte und Strategien*, 8 February. (http://www.ndrinfo.de/ndrinfo_pages_std/0,2758,OID68144,00. html, accessed 8 November 2004).

Inbar, Efraim. 1991. Israel's Small War: The Military Response to the Intifada. *Armed Forces & Society*, vol. 18, no. 1 (Fall), 29–50.

International Alert (Ed.). 1999. *The Privatization of Security: Framing a Conflict Prevention and Peacebuilding Policy Agenda.* London: International Alert.

International Commission on Intervention and State Sovereignty. 2001. *The Responsibility to Protect.* (www.iciss-ciise.gc.ca, accessed 26 October 2004).

International Committee of the Red Cross. 2004. *ICRC to Expand Contacts with Private Military and Security Companies*, 17 May. (http://www.icrc.org/Web/Eng/siteeng0.nsf/iwpList74/21414DE8FCAF2645C1256EE50038A631, accessed 8 November 2004).

International Institute for Strategic Studies. 2004. The US Global Posture Review. *Strategic Comments*, vol. 10, no. 7 (September).

International Peace Operations Association. 2003. *Supporting the MONOC Mandate with Private Services in the Democratic Republic of Congo.* (www.ipoaonline.org, accessed 15 August 2004).

International Peace Operations Association. 2004. IPOA's Mission is to End Wars. (www.ipoaonline.org, accessed 26 October 2004).

Isenberg, David. 2004. A Fistful of Contractors: The Case for a Pragmatic Assessment of Private Military Companies in Iraq. In *BASIC*, Research report, September.

Jablonsky, David. 2001. Army Transformation: A Tale of Two Doctrines. *Parameters*, vol. XXXI, no. 3 (Fall), 43–62.

Jakobsen, Peter Viggo. 2002. The Transformation of United Nations Peace Operations in the 1990s. *Cooperation and Conflict*, vol. 37, no. 3, 268–282.

Janowitz, Morris. 1960. *The Professional Soldier: A Social and Political Portrait.* New York: Free Press.

Jean, François and Jean-Christophe Ruffin (Eds). 1999. *Ökonomie der Bürgerkriege.* Hamburg: Hamburger Institut für Sozialforschung. Hamburger Edition.

Jenkins, Brian. 2003. The US Response to Terrorism and its Implications for Transatlantic Relations. In Lindstrom, Gustav (Eds). 2003. *Shift or Rift. Assessing US–EU Relations after Iraq.* Paris: EU Institute for Security Studies, 207–229.

Kagan, Robert. 2002. Power and Weakness. *Policy Review*, no. 113, June/July. (http://www.policyreview.org/JUN02/kagan_print.html, accessed 8 November 2004).

Kahn, Mafruza. 2002. *Business on the Battlefield: The Role of Private Military Companies.* Corporate Research Project. Corporate Research E-Letter, no. 30, December. (www.corp-research.org/dec02.htm, accessed 8 November 2004).

Kaldor, Mary. 1981. *The Baroque Arsenal.* New York: Hill and Wang.

Kaldor, Mary. 1997. Introduction. In Mary Kaldor and Basker Vashee (Eds). 1997. *Restructuring the Global Military Sector.* London and Washington: Pinter, 3–33.

Kaldor, Mary. 1999. *New and Old Wars, Organized Violence in a Global Era.* Cambridge, UK: Polity Press.

Karkoszka, Andrzej. 2003. Defence Reforms for Democracy in Eastern Europe from 1989 to 2002. In Bryden, Alan and Philipp Fluri (Eds). 2003. *Security Sector Reform: Institutions, Society and Good Governance.* Baden-Baden: Nomos Verlag, 47–60.

Karsten, Peter. 2001. The US Citizen-Soldier's Past, Present, and Likely Future. *Parameters*, vol. XXXI, no. 2 (Summer), 61–73.

Keane, Rory. 2004. The EU's African Peace Facility Uncovered: Better Late than Never? *European Security Review*, no. 24, October. (http://www.isis-europe.org/ftp/Download/ESR%2024-%20final.PDF, accessed 25 October 2004).

Keen, David. 1998. *The Economic Functions of Violence in Civil Wars*. London: The International Institute for Strategic Studies: Adelphi paper no. 320.

Kent, Vanessa and Mark Malan. 2003. *Decisions, Decisions. South Africa's Foray into Regional Peace Operations*. Pretoria: Institute for Security Studies. Occasional paper 72. April.

Keohane, Robert O. 1998. International Institutions: Can Interdependence Work? *Foreign Policy*, no. 110 (Spring), 82–96.

Kingma, Kees (Ed.). 2000. *Demobilization in Sub-Saharan Africa: The Development of Security Impacts*. Basingstoke: Macmillan.

Kohn, Richard H. 1997. How Democracies Control the Military. *Journal of Democracy*, vol. 8, no. 4 (October), 140–153.

Kosnik, Mark E. 2000. The Military Response to Terrorism. *Naval War College Review*, vol. LIII, no. 2, 13–39.

Ku, Charlotte and Harold K. Jacobson. 2001. Using Military Forces Under International Auspices and Democratic Accountability. *International Relations of the Asia–Pacific*, vol. 1, 21–50.

Ku, Charlotte and Harold K. Jacobson (Eds). 2003a. *Democratic Accountability and the Use of Force in International Law*. Cambridge, UK: Cambridge University Press.

Ku, Charlotte and Harold K. Jacobson. 2003b. Broaching the Issues. In Ku, Charlotte and Harold K. Jacobson (Eds). 2003. *Democratic Accountability and the Use of Force in International Law*. Cambridge, UK: Cambridge University Press, 3–35.

Kühne, Winrich (Ed.). 1993. *Blauhelme in einer turbulenten Welt*. Baden-Baden: Nomos Verlag.

Kurtenbach, Sabine and Peter Lock (Eds). 2004. *Kriege als (Über)Lebenswelten*. Bonn: Dietz Verlag.

Lanman, Eric. 1998a. Peacekeeping's Toll: High Personnel Tempo Eroding Readiness on Several Fronts. *Armed Forces Journal International*, March, 18–19.

Lanman, Eric. 1998b. 'Wither the Warrior?' *Proceedings*, April, 26–29.

Laurance, Edward J., Hendrik Wagenmakers and Herbert Wulf. 2005. Managing the Global Problems Created by the Conventional Arms Trade: An Assessment of the United Nations Register of Conventional Arms. *Global Governance*, vol. 11, no. 2, 225–246.

Leriche, Matthew. 2004. Unintended Alliance: The Co-option of Humanitarian Aid in Conflicts. *Parameters*, vol. XXXIV, no. 1 (Spring), 104–120.

Lilly, Damian. 2000a. *The Privatization of Peacekeeping: Prospects and Realities*. Geneva: UNIDIR, Disarmament Forum 3, 53–62.

Lilly, Damian. 2000b. *The Privatization of Security and Peacebuilding*. London: International Alert.

Lilly, Damian and Michael von Tangen Page (Eds). 2002. *Security Sector Reform: The Challenges and Opportunities of the Privatisation of Security*. London: International Alert.

Lindstrom, Gustav. 2004. Im Einsatzgebiet: ESVP-Operationen. In Gnesotto, Nicole (Ed.). 2004. *Die Sicherheits- und Verteidigungspolitik der EU*. Paris: EU Institute for Security Studies, 131–153.

Lischer, Sarah Kenyon. 2003. Collateral Damage. Humanitarian Assistance as a Cause of Conflict. *International Security*, vol. 28, no. 1 (Summer), 79–109.

Lock, Peter. 2001. Sicherheit á la Carte? Entstaatlichung, Gewaltmärkte und die Privatisierung des staatlichen Gewaltmonopols. In Brühl, Tanja, Tobias Debiel, Brigitte Hamm, Hartwig Hummel and Jens Martens (Eds). 2001. *Die*

Privatisierung der Weltpolitik. Entstaatlichung und Kommerzialisierung im Globalisierungsprozess. Bonn: Dietz Verlag, 200–229.

Lock, Peter. 2004. Gewalt als Regulation: Zur Logik der Schattenglobalisierung. In Kurtenbach, Sabine and Peter Lock (Eds). 2004. *Kriege als (Über)Lebenswelten.* Bonn: Dietz Verlag, 40–61.

Luckham, Robin. 2003. Democratic Strategies for Security in Transition and Conflict. In Cawthra, Gavin and Robin Luckham (Eds). 2003. *Governing Insecurity.* London: Zed Books, 3–28.

MacFarlane, S. Neil. 1997. Peace Support Operations and Humanitarian Action: A Conference Report. Oxford University. Oxford Center for International Studies, 9 August.

MacFarlane, S. Neil. 2002. *Intervention in Contemporary World Politics.* London: The International Institute for Strategic Studies: Adelphi paper no. 350.

Mair, Stefan. 2004. Die Rolle von *Private Military Companies* in Gewaltkonflikten. In Kurtenbach, Sabine and Peter Lock (Eds). 2004. *Kriege als (Über)Lebenswelten.* Bonn: Dietz Verlag, 260–273.

Malan, Mark. 2004. New Tools in the Box? Towards a Standby Force for the AU. In Field, Shannon (Ed.). 2004. *Peace in Africa.* Johannesburg: Institute for Global Dialogue, 193–223.

Mandel, Robert. 2001. The Privatization of Security. *Armed Forces & Society,* vol. 28, no. 1 (Fall), 129–151.

Manigart, Philippe. 2001. Defense Restructuring: Comparative Survey Among Military Personnel in Four European Countries. International Conference on Disarmament and Conversion, Bremen: (unpublished).

Markusen, Ann R. 2003. The Case Against Privatizing National Security. *Governance,* vol. 16, no. 4 (October), 471–501.

Markusen, Ann R. and Sean S. Costigan. 1999. The Military Industrial Challenge. In Markusen, Ann R. and Sean S. Costigan (Eds). 1999. *Arming the Future: A Defense Industry for the 21st Century.* New York: Council on Foreign Rations Press, 3–34.

Matthies, Volker (Ed.). 1995. *Vom Krieg zum Frieden. Kriegsbeendigung und Friedenskonsolidierung.* Bremen: Temmen.

Mawdsley, Jocelyn. 2004. The Policy Choices Ahead for the EU on Armaments. In Mawdsley, Jocelyn, Marta Martinelli and Eric Remacle (Eds). *Europe and the Global Arms Agenda: Security, Trade and Accountability 2004.* Baden-Baden: Nomos Verlag, 41–49.

Mayhew, Barney. 2000. *CARE International's Relationship with the Military: A Draft Discussion Paper.* Brüssel: CARE International.

McPeak, Michael and Sandra N. Ellis. 2004. Managing Contractors in Joint Operations: Filling the Gaps in Doctrine. *Army Logistician,* vol. 36, no. 2, 6–9.

Medico International (Ed.). *Macht und Ohnmacht der Hilfe,* Frankfurt/Main: Medico Report 25.

Mendez, Ruben P. 1999. Peace as a Global Public Good. In Kaul, Inge, Isabelle Grunberg and Marc Stern (Eds). 1999. *Global Public Goods.* Oxford: Oxford University Press. 382–416.

Messner, Dirk and Franz Nuscheler. 1997. Global Governance. Herausforderungen an der Schwelle zum 21. Jahrhundert. In Dieter Senghaas (Ed.). 1997. *Frieden machen,* Frankfurt/Main: Suhrkamp, 337–361.

Miller, Laura, L. 1997. Do Soldiers Hate Peacekeeping? The Case of Preventive Diplomacy Operations in Macedonia. *Armed Forces & Society,* vol. 23, no. 3 (Spring) 415–450.

Milliken, Jennifer (Ed.). 2003. *State Failure, Collapse & Reconstruction*. Oxford: Blackwell.

Minear, Larry and Phillipe Guillot. 1996. *Soldiers to the Rescue: Humanitarian Lessons from Rwanda*. Paris: Organisation for Economic Co-operation and Development.

Minear, Larry, Ted van Baarda and Marc Sommers. 2000. *NATO and Humanitarian Action in the Kosovo Crisis*. Humanitarian & War Project, Providence, Rhode Island: Brown University.

Mingst, Karen A. 2003. Domestic Political Factors and Decisions to Use Military Forces. In Ku, Charlotte and Harold K. Jacobson. (Eds). 2003. *Democratic Accountability and the Use of Force in International Law*. Cambridge, UK: Cambridge University Press, 61–80.

Misereor, EED and Brot für die Welt. 2003. *Entwicklungspolitik im Windschatten militärischer Intervention*. Position paper. Aachen, Bonn, Stuttgart: 31 July. (www.misereor.de/allgemein_4459.php, accessed 8 November 2004).

Mockaitis, Thomas R. 1993. Low-intensity Conflict: The British Experience. *Conflict Quarterly*, vol. 13, no. 1 (Winter), 7–16.

Monaco, Analisa. 2003. NATO Response Force: More Than a 'Paper Army'? *NATO Notes* (ISIS Europe), vol. 5, no. 7 (October) 1–3. (http://.isis-europe.org/ftp/download/nato%20notes%20vol.%205%20no%20.7.pdf, accessed 7 November 2004).

Moskos, Charles C. 1976. *Peace Soldiers*. Chicago: University of Chicago Press.

Moskos, Charles C., John Allen Williams and David R. Segal (Eds). 2000a. *The Postmodern Military*. New York and London: Oxford University Press.

Moskos, Charles C., John Allen Williams and David R. Segal. 2000b. Armed Forces After the Cold War. In Moskos, Charles C., John Allen Williams and David R. Segal (Eds). 2000. *The Postmodern Military*. New York and London: Oxford University Press, 1–13.

Münkler, Herfried, 2001. Die brutale Logik des Terrors. *Süddeutsche Zeitung am Wochende*, Feuilleton-Beilage, 29/30 1 September.

Münkler, Herfried. 2002. *Neue Kriege*. Hamburg: Rowohlt Verlag.

Musah, Abdel-Fatau and J.`Kayode Fayemi (Eds). 2000. *Mercenaries. An African Security Dilemma*. London and Sterling, Virginia: Pluto Press.

Mutz, Reinhard. 2004. Verteidigung am Hindukusch? Gratwanderung deutscher Sicherheitspolitik. In Weller, Christoph, Ulrich Ratsch, Reinhard Mutz, Bruno Schoch and Corinna Hauswedell (Eds). 2004. Lit Verlag, Münster, 251–259.

Nathan, Laurie. 2001. 'The Four Horsemen of the Apocalypse'. Structural Causes of Crisis and Violence in Africa. *Track Two*, vol. 10, no. 2 (August), 3–24.

Nathan, Laurie. 2004. *The Absence of Common Values and Failure of Common Security in Southern Africa, 1992–2003*. London: Crisis States Programme. Working paper no. 50. (www.crisisstates.com/publications/wp/wpregion.htm, accessed 4 November 2004).

NATO. *Military Commission Doctrine* MC 411/1. no year. (http://www.nato.int/ims/docu/mc411-1-e.htm, accessed 8 November 2004).

NATO. 1999. *Strategisches Konzept*, Brüssel. (www.NATO/inf/docu/pr/1999/p99–065e.html, accessed 20 February 2002).

NATO. 2001. Can Soldiers be Peacekeepers and Warriors? *NATO Review*, Web edition, vol. 49, no. 2 (Summer), 16–20.

NATO. 2003. Fact Sheet. *The NATO Response Force – NRF*. (www.nato.int/shape/issues/shape_nrf/030820.htm, accessed 25 September 2003).

Neethling, Theo. 2002. The Emerging South African Profile in Africa. Reflection on the Significance of South Africa's Entrance into Peacekeeping. *Africa Journal in Conflict Resolution*, no. 1. (www.accord.org.za, accessed 28 February 2004).

Nhara, William. 1998. Conflict Management and Peace Operations: The Role of the Organisation of African Unity and Subregional Organisations. In Malan, Mark (Ed.). *Resolute Partners. Building Peacekeeping Capacity in Southern Africa.* Pretoria: ISS Monograph Series, no. 21, February, 32–42.

Nieuwkerk, Anthoni van. 2004. The Role of the AU and NEPAD in Africa's New Security Regime. In Field, Shannon (Ed.). 2004. *Peace in Africa.* Johannesburg: Institute for Global Dialogue, 41–61.

Nolte, Georg. 2003. Die USA und das Völkerrecht. *Friedenswarte.* vol. 78, no. 2–3, 119–140.

Nuscheler, Franz. 2000a. Global Governance, Entwicklung und Frieden. Zur Interdependenz globaler Ordnungsstrukturen. In Franz Nuscheler (Ed.). 2000. *Entwicklung und Frieden im 21. Jahrhundert.* Bonn: Sonderband der Stiftung Entwicklung und Frieden, 471–507.

Nuscheler, Franz. 2000b. Kritik der Kritik am Global Governance-Konzept. *PROKLA. Zeitschrift für kritische Sozialwissenschaft*, vol. 30, no. 118, 151–156.

O'Brian, Kevin A. 1998. Military-Advisory Groups and African Security: Privatized Peacekeeping? *International Peacekeeping*, vol. 5, no. 3 (Autumn), 78–105.

O'Hanlon, Michael and Peter W. Singer. 2004. The Humanitarian Transformation: Expanding Global Intervention Capacity. *Survival*, vol. 46, no. 1 (Spring), 77–100.

Ogata, Sadako and Amartya Sen. 2003. *Final Report of the Commission on Human Security.* (http://www.humansecurity-chs.org/finalreport/FinalReport.pdf, accessed 8 November 2004).

Operation Eagle Claw. (www.specwarnet.com/miscinfo/eagleclaw.html, accessed 4 March 2002).

Organisation for Economic Co-operation and Development/DAC. 1997. *Civilian and Military Means of Providing and Supporting Humanitarian Assistance During Conflict: A Comparative Analysis.* Paris: Document DCD/DAC(97)19.

Organisation for Economic Co-operation and Development/DAC. 2001. *Helping Prevent Violent Conflict. Orientations for External Partners. Supplement to the DAC Guidelines on Conflict, Peace and Development Co-operation on the Threshold of the 21st Century*, Paris. (http://www.oecd.org/dac/pdf/G-con-e.pdf, accessed 17 November 2002).

Organisation for Economic Co-operation and Development/DAC. 2004. *Security System Reform and Governance. DAC Guidelines and Reference Series.* Paris. (www.oecd.org/dac/conflict, accessed 7 November 2004).

Orsini, Eric A. and Gary T. Bublitz. 1999. Contractors on the Battlefield: Risks on the Road Ahead? *Army Logistician*, vol. 31, no. 1, 130–132.

OXFAM. 2000. The Roles of Civilian Humanitarian Agencies and the Military in Humanitarian Crises. Dicussion paper (unpublished). Oxford. 26 July.

OXFAM. 2003. *Iraq: Humanitarian–Military Relations.* Oxford: OXFAM Briefing paper 41, February.

OXFAM. 2004. *Oxfam Suspends all Direct Operations in Iraq.* Oxford. (www.Oxfam.org.uk/what_we_do/where_we_work/iraq/update0404, accessed 8 November 2004).

Pape, Matthias. 1997. *Humanitäre Intervention. Zur Bedeutung der Menschenrechte in den Vereinten Nationen.* Baden-Baden: Nomos Verlag.

Pelton, Emily. 2000. Mission Creep? Peacekeepers' Influence on Humanitarian Aid Delivery in Kosovo and East Timor. CARE, Policy and Advocacy Unit. Discussion paper (unpublished).

Pugh, Michael. 2003. Protectorates and Spoils of Peace: Political Economy in South-East Europe. In Jung, Dietrich (Ed.). 2003. *Shadow Globalization, Ethnic Conflicts and New Wars*. London: Routledge, 47–69.

Pugh, Michael. 2004. Peacekeeping and Critical Theory. *International Peacekeeping*, vol. 11, no. 1 (Spring), 39–58.

Pugh, Michael and Neil Cooper. 2004. *War Economies in a Regional Context.* Boulder, Co and London: Lynne Rienner.

Reno, William. 2000. Shadow States and the Political Economy of Civil War. In Berdal, Mats and David M. Malone (Eds). 2000. *Greed and Grievances: Economic Agendas in Civil Wars*. Boulder, Co and London: Lynne Rienner, 43–68.

Republic of South Africa. 1996. *Defence in a Democracy. White Paper on National Defence for the Republic of South Africa*, May. (www.gov.za/whitepaper/1996/defencewp.htm#inter_peace, accessed 20 February 2004).

Republic of South Africa. 1999. *White Paper on South African Participation in International Peace Missions.* February. (www.gov.za/whitepaper/1999/peace_missions.htm, accessed 20 February 2004).

Rice, Condoleeza. 2000. Promoting the National Interest. *Foreign Affairs*, vol. 79, January/February, 45–62.

Roberts, Adam. 1996. *Humanitarian Action in War – Aid, Protection and Impartiality in a Policy Vacuum*. London: The International Institute for Strategic Studies: Adelphi paper No. 305.

Sandler, Todd and Keith Hartley. 1995. *The Economics of Defense*. Cambridge, UK: Cambridge University Press.

Sandline International. 1998. *Private Military Companies – Independent or Regulated?* (www.sandline.com/site/index.html. September, accessed 14 June 2001), 1.

Sandoz, Yves. 1999. Perspectives on Suitable Policy Frameworks. In International Alert (Ed.). 1999. *The Privatization of Security: Framing a Conflict Prevention and Peacebuilding Policy Agenda*. London: International Alert, 19–22.

Schiff, Rebecca L. 1995. Civil–Military Relations Reconsidered: A Theory of Concordance. *Armed Forces & Society*, vol. 22, no. 1 (Fall), 7–24.

Schlichte, Klaus. 1996. *Krieg und Vergesellschaftung in Afrika. Ein Beitrag zur Theorie des Krieges*. Münster/Hamburg/London: Lit Verlag.

Schlichte, Klaus. 1998. *Why States Decay. A Preliminary Assessment*. Hamburg: Universität Hamburg, Forschungsstelle Kriege, Rüstung und Entwicklung. Arbeitspapier no. 2.

Schmitt, Burkard. 2004. Europas Fähigkeiten – Wie viele Divisionen? In Gnesotto, Nicole (Ed.). 2004. *Die Sicherheits- und Verteidigungspolitik der EU*. Paris: EU Institute for Security Studies, 105–130.

Schreier, Fred and Marina Caparini. 2005. Law, Practice and Governance of Private Military and Security Companies. Geneva Centre for the Democratic Control of the Armed Forces, Geneva: Occasional Paper, no. 6, March.

Schwartz, Nelson D. 2003. The War Business. The Pentagon's Private Army. *Fortune*, 3 March. (www.fortune.com/fortune/articles/0,15114,427948,00.html, accessed 8 November 2004).

Shaw, Mark and Jakkie Cilliers (Ed.). 1995. *South Africa and Peacekeeping in Africa*. Midrand: Institute for Defence Policy.

Shawcross, William. 2000. *Deliver us from Evil: Peacekeepers, Warlords, and a World of Endless Conflict*. London: Bloomsbury.

Shearer, David. 1998. *Private Armies and Military Intervention*. London: The International Institute for Strategic Studies: Adelphi paper no. 316.

Shultz, George P. 1984. *Terrorism and the Modern World*. Department of State Bulletin, December.

Singer, Peter W. 2001/02. Corporate Warriors: The Rise and Ramifications of the Privatized Military Industry. *International Security*, vol. 26, no. 3 (Winter), 186–220.

Singer, Peter W. 2003. *Corporate Warriors. The Rise of the Privatized Military Industry*. Ithaka: Cornell University Press.

Sloan, Stephen. 1986. In Search of a Counterterrorism Doctrine. *Military Review*, January, 44–48.

Slocombe, Walter B. 2003. Terrorism/Counter-Terrorism: Their Impact on Security Sector Reform and Basic Democratic Values. In Bryden, Alan and Philipp Fluri (Eds). 2003. *Security Sector Reform: Institutions, Society and Good Governance*. Baden-Baden: Nomos Verlag, 291–301.

Smillie, Ian. 2000. Inside the Wire? Civil–Military Cooperation in Complex Emergencies. Discussion paper (unpublished) CARE Canada.

Smith, Edwin M. 2003. Collective Security, Peacekeeping, and ad hoc Multilateralism. In Ku, Charlotte and Harold K. Jacobson (Eds). 2003. *Democratic Accountability and the Use of Force in International Law*. Cambridge, UK: Cambridge University Press, 81–103.

Smith, Eugene B. 2002/03. The New Condottieri and US Policy: The Privatization of Conflict and Its Implications. *Parameters*, vol. XXXII, no. 4 (Winter), 104–119.

Solana, Javier. 2003. *A Secure Europe in a Better World*. European Council. Thessaloniki, 20 June. (http://ue.eu.int/newsroom, accessed 21 February 2004).

Sorensen, Henning. 2000. Denmark: From Obligation to Option. In Moskos, Charles C., John Allen Williams and David R. Segal (Eds). 2000. *The Postmodern Military*. New York and London: Oxford University Press, 121–136.

Spicer, Tim. 1998. Why We can Help Where Governments Fear to Tread. *Sunday Times*, 24 May.

Steyn, Pierre. 1998. South Africa and Peace Support Operations: Limitations, Options and Challenges. *African Security Review*, vol. 7, no. 1, 26–36.

Stockholm International Peace Research Institute. 2001–2004. *SIPRI Yearbook (annual). Armaments, Disarmament and International Security*. Oxford: Oxford University Press.

Studer, Meinrad. 2000. Civil-Military Relations in Humanitarian Emergencies – An ICRC Perspective. (www.isn.ethz.ch/4isf/3/elements/w_II-5_ab_studer.htm).

Studer, Meinrad. 2001. The ICRC and Civil–Military Relations in Armed Conflict. *International Review of the Red Cross*, no. 842, 367–391.

Study Group on Europe's Security Capabilities. 2004. *A Human Security Doctrine for Europe*. Barcelona, 15 September. (http://www.gfn-ssr.org/edocs/lse_human_security_report.pdf, accessed 8 November 2004).

Tauxe, Jean-Daniel. 2000. The ICRC and Civil–Military Cooperation in Situations of Armed Conflict. Paper presented at the 45th Rese-Roth Seminar, Montreux, 2 March.

Thakur, Ramesh and Dipankar Banerjee. 2003. India: Democratic, Poor, Internationalist. In Ku, Charlotte and Harold K. Jacobson (Eds). 2003. *Democratic Accountability and the Use of Force in International Law*. Cambridge, UK: Cambridge University Press, 176–204.

The Center for Public Integrity. 2004. *Windfalls of War*. (www.publicintegrity. org/wow/bio.aspx?act=prod&ddlC=31, accessed 8 November 2004).

Thomson, Janice. 1994. *Mercenaries, Pirates, and Sovereigns: State-building and Extraterritorial Violence in Early Modern Europe*, Princeton, NJ: Princeton University Press.

Tilly, Charles. (Ed.). 1990. *Coercion, Capital, and European States*. Cambridge, MA: Basil Blackwood.

Tomuschat, Christian. 2003. Iraq – Demise of International Law? *Friedenswarte*, vol. 78, nos. 2–3, 141–160.

Trotha, Trutz von. 1996. From Administrative to Civil Chieftaincy. Some Problems and Prospects of African Chieftaincy. *Journal of Legal Pluralism and Unofficial Law*, no. 37/38, 79–107.

Trotha, Trutz von. 1997. Zur Soziologie der Gewalt. In Trotha, Trutz von (Ed.). 1997. *Soziologie der Gewalt, Kölner Zeitschrift für Soziologie und Sozialpsychologie*, Sonderheft 37, Opladen and Wiesbaden: Westdeutscher Verlag, 9–56.

Tuzmukhamedov, Bakhtiyar. 2000. The Legal Framework of CIS Regional Peace Operations. *International Peacekeeping*, vol. 6, no. 1 (January/February), 1–6.

UK Government. 2002. *Private Military Companies: Options for Regulation*. 12 February. (www.fco.gov.uk/files/kfile/mercenaries,0.pdf, accessed 15 January 2004).

UK Government. 2004a. *Public Private Partnerships. Changing the Way We do Business. Elements of PPP in Defence*. (http://mod.uk/business/ppp_defence.htm, accessed 14 August 2004).

UK Government. 2004b. *Public Private Partnerships: Changing the Way We do Business. Sponsored Reserves*. (http://mod.uk/business/ppp/reserves.htm, accessed 14 August 2004).

UK Government. 2004c. *Public Private Partnerships. Changing the Way We do Business. PFI Guidelines*. London. (http://mod.uk/business/ppp/guidelines/ intro.htm, accessed 14 August 2004).

UK Government. 2004d. *Ministry of Defence: Signed PPP Projects*. (http://www.mod.uk/business/ppp/database.htm, accessed 14 August 2004).

UK Government. 2004e. *Ministry of Defence: PPP Projects in Procurement*. (http://www.mod.uk/business/ppp/database.htm, accessed 14 August 2004).

UK Parliament. 2003. *Seventh Report*. Select Committee on European Union Seventh Report. 11 February. (http://www.publications.parliament.uk/ pa/ld200203/idselect/ldeucom/53/5301.htm, accessed, 7 January 2004).

UN Department of Humanitarian Assistance. 1994. *Guidelines on the Use of Military and Civil Defense Assets in Disaster Relief*. Geneva: May.

UN Economic and Social Council. 2001a. *The Right of Peoples to Self-determination and Its Application to Peoples Under Colonial or Alien Domination or Foreign Occupation*. Geneva: E/CN.4/2001/18, 14 February.

UN Economic and Social Council. 2001b. *Commission on Human Rights*. Geneva: E/CN.4/2001/19, 11 January.

UN Economic and Social Council. 2002. *The Right of Peoples to Self-determination and Its Application to Peoples Under Colonial or Alien Domination or Foreign Occupation (UN Commission on Human Rights)*. E/CN.4/2002/20, 10 January.

UN Economic and Social Council. Release 2002. *UN Expert Meeting Recommends Clearer Definitions of Mercenaries; Calls for Increased Accountability of Private Security Companies.* 22 May.

United Nations Development Programme. 2002. *Human Development Report. Deepening Development in a Fragmented World.* New York: Oxford University Press.

United Nations Development Programme. 2003. *Human Development Report. Millennium Development Goals: A Compact Among Nations to End Human Poverty.* New York: Oxford University Press.

United Nations General Assembly. 1999. *Report of the Secretary General, The Fall of Srebrenica.* New York: November. (http://www.srebrenica.nl/en/munulinks. htm, accessed 20 January 2002).

United Nations General Assembly. 2001a. *Comprehensive Review of the Whole Question of Peacekeeping Operations in all their Aspects.* Report of the Special Committee on Peacekeeping Operations. New York: (A/55/1024), 31 July. [Brahimi Report].

United Nations General Assembly. 2001b. *Prevention of Armed Conflict. Report of the Secretary General.* New York: (A/55/985 and S/2001/574), 7 June.

United Nations High Commissioner for Human Rights. 2002. *The Impact of Mercenary Activities on the Right of Peoples to Self-Determination.* Geneva: Office of the United Nation High Commissioner for Human Rights, Fact Sheet No. 28, GE.01-46674.

United Nations High Commissioner for Refugees. 2003. *Refugees by Numbers.* (www.unhcr.ch/cgi-bin/texis/vtx/basics, accessed 8 November 2004).

United Nations High Commissioner for Human Rights. 2004. *Maintaining the Civlian and Humanitarian Character of Asylum.* Geneva: PPLA Series, no. 2, June.

United Nations High-level Panel on Threats, Challenges and Change. 2004. *A More Secure World: Our Shared Responsibility.* New York: Report of the High-level Panel on Threats, Challenges and Change.

United Nations Inter-Agency Standing Committee Work Group. 2004. *Civil–Military Relationship in Complex Emergencies.* New York: An IASC Reference paper, 28 June.

United Nations Secretary General. 2000. *'We the Peoples'.* New York: (A/54/2000). [Millennium Report].

United States General Accounting Office. 1997a. *Contingency Operations. Opportunities to Improve the Logistics Civil Augmentation Program.* Washington: GAO/NSIAD-97–63, February.

United States General Accounting Office. 1997b. *DoD Competitive Sourcing. Savings are Occurring, But Actions are Needed to Improve Accuracy of Savings Estimates.* Washington: GAO/NSIAD-00–107.

United States General Accounting Office. 1999a. *DoD Competitive Sourcing. Results of Recent Competitions.* Washington: GAO/NSIAD-99–44.

United States General Accounting Office. 1999b. *DoD Competitive Sourcing. Questions About Goals, Pace, and Risks of Key Reform Initiatives.* Washington: GAO/NSIAD-99–46.

United States General Accounting Office. 2000. *DoD Competitive Sourcing. Some Progress, but Continuing Challenges Remain in Meeting Program Goals.* Washington: GAO/NSIAD-00–106.

United States General Accounting Office. 2003a. *DoD Faces Challenges Implementing Its Core Competency Approach and A-76.* Washington. GAO-03–818.

United States General Accounting Office. 2003b. *Major Management Challenges and Program Risks*. Washington: GAO-03-98.

US Department of Defense. 1990. *Annual Defense Report to the President and Congress*. Washington, DC: US Government Printing Office (GPO).

US Department of Defense. 1997. *Annual Defense Report to the President and Congress*. (www.defenselink.mil/execsec/adr-97/chap9.html, accessed 4 March. 2002).

US Department of Defense. 2001a. *Annual Defense Report to the President and Congress*. (www.dtic.mil/execsec/adr-2001/, 26, accessed 4 March 2002).

US Department of Defense. 2001b. *Secretary of Defense Donal H. Rumsfeld, Quadrennial Defense Review Report*. (www. defenselink.mil/pubs/qudr2001.pdf, accessed 4 March 02).

US Department of State. 2004a. *Patterns of Global Terroism*. (www.state.gov/s/ct/rls/pgtrpt/2003/33771.htm, accessed 8 November 2004).

US Department of State. 2004b. *US Global Posture Review*. (http://fpc.state.gov/fpc/35246.htm, accessed 20 October 2004).

US Government. White House. 2002a. *National Security Strategy*. Washington. (www.whitehouse-gov/nsc/nssall.html, accessed 22 May 2003).

US Government. White House. 2002b. *President George W. Bush, The Global War on Terrorism. The First 100 Days*. Washington. (www.whitehouse.gov/news/releases/2001/12/print/100ddayreport.html, 7, accessed 4 March 2002).

Vaux, Tony, Chris Seiple, Greg Nakano and Koenraad van Brabant. 2002. *Humanitarian Action and Private Security Companies*. London: International Alert.

VENRO. 2003. *Streitkräfte als humanitäre Helfer?* Bonn: VENRO Position paper, May.

Verlöy, André and Daniel Politi. 2004. *Contracting Intelligence*. The Center for Public Integrity. (www.publicintegrity.org/wow/report.aspx?aid=361, accessed 8 November 2004).

Vines, Alex. 2000. Mercenaries, Human Rights and Legality. In Musah, Abdel-Fatau and J. `Kayode Fayemi (Eds). 2000. *Mercenaries. An African Security Dilemma*. London and Sterling, Virginia: Pluto Press, 169–197.

Wagner, Wolfgang. 2004. *Für Europa sterben? Die demokratische Legitimität der Europäischen Sicherheits- und Verteidigungspolitik*. HSFK-Report no. 3, Frankfurt/Main: Hessische Stiftung Friedens- und Konfliktforschung.

Wallace, J. J. A. 1996. Manoeuvre Theory in Operations Other Than War. *Journal of Strategic Studies*, vol. 19, no. 4 (December), 207–226.

Weber, Max. 1919. Politik als Beruf. In Max Weber. 1992. *Gesamtausgabe*, vol. 17, Tübingen: J.C.B. Mohr/Paul Siebeck, 157–252.

Weiss, Aaron. 2001. When Terror Strikes, Who Should Respond? *Parameters*, vol. XXXI, no. 3 (Autumn), 117–133.

Weiss, Thomas George. 1999. *Military–Civilian Interactions*. Lanham: Rowman and Littlefield.

Weiss, Thomas George. 2000. Governance, Good Governance and Global Governance. *Third World Quarterly*, vol. 21, no. 5 (October), 795–814.

Western, Jon. 2002. Sources of Humanitarian Intervention. *International Security*, vol. 26, no. 4 (Spring), 112–142.

Wilkinson, Paul. 2002. *Terrorism versus Democracy. The Liberal State Response*. London and Portland: Frank Cass Publisher, 19–20.

Williams, Rocky. 2000. From Peacekeeping to Peacebuilding? South African Policy and Practice in Peace Missions. *International Peacekeeping*, vol. 7, no. 3 (Autumn), 84–104.

Wilson, Gary. 2003. UN Authorized Enforcement: Regional Organizations versus 'Coalitions of the Willing'. *International Peacekeeping*, vol. 10, no. 2 (Summer), 89–106.

Wright, Neill. 2000. Civil–Military Relations in Humanitarian Emergencies – A UNHCR Perspective. Paper presented at the 4th International Security Forum, Workshop II.5. Geneva, 17 November.

Wulf, Herbert. 2002. Change of Uniform – but no Uniform Change in Function. Soldiers in Search of a New Role. In *BICC Conversion Survey 2002*. Baden-Baden: Nomos Verlag, 92–109.

Wulf, Herbert. 2003. 'Rent-a-Soldier'. Die Privatisierung des Militärs. *Wissenschaft und Frieden*, vol. 21, no. 3, 7–12.

Wulf, Herbert. 2004a. Security Sector Reform in Developing and Transitional Countries. In McCartney, Clem, Martina Fischer and Oliver Wils (Eds). 2004. *Security Sector Reform Potentials and Challenges for Conflict Transformation.* Berlin: Berghof Foundation, 9–28. (http://www.berghof-handbook.net/articles/ ssr_ complete.pdf, accessed 8 November 2004).

Wulf, Herbert. 2004b. Have the European Union and Its Member States Put Arms Control on the Backburner? *European Security*, no. 12, 113–128.

Wulf, Herbert. 2005. *Internationalisierung und Privatisierung von Krieg und Frieden.* Baden-Baden: Nomos Verlag.

Zamparelli, Steven J. 1999. Contractors on the Battlefield: What Have We Signed up for? *Air Force Journal of Logistics*, vol. 23, no. 3 (Fall), 11–14.

Zartman, I. William (Ed.). 1995. *Collapsed States: The Disintegration and Restoration of Legitimate Authority.* Boulder, Co and London: Lynne Rienner.

Index